Philip Gamaghelyan

CONFLICT RESOLUTION BEYOND THE INTERNATIONAL RELATIONS PARADIGM

Evolving Designs as a Transformative Practice in Nagorno-Karabakh and Syria

With a foreword by Susan Allen

ibidem-Verlag
Stuttgart

Bibliografische Information der Deutschen Nationalbibliothek
Die Deutsche Nationalbibliothek verzeichnet diese Publikation in der Deutschen Nationalbibliografie; detaillierte bibliografische Daten sind im Internet über http://dnb.d-nb.de abrufbar.

Bibliographic information published by the Deutsche Nationalbibliothek
Die Deutsche Nationalbibliothek lists this publication in the Deutsche Nationalbibliografie; detailed bibliographic data are available in the Internet at http://dnb.d-nb.de.

Cover picture: © Jahangir Yusuf. Reprint with kind permission.

∞

Gedruckt auf alterungsbeständigem, säurefreien Papier
Printed on acid-free paper

ISSN: 1614-3515

ISBN-13: 978-3-8382-1057-5

© *ibidem*-Verlag
Stuttgart 2017

Alle Rechte vorbehalten

Das Werk einschließlich aller seiner Teile ist urheberrechtlich geschützt. Jede Verwertung außerhalb der engen Grenzen des Urheberrechtsgesetzes ist ohne Zustimmung des Verlages unzulässig und strafbar. Dies gilt insbesondere für Vervielfältigungen, Übersetzungen, Mikroverfilmungen und elektronische Speicherformen sowie die Einspeicherung und Verarbeitung in elektronischen Systemen.

All rights part of this publication may be reproduced, stored in or introduced into a retrieval system, or transmitted, in any form, or by any means (electronic, mechanical, photocopying, recording or otherwise) without the prior written permission of the publisher. Any person who does any unauthorized act in relation to this publication may be liable to criminal prosecution and civil claims for damages.

Printed in the EU

Table of Contents

Abstract 9
Acknowledgments 11
Foreword by Susan Allen 15
Abbreviations 19
Introduction 21
    Questions I am aiming to address 24
    The organization of the text 26
Part I 29
Chapter 1: Critical review of conflict resolution theories 31
    Binary frames in conflict resolution 32
        Realist theories of international relations 33
        Liberal theories of international relations 34
        In the shadow of Track 1: interactive problem solving 40
    Alternative to binary frames in conflict resolution 44
        Multitrack models of conflict resolution 44
        Network theory 45
        The third side 47
    Constructivist trends in conflict analysis 47
        Reflective and elicitive practice 51
        Theories of ethnicity and nationalism 52
        Critical theory 56
        Structuration theory: segue into participatory research design 59
Chapter 2: Methodology 63
    Participatory action research 63
        Case selection 66
        Auto-ethnography 68
        First-person action research and collective auto-ethnography 68
        Second-person action research 73
    Ethical considerations and limitations 78

Chapter 3: Auto-ethnographic sketch 85
    My background, the resulting perspective and subjectivity,
    and their role in this research 85

Part II 97

**Chapter 4: On ethical and methodological challenges of
leading a Syrian dialogue program in the middle of a civil war:
from exclusion to inclusion** 99
    The program design and implementation 104
        Program design vs. program reality *109*
        Intermission *111*
        Back to dialogue *112*
        Methodological agony *113*
        Reframing *115*
        Getting real *119*
        Closure *123*
    Implications of the Syrian dialogue for this research: toward
    inclusive frames that do not privilege the violent extremes 125

**Chapter 5: On methodological challenges of leading an analytic
initiative in the context of the long-lasting Nagorno-Karabakh
conflict: from inclusion to exclusion** 129
    The Nagorno-Karabakh Analytic Initiative 129
        The first meeting *132*
        The first full symposium *133*
        The second full symposium *135*
        Working group *139*
    Implications of the Nagorno-Karabakh Analytic Initiative for
    recognizing power dynamics and resulting exclusion, and
    marginalization 147
        Part II postscript *150*

Soviet and Post-Soviet Politics and Society (SPPS) Vol. 171
ISSN 1614-3515

General Editor: Andreas Umland,
Institute for Euro-Atlantic Cooperation, Kyiv, umland@stanfordalumni.org

Commissioning Editor: Max Jakob Horstmann,
London, mjh@ibidem.eu

EDITORIAL COMMITTEE*

DOMESTIC & COMPARATIVE POLITICS
Prof. **Ellen Bos**, *Andrássy University of Budapest*
Dr. **Ingmar Bredies**, *FH Bund, Brühl*
Dr. **Andrey Kazantsev**, *MGIMO (U) MID RF, Moscow*
Prof. **Heiko Pleines**, *University of Bremen*
Prof. **Richard Sakwa**, *University of Kent at Canterbury*
Dr. **Sarah Whitmore**, *Oxford Brookes University*
Dr. **Harald Wydra**, *University of Cambridge*

SOCIETY, CLASS & ETHNICITY
Col. **David Glantz**, *"Journal of Slavic Military Studies"*
Dr. **Marlène Laruelle**, *George Washington University*
Dr. **Stephen Shulman**, *Southern Illinois University*
Prof. **Stefan Troebst**, *University of Leipzig*

POLITICAL ECONOMY & PUBLIC POLICY
Prof. em. **Marshall Goldman**, *Wellesley College, Mass.*
Dr. **Andreas Goldthau**, *Central European University*
Dr. **Robert Kravchuk**, *University of North Carolina*
Dr. **David Lane**, *University of Cambridge*
Dr. **Carol Leonard**, *Higher School of Economics, Moscow*
Dr. **Maria Popova**, *McGill University, Montreal*

FOREIGN POLICY & INTERNATIONAL AFFAIRS
Dr. **Peter Duncan**, *University College London*
Prof. **Andreas Heinemann-Grüder**, *University of Bonn*
Dr. **Taras Kuzio**, *Johns Hopkins University*
Prof. **Gerhard Mangott**, *University of Innsbruck*
Dr. **Diana Schmidt-Pfister**, *University of Konstanz*
Dr. **Lisbeth Tarlow**, *Harvard University, Cambridge*
Dr. **Christian Wipperfürth**, *N-Ost Network, Berlin*
Dr. **William Zimmerman**, *University of Michigan*

HISTORY, CULTURE & THOUGHT
Dr. **Catherine Andreyev**, *University of Oxford*
Prof. **Mark Bassin**, *Södertörn University*
Prof. **Karsten Brüggemann**, *Tallinn University*
Dr. **Alexander Etkind**, *University of Cambridge*
Dr. **Gasan Gusejnov**, *Moscow State University*
Prof. em. **Walter Laqueur**, *Georgetown University*
Prof. **Leonid Luks**, *Catholic University of Eichstaett*
Dr. **Olga Malinova**, *Russian Academy of Sciences*
Prof. **Andrei Rogatchevski**, *University of Tromso*
Dr. **Mark Tauger**, *West Virginia University*

ADVISORY BOARD*

Prof. **Dominique Arel**, *University of Ottawa*
Prof. **Jörg Baberowski**, *Humboldt University of Berlin*
Prof. **Margarita Balmaceda**, *Seton Hall University*
Dr. **John Barber**, *University of Cambridge*
Prof. **Timm Beichelt**, *European University Viadrina*
Dr. **Katrin Boeckh**, *University of Munich*
Prof. em. **Archie Brown**, *University of Oxford*
Dr. **Vyacheslav Bryukhovetsky**, *Kyiv-Mohyla Academy*
Prof. **Timothy Colton**, *Harvard University, Cambridge*
Prof. **Paul D'Anieri**, *University of Florida*
Dr. **Heike Dörrenbächer**, *Friedrich Naumann Foundation*
Dr. **John Dunlop**, *Hoover Institution, Stanford, California*
Dr. **Sabine Fischer**, *SWP, Berlin*
Dr. **Geir Flikke**, *NUPI, Oslo*
Prof. **David Galbreath**, *University of Aberdeen*
Prof. **Alexander Galkin**, *Russian Academy of Sciences*
Prof. **Frank Golczewski**, *University of Hamburg*
Dr. **Nikolas Gvosdev**, *Naval War College, Newport, RI*
Prof. **Mark von Hagen**, *Arizona State University*
Dr. **Guido Hausmann**, *University of Munich*
Prof. **Dale Herspring**, *Kansas State University*
Dr. **Stefani Hoffman**, *Hebrew University of Jerusalem*
Prof. **Mikhail Ilyin**, *MGIMO (U) MID RF, Moscow*
Prof. **Vladimir Kantor**, *Higher School of Economics*
Dr. **Ivan Katchanovski**, *University of Ottawa*
Prof. em. **Andrzej Korboński**, *University of California*
Dr. **Iris Kempe**, *"Caucasus Analytical Digest"*
Prof. **Herbert Küpper**, *Institut für Ostrecht Regensburg*
Dr. **Rainer Lindner**, *CEEER, Berlin*
Dr. **Vladimir Malakhov**, *Russian Academy of Sciences*

Dr. **Luke March**, *University of Edinburgh*
Prof. **Michael McFaul**, *Stanford University, Palo Alto*
Prof. **Birgit Menzel**, *University of Mainz-Germersheim*
Prof. **Valery Mikhailenko**, *The Urals State University*
Prof. **Emil Pain**, *Higher School of Economics, Moscow*
Dr. **Oleg Podvintsev**, *Russian Academy of Sciences*
Prof. **Olga Popova**, *St. Petersburg State University*
Dr. **Alex Pravda**, *University of Oxford*
Dr. **Erik van Ree**, *University of Amsterdam*
Dr. **Joachim Rogall**, *Robert Bosch Foundation Stuttgart*
Prof. **Peter Rutland**, *Wesleyan University, Middletown*
Prof. **Marat Salikov**, *The Urals State Law Academy*
Dr. **Gwendolyn Sasse**, *University of Oxford*
Prof. **Jutta Scherrer**, *EHESS, Paris*
Prof. **Robert Service**, *University of Oxford*
Mr. **James Sherr**, *RIIA Chatham House London*
Dr. **Oxana Shevel**, *Tufts University, Medford*
Prof. **Eberhard Schneider**, *University of Siegen*
Prof. **Olexander Shnyrkov**, *Shevchenko University, Kyiv*
Prof. **Hans-Henning Schröder**, *SWP, Berlin*
Dr. **Yuri Shapoval**, *Ukrainian Academy of Sciences*
Prof. **Viktor Shnirelman**, *Russian Academy of Sciences*
Dr. **Lisa Sundstrom**, *University of British Columbia*
Dr. **Philip Walters**, *"Religion, State and Society", Oxford*
Prof. **Zenon Wasyliw**, *Ithaca College, New York State*
Dr. **Lucan Way**, *University of Toronto*
Dr. **Markus Wehner**, *"Frankfurter Allgemeine Zeitung"*
Dr. **Andrew Wilson**, *University College London*
Prof. **Jan Zielonka**, *University of Oxford*
Prof. **Andrei Zorin**, *University of Oxford*

* While the Editorial Committee and Advisory Board support the General Editor in the choice and improvement of manuscripts for publication, responsibility for remaining errors and misinterpretations in the series' volumes lies with the books' authors.

Soviet and Post-Soviet Politics and Society (SPPS)
ISSN 1614-3515

Founded in 2004 and refereed since 2007, SPPS makes available affordable English-, German-, and Russian-language studies on the history of the countries of the former Soviet bloc from the late Tsarist period to today. It publishes between 5 and 20 volumes per year and focuses on issues in transitions to and from democracy such as economic crisis, identity formation, civil society development, and constitutional reform in CEE and the NIS. SPPS also aims to highlight so far understudied themes in East European studies such as right-wing radicalism, religious life, higher education, or human rights protection. The authors and titles of all previously published volumes are listed at the end of this book. For a full description of the series and reviews of its books, see
www.ibidem-verlag.de/red/spps.

Editorial correspondence & manuscripts should be sent to: Dr. Andreas Umland, Institute for Euro-Atlantic Cooperation, vul. Volodymyrska 42, off. 21, UA-01030 Kyiv, Ukraine

Business correspondence & review copy requests should be sent to: *ibidem* Press, Leuschnerstr. 40, 30457 Hannover, Germany; tel.: +49 511 2622200; fax: +49 511 2622201; spps@ibidem.eu.

Authors, reviewers, referees, and editors for (as well as all other persons sympathetic to) SPPS are invited to join its networks at
www.facebook.com/group.php?gid=52638198614
www.linkedin.com/groups?about=&gid=103012
www.xing.com/net/spps-ibidem-verlag/

Recent Volumes

163 *Alexandra Cotofana, James M. Nyce (eds.)*
Religion and Magic in Socialist and
Post-Socialist Contexts I
Historic and Ethnographic Case Studies of Orthodoxy,
Heterodoxy, and Alternative Spirituality
With a foreword by Patrick L. Michelson
ISBN 978-3-8382-0989-0

164 *Nozima Akhrarkhodjaeva*
The Instrumentalisation of Mass Media in
Electoral Authoritarian Regimes
Evidence from Russia's Presidential Election
Campaigns of 2000 and 2008
ISBN 978-3-8382-1013-1

165 *Yulia Krasheninnikova*
Informal Healthcare in Contemporary Russia
Sociographic Essays on the Post-Soviet Infrastructure
for Alternative Healing Practices
ISBN 978-3-8382-0970-8

166 *Peter Kaiser*
Das Schachbrett der Macht
Die Handlungsspielräume eines sowjetischen Funktionärs
unter Stalin am Beispiel des
Generalsekretärs des Komsomol
Aleksandr Kosarev (1929-1938)
Mit einem Vorwort von Dietmar Neutatz
ISBN 978-3-8382-1052-0

167 *Oksana Kim*
The Effects and Implications of Kazakhstan's Adoption of International Financial Reporting Standards
A Resource Dependence Perspective
With a foreword by Svetlana Vlady
ISBN 978-3-8382-0987-6

168 *Anna Sanina*
Patriotic Education in
Contemporary Russia
Sociological Studies in the Making
of the Post-Soviet Citizen
With a foreword by Anna Oldfield
ISBN 978-3-8382-0993-7

169 *Rudolf Wolters*
Spezialist in Sibirien
Faksimile der 1933 erschienenen
ersten Ausgabe
Mit einem Vorwort von Dmitrij Chmelnizki
ISBN 978-3-8382-0515-1

170 *Michal Vít, Magdalena M. Baran (eds.)*
Transregional versus National Perspectives on
Contemporary Central European History
Studies on the Building of Nation-States and Their
Cooperation in the 20th and 21st Century
With a foreword by Petr Vágner
ISBN 978-3-8382-1015-5

Part III **153**

Chapter 6: Influence of macro-frames on conflict resolution practice. Addressing exclusion perpetuated by binary conflict discourses of international relations................................**155**

   In the shadow of the international relations discourse 156
      Practical implications of naming initiatives "Track 2":
      impact on selection 157
      Practical implications of naming initiatives "Track 2":
      impact on dialogue..163
   Leaving the shadow: addressing patterns of marginalization
   influenced by the international relations discourse 168
      Conceptual alternatives 168
      Evolving Designs: rethinking the language of mediation................173
      Evolving Designs: rethinking dialogue and PSW............................177
      Evolving Designs in practice: transforming the Analytic Initiative...184
   Chapter 6 postscript: gender and other binaries
   that affect conflict resolution practice 192
   Chapter conclusions...195

Chapter 7: Marginalization specific to conflict resolution initiatives. Addressing the formation of dominant factions **197**

   Formation of a single dominant faction within initiatives 198
      Cultural intelligibility to the organizers 198
      Reliance on a dominant discourse external to the initiative 200
   Competition for domination and shifting marginalization..........203
   Recognizing and addressing domination and resulting
   marginalization 207
   Chapter conclusions...215

Chapter 8: Addressing marginalization patterns within the conflict resolution community **217**

   Competition among organizations 217
      Walking the talk: the case for the organizations
      preaching cooperation to lead by example......................................225
   Power struggles within teams 233

  Addressing marginalization within teams 242
 Chapter conclusions 247
Chapter 9: Lessons learned **249**
 Reflection: the learning and the key findings 250
 Action: Evolving Designs in Imagine Center's recent
 initiatives 255
 Questions for further research 261
 Postscript 263
Bibliography **267**
Index **277**

Abstract

The field of conflict resolution holds the promise of freeing approaches and policies concerning politics of identity from the fatalistic grip of realism. While the conceptual literature on conflicts has moved in this alternative direction, conflict resolution practice continues to rely on realist frames and acts as an unwanted auxiliary to official processes. Perpetuation of conflict discourses, marginalization, and exclusion of affected populations are widespread, caused by the overreliance of conflict resolution practice on the binary frames of classic international relations paradigms and also by the competitive and hierarchical relationships within the field itself.

This book learns from the reflection and action cycles customary for participatory action research (PAR) and collective auto-ethnography to expose patterns of exclusion and marginalization as well as the paradoxical reproduction of conflict-promoting frames in current conflict resolution practices applied to the Nagorno-Karabakh and Syrian cases. It builds on the work of postmodernist scholars, reflective practice, and discourse analysis to explore alternative and inclusive strategies and to propose the flexible methodology of Evolving Designs that carries a transformative potential for conflict resolution.

Acknowledgments

It is hard to find words to describe the depth of gratitude I feel to my family, friends, colleagues, and mentors for years of unwavering support that allowed me to complete this book that developed out of my dissertation.

First and foremost, I am grateful to my mentor, colleague, and dissertation committee chair Dr. Susan Allen for her advice, challenge, ongoing communication, feedback, and suggestions on numerous drafts of each chapter. I am particularly grateful to Susan for encouraging me to develop my own voice in the field and to stay true to my constructivist belief system, for her support to my choice of a not-very-traditional to conflict resolution action research methodology that proved to be invaluable and innovative both for the findings in this book and the practices that it touched.

I am thankful to my dissertation committee member Dr. Susan Hirsch for her amazing deconstructive and reconstructive touch that helped me to rethink the entire organization and structure of this book. I am grateful to Susan for her support in helping me develop the ethnographic angle of my research. And I am grateful to her for my times as a Graduate Teaching Assistant in the School for Conflict Analysis and Resolution (S-CAR) undergraduate program, where thanks to Susan's collegial approach, I felt a valued and integral part of the team working on innovation of curricula and teaching methods.

I am fascinated and feel extremely lucky to have worked with my dissertation committee member Dr. Jessica Srikantia, who effortlessly combined in her approach utmost care, emotional and intellectual support for my work, with an equally blunt challenge to the patriarchy, racism, classism, and many other "isms" subconsciously held by me and present in my writing. A great many of Jessica's comments made me pause my work, re-engage in reading, reflection, and self-questioning, very often leading to cardinal changes in my approaches to this book, practice, and life in general.

I am grateful to the School of Conflict Analysis and Resolution of George Mason University (GMU) for serving as my academic home during my PhD studies, and for the Dissertation Completion Grant that allowed me to concentrate on writing in the most intense stage of the research.

I am forever indebted to my close friend and colleague from the Imagine Center for Conflict Transformation (Imagine Center), linguist, Maria Karapetyan, who fully deserves to be named the chief editor of this book. From the very first line of the proposal to the very last line of this book, Maria has been the person with whom I discussed every section of every draft of this book; she was the first reader, the main critic, and the adviser. No time did Maria show that this work has been a burden for her, though it took weeks if not months of her time. I cannot imagine finishing the book without Maria's friendship and support.

I am very lucky to be surrounded in my work by a great team of friends and colleagues who are always supportive, always challenging, extremely smart and courageous, devoted to each other and the vision of peace. In addition to Maria Karapetyan, our team of current and former colleagues who supported me in writing this book includes Sona Dilanyan, Veronika Aghajanyan, Sergey Rumyansev, Pinar Sayan, Christopher Littlefield, Arzu Geybullayeva, Hamida Giyasbaily, Sevil Huseynova, and Zamira Abbasova. I want to thank them for their dedication, support, and the time spent reflecting, hearing, questioning, and advising. Most importantly, I am appreciative for their openness in allowing us to experiment in our practice with the insights gained through the action research process of my research. Without such support from the team, it would have been impossible to complete the "action" part of the reflection and action cycles of the research that resulted in this book. A particularly strong "thank you" goes to Sona Dilanyan on whose judgment and advice I relied when working through particularly sensitive passages.

I am grateful to my fellow students, Jacquelyn Greiff and Matthew Graville, in the Reflective Practice class at S-CAR, GMU, for all the time they devoted to reflection sessions that would support the research that resulted in this book. During the year-long period of our joint work on some of the Imagine Center's projects, Jacquelyn's perspicacity through all our reflective conversations in her office and on our flights to and from the project locations shaped many of the core ideas of this book.

I thank all the colleagues working in the Nagorno-Karabakh and Syrian conflict contexts who participated in this research and particularly its reflection and action part, yet who I cannot name in the interest of preserving their anonymity. The insights, findings, and innovations suggested here belong to them as much as they belong to me.

And I am most appreciative of the opportunity to express how incredibly lucky I am to have near me Zara Papyan—my best friend, my life partner, and my spouse—and my two boys Mark and Mikael, who tolerated me despite my continuous evening disappearances in the bedroom with books, papers, and laptops. I am deeply touched by the care, not least in form of an ongoing supply of tea and fruit, that kept me going through hours of writing, and for all the love expressed through undeserved hugs and cheers as I would emerge from my cave. I love you!

Foreword

Philip Gamaghelyan is not only the author of this book, but also an expert conflict resolution practitioner. The book you hold now represents a synthesis of expert insights from his years of practical engagement in conflict processes, presented with careful reflection. By pairing his own experience of over a decade of facilitation with reflective practice with colleagues and in-depth study of other conflict transformation literature, Philip offers us important insights that will inspire needed developments in the field of conflict resolution.

This book challenges us to create truly inclusive conflict transformation processes. So much of conflict is about exclusion. In deeply divided conflicts, the "other" is dehumanized, and their stories and perspectives dismissed. When we start to engage in these conflicts, getting to know them and their conversations, we begin to speak the conflict's language. That language risks perpetuating the conflict. The book challenges us to ask how dialogues on conflict issues can avoid perpetuating these exclusionary dynamics?

I have faced the struggle with exclusionary dynamics in my own work. When Philip came to the School for Conflict Analysis and Resolution, he worked with me on a dialogue series called Point of View. The first of these dialogues had taken place at George Mason University's conflict resolution retreat center, Point of View, just after the August 2008 war over South Ossetia. People from Tbilisi and Tskhinval(i) came together there and considered ways to address the ongoing humanitarian needs after the war. They needed each other to address issues such as missing persons (where information from the other side of the ceasefire line was helpful), prisoners held across the ceasefire line, etc. By the time Philip joined us in 2010, the dialogues had developed into a phase of increasing understanding across the dividing line. Philip was quick to point out to me that we had framed the dialogues as Georgian-South Ossetian dialogues. But, we also had people of mixed heritage participating in the dialogues. What of the participants who were part-Georgian and part-South Ossetian? Did the dialogues make them choose a side? Yes, they traveled to the dialogues from one side of the ceasefire line, but were they being constrained by the framing of the discussion as a two-sided conversation? Could they not also have unique perspectives, drawn from conversations with relatives across the dividing line? In fact, everyone on the dialogues each brought their own unique perspectives. With Philip's encouragement, we incorporated more thematic discussions that did not need to be framed as two-sided. As we turned to look at what would make prisoner release possible, we became a group of individuals, each with his/her own connections to the prisoner release efforts, each with his/her own expertise, and we worked on solving a shared problem. Yes, some of the group could meet only with the leadership in South Ossetia, and, yes, some of the group could meet only with the leadership in Georgia, but these were not the only defining aspects of the expertise participants brought. Some were legal experts, some were media experts, some worked with displaced people who had vocal opinions on the prisoner release issues, and some visited prisoners to monitor human rights. Drawing on these various kinds of expertise was important to allow the dialogue group to lay the groundwork that made the eventual prisoner release possible. By seeing the complexity of each participant's identity, we drew on the many strengths in the group.

All this points out that the suggestions offered by this book are timely and pragmatic. The book touches the core of the field of conflict analysis and resolution, asking us to improve our theory and our practices, and, ultimately, the structure of our field. Starting with how we conceive of conflict transformation dialogues, and how we invite individuals to join these dialogues, moving on to how a conflict mapping organically represents the people gathered in the room, based on their own ways of categorizing themselves, and then considering how to prevent dominant factions from commandeering conversations. Our field must build more inclusive structures, overcome the competition for funding that in practice makes a mockery of our theory of collaboration, and build teams that engage all members' voices with respect. Philip's many years of conflict resolution work allow him to speak with authority about approaches that have worked in practice.

The Participatory Action Research (PAR) methodology that informs this work was also essential to its success. Philip writes not only from his own experience, but also from that of the colleagues that joined him as co-researchers, reflecting together on their experiments with more inclusive conflict resolution practices. By engaging colleagues as co-researchers, Philip assured he was not only examining others' assumptions, but also putting his own assumptions up for examination. Philip's own auto-ethnography is a core part of the book, allowing him to tell his own stories of his forays into conflict transformation. In addition, a major strength here is the collective auto-ethnography he captures based on group reflection of their shared work. I hope Philip's work will be read not only for the important theoretical and practical insights offered here, but also as an example of methodological innovation that offers our field new possibilities in research. I see many more possibilities for the expansion of Participatory Action Research (PAR) in conflict resolution research.

In conclusion, I urge colleagues and students of conflict resolution to read this book attentively. Philip offers us guidance as we develop practices that more closely align with our constructivist and inclusive theories. And, he offers guidance on how to do conflict-appropriate research with PAR. There is, of course, still more to do in this direction. Philip is already working on more in-depth consideration of gender inclusivity in conflict transformation processes. And, I encourage readers to find additional ways to build on this revolutionary work.

Susan Allen, Ph.D.
Director, Center for Peacemaking Practice
Associate Professor, School for Conflict Analysis and Resolution
George Mason University

Abbreviations

ADR	Alternative Dispute Resolution
CDA	Critical Discourse Analysis
GMU	George Mason University
HSRB	Human Subjects Review Board
ICG	International Crisis Group
Imagine Center	Imagine Center for Conflict Transformation
ISIL	Islamic State of Levant
LGBTI	Lesbian, Gay, Bisexual, Transgender, Intersex
NATO	North Atlantic Treaty Organization
NGO	Non-Governmental Organization
NK	Nagorno-Karabakh
NKAO	Nagorno-Karabakh Autonomous Oblast
OSCE	Organization for Security and Cooperation in Europe
PAR	Participatory Action Research
PSW	Problem-Solving Workshop
S-CAR	School for Conflict Analysis and Resolution
SSR	Soviet Socialist Republic

Introduction

I entered the field of conflict analysis and resolution in 2004, and soon encountered interactive problem solving, also known as problem-solving workshop (PSW) and dialogue with their variations and adaptations as central methods of conflict resolution practice. Ever since, my career has been devoted to advancing conflict resolution practice in various areas of the world, primarily in the South Caucasus. At the initial stages of my conflict resolution career, I tried to learn the conventional methods of the field and apply them in conflict contexts where I worked. Later, I grew critical of some of the conventions. Among the first, I questioned the presumed need for the neutrality or impartiality of the facilitator and the suggestion to stay away from the history of conflict seen as a dividing phenomenon, and I worked on developing respective adaptations of the PSWs and dialogue. I strove to keep to their core, while experimenting with new elements, such as methods for working with memory and history or encouraging facilitation by insider-partials. Devotee to conflict resolution and believer in its inherent goodness, I would question the *effectiveness* of the practices employed, but not the *rationale* of specific practices themselves.

It was not until 2013, when I had an opportunity to work with a group of Syrian peace activists when I started suspecting that conflict resolution practices approached uncritically can sometimes not only fail to do good but could do harm. To quote Avruch, "concern with making our conflict interventions instrumentally effective raises—or should raise—ethical questions: efficiency for whom, in the service of what?" (Avruch 2012, 29). I saw the need to rethink my work, to rethink what I knew about conflict resolution and how I knew it.

From a conceptual standpoint, the conflict analysis and resolution theories do not always define conflict as a disagreement between or among preestablished sides. In conflict resolution practice, however, "sides" are central to our understanding of conflict. PSWs and dialogues are methods focused on the process of relationship building between or among the conflict sides and on interactive forms of imagining new solutions for addressing existing problems between or among them. The taken-for-granted assumption in these methods is the presence of a specific number of identifiable sides to conflict, typically of two sides. We commonly understand any conflict as a clash between them. From the beginning of the current Syrian conflict in 2011 and until 2013, when I started working on this book, the US and Western European media routinely portrayed it as a conflict between the Bashar Assad regime and the "opposition," by 2014 adding the Islamic State of Levant (ISIL) as a "side" and later yet started framing Syria as a multilateral conflict. In these early days, however, the binary frames prevailed. The analyses of international think tanks were more nuanced than that of media and acknowledged the presence of multiple identity groups, such as Alewites, Sunnis, Christians, Kurds, the Syrian Army, the Free Syrian Army, and various non-armed opposition groups. The think tanks also, however, framed the conflict itself as a struggle between the regime and the opposition and tried to fit the identity groups into one or the other. A report on Syria produced by the International Crisis Group (ICG) in 2013 consistently referred to "the regime" and "the opposition" as units of analysis. It described Alewites as supporters of the regime, Sunnis as supporters of the opposition and used phrases such as "the opposition should," showing that to the ICG, "the opposition" is an identifiable party to the conflict that is the binary opposite of the regime ("Syria's Mutating Conflict — International Crisis Group" 2013). Such framings dictated approaches to respective conflict resolution efforts. As the conflict was framed to be between a dictatorial regime and a fragmented opposition, the early intervention efforts led by the United States and its allies were directed at supporting and consolidating the opposition. Further, as the fragmentation of opposition was often framed as consisting of one wing leaning toward Islamic fundamentalism and another leaning toward democratic reform, the efforts were directed at the strengthening of the democratic wing. Other interventions, such as former UN Secretary General Kofi Annan's effort, were attempting to find a mediated solution between the "two sides" (Annan 2012).

In 2013, the binary framing seemed natural to me as well. When invited to facilitate a workshop for a group of Syrian peace activists, my colleagues and I initially followed the convention and framed the initiative as a dialogue between Assad and opposition supporters, before discovering that only the small minority of those present self-identified as belonging to either of these sides. It dawned on me then that I knew of no method that would help me integrate a group of Syrians of no side into a conflict resolution process. When describing conflict, I had learned to use the binary framing by default, without questioning the influence that such framing and subsequent interventions can have on the conflict. On the example of Syria, as we framed it as a conflict between two sides, the support for a particular side or a mediation that brought the sides together was appropriate. However, were we to frame the Syrian context as a fluid and chaotic struggle of numerous agendas and cross-cutting identities still united under the umbrella of the overarching Syrian identity, then boiling it all down to an over-simplified notion of "regime vs. opposition" would do little to help the situation. Such an approach would arbitrarily assign individuals and identity groups to one side or the other exacerbating the dichotomy that might not have been otherwise clearly pronounced, and then in a manifestation of a self-fulfilling prophecy, tried to bridge the divide it had itself created.

This is not to say, of course, that it is the mediators or the conflict resolution practitioners who construct conflicts or that the binary frames are never acceptable. Conflicts are typically in place well before we intervene. However, we should be open to a possibility that our framing and interventions could do further damage; that assuming a binary every time we see a conflict can pave the way for solidifying one. Yes, starting from 2011, Syria had some defined conflict sides, such as the Assad regime and specific armed groups opposing the regime. Nevertheless, large parts of the population did not identify with any of these actors. Many Alewites and Christians, routinely considered by commentators of that time as pro-regime, were opposed to it while they also feared the armed opposition. Moreover, many of those opposing the regime included groups, such as various nonviolent movements, ethnic minorities, nonaligned youth groups, intellectuals, to name just a few, who were opposing the armed rebels just as much. More importantly, a great many people still identified themselves as Syrians, a shared identity, and strongly resisted any attempt to classify them as pro-regime, anti-regime, Alewite, Sunni,

Kurdish, Islamist, or anything else that could suggest a division. Yet these voices were rarely heard, as they were neither "the regime" nor "the opposition." They were excluded and marginalized, among others, by the conflict resolution community.[1]

My questioning started from my inability to apply the concept of "sides" in the context of a particular initiative that defied all analytic frames I was familiar with. It seemed a minor inconvenience at first, but at a closer look, turned out that "sides" were central to the literature on conflict resolution practice — the first fallen domino that would bring down many others as my research progressed.

Questions I am aiming to address

At the time of my involvement with the Syrian dialogue mentioned above, I was working actively on a research project titled "How is Change Sustained?" Convinced that conflict resolution practices inherently do good, I was concerned with improving their effectiveness and longer-term influence of the change they produce. Yet I was suddenly confronted with the realization that in the Syrian case, the conventional binary frame of the conflict resolution practices that I aimed to make more effective resulted in marginalization of the majority of Syrians.

This realization prompted me to explore whether the marginalization embedded in binary frames was unique to the evolving context of Syria, and whether the contexts where the binary frame had long been established, such as the Nagorno-Karabakh conflict, were better

---

[1] I do not use the words "marginalization" and "exclusion" from conflict resolution processes interchangeably. By "marginalization" I refer to a context when the voice of an individual or a group affected by the conflict is silenced or continually dismissed. By "exclusion" I refer to a relationship where an individual or a group is actively precluded from physically taking part in the conflict resolution process. One can be excluded from a process but not marginalized as her voice finds a way to break through, often thanks to access to external to the context academic or media resources influencing the process. At the same time, one can be included and physically present in the conflict resolution process and yet dismissed or silenced and therefore marginalized. As it is not practically possible to always involve everyone in conflict resolution initiatives, exclusion in itself can be neutral. It becomes problematic, however, when its intention or impact is the marginalization of communities or individuals affected by the conflict.

suited for conventional and binary dialogue designs. Or was it possible that binary frames could marginalize affected populations there too? And were the binary frames the only trap in the conflict resolution discourse that had the potential to marginalize? I did not know the answers, but I knew that I could no longer assume that change produced by conflict resolution practice was necessarily positive and ask, "How is Change Sustained?" I now had a prior question: what were the possible variants of that change and was it possible that some of the change produced marginalization or other harm?

My main intention for this book is not solely to be critical. I continue to be devoted to the conflict resolution field and believe in its promise and potential for changing societies for the better. I also remain and plan to remain a scholar-practitioner in this field, working on its theory and practice. My research questions, therefore, have the goal of reflecting on my own practice and that of my colleagues, identifying patterns that could be marginalizing or otherwise harmful of affected populations, raising the awareness of my colleagues in regard to such practices, and, most importantly, exploring possible inclusive alternatives.

The following questions drive this inquiry:

- Are binary frames problematic in the Syrian conflict only or do they adversely affect conflict resolution practice in other conflict contexts as well?
- Are there other patterns of conflict resolution practice that (re)produce conflict or that contribute to exclusion from the peace processes of populations affected by conflict and marginalization of peace constituencies?
- Do we need to rethink not only conflict resolution but conflict itself in order to develop adequate responses to today's challenges?
- If the answer to any of to the above questions is positive, what can be the alternative approaches that help us conceive inclusive conflict resolution practices?

The organization of the text

The book is organized into three parts and nine chapters, including the conclusions. Following this introduction, Part I contains three chapters. Chapter 1 is a critical review of the theories that traditionally informed policymaking and conflict resolution practice. It is also an exploration of alternative theories that can help us rethink conflict. I start with theories most often used by the policymaking community in understanding and addressing conflicts, namely with realist and liberal theories of international relations and criticize their rigid and binary frames that contribute to the reproduction of conflicts. I then examine conflict resolution theories that position themselves as a critique and alternative to international relations, yet in practice borrow its frames, as a result similarly contributing to the reproduction of the conflict discourses.

The contemporary conflict analysis and resolution theories, however, are much broader than its segments that take after international relations. They range from the long-known in the field positivist social-psychological needs theories of Burton and his colleagues and followers and post-positivist structural theories of Galtung to increasingly popular critical and hermeneutic paradigms and to post-structuralist and postmodernist approaches that either implicitly or explicitly reject dichotomies and the very notion of bounded groups as units of analysis. The discussion of the potential of the latter schools, as well as of various directions of critical theory, in transforming not only conflict analysis theories but also conflict resolution practice concludes the chapter, setting the stage for the discussion of methodology.

As one of the aims of this book was to redefine my practice and that of my colleagues who agreed to engage in this journey with me, I relied on participatory action research (PAR) as the primary methodological choice that has a transformative potential. The methodology of this project, therefore, was never only a tool for inquiry. It was an evolving intervention in itself that helped me rethink the concept of conflict and the practices of conflict resolution, and therefore deserves its own chapter. Chapter 2 details the development of the methodology for this book with a hope that it might be useful in future conflict resolution research.

Chapter 3 is short and auto-ethnographic. I reflect there on the events in my life that led me to conflict resolution work and to this book. I expose my biases and epistemological standing to your (my reader's) judgment.

Part II of the book that contains Chapters 4 and 5, I wrote from the position of collective auto-ethnography, and in a form of a thick description of two initiatives led by teams that I was part of. These cases present a close-up view of patterns of exclusion and marginalization perpetrated by conflict resolution practice in the contexts of Nagorno-Karabakh and Syria. The Syrian initiative discussed in Chapter 4 is a dialogue project with an initial exclusionary frame where the workshop design created a binary that deprived of voice the majority of participants who did not see themselves as part of the conflict sides, yet where the facilitators and the participants worked together to find new and inclusive frames. An initiative from the Nagorno-Karabakh context presented in Chapter 5 followed the reversed trajectory: started with an aim to include all possible conflict voices, it demonstrated an unlimited potential in producing exclusion and marginalization as it progressed.

In Part II, I look deep into two particular cases. In Part III that contains Chapters 6–8, to the contrary, I zoom out and focus on patterns of exclusion and marginalization as learned from the analysis of over 30 conflict resolution initiatives conducted in Syria, Nagorno-Karabakh, and other contexts. The critique is followed by a discussion of alternative and inclusive models of conflict resolution practices.

Chapter 6 explores how the macro-frames external to conflict resolution practice influence that practice in ways that contribute to the marginalization and exclusion of key groups affected by conflict and to the perpetuation of conflict discourses. The specific macro-frames discussed in the chapter are the binary frames of international relations and their influence on conflict resolution initiatives, as well as possible alternative frames and approaches to conflict. A number of other binaries, particularly the gender binary, are also discussed although in less detail. I conclude that these frames advance narrow definitions of conflict and identity and that they privilege the violent or nationalist extremes while marginalizing many of those affected by conflict yet not fitting neatly into predefined ethnic or gender roles.

Chapter 7 looks into exclusion and marginalization specific to conflict resolution initiatives. It looks into hierarchical relations between conflict resolution professionals and participants, and into the emergence of dominant factions within conflict resolution initiatives that coalesce around a common discourse pushing forward a particular exclusivist agenda and marginalizing others. Such factions can get formed around a macro-frame located outside the initiative, such as the international human rights regime, or around an affiliation with a source of power external to the initiative, such as belonging to a government, or through a greater cultural intelligibility of some of the participants to the organizers. The patterns of marginalization covered by this chapter are highly context-specific and are, therefore, amenable to change more easily than the ones discussed in Chapter 6.

Finally, Chapter 8 discusses patterns of exclusion and marginalization within the community of conflict resolution practitioners facilitated by such common to capitalist organization of the society practices as competition over resources, gate-keeping, or strict hierarchies within teams that suppress creativity and participation. After exposing the contradiction between these common practices and the values of cooperation and inclusivity advanced by that same practice in conflict zones, I explore alternative approaches to interorganizational and team relations.

Part I

Part I of this book lays the ground for the main arguments presented in Parts II and III. I start Part I with the critical review of the mainstream conflict resolution theories, which as I argue serve to reproduce rather than solve conflicts, followed by discussion of their conceptual alternatives. These alternatives point toward participatory research methods positioned at the intersection of research, theory, and practice and are discussed in Chapter 2. I end Part I with a short autoethnographic sketch intended to explain why and how I came to this work, and what are the values and personal and methodological bias that guide my writing.

Chapter 1
Critical review of conflict resolution theories

Conflict resolution practice has been rapidly diversifying and can have many shapes, ranging from negotiations to collaborations between artists, and a number of these interventions move away from binary frames. The interventions that explicitly aim at analyzing or addressing the ethnically or ethno-religiously framed violent conflicts in search of sustainable solutions, however, traditionally follow the lead of international relations field and frame conflicts in binary terms. Many of these theories and practices, including PSWs, consultations, and multitrack diplomacy, explicitly position themselves as auxiliary to international relations and borrow the preestablished binary frames of the latter. Researchers at Uppsala University, one of the leading research institutions in the field, define armed conflict as "a contested incompatibility that concerns government or territory or both, where the use of force *between two parties* [emphasis added] results in at least 25 battle-related deaths a year" (Themnér and Wallensteen 2011).

As the field of conflict resolution developed, certain theories and respective practices aimed to break away from the binary frames of international relations. Some did so more successfully than others. Parts of conflict analysis and resolution theories reproduced the binary frames of international relations. Other parts of conflict analysis and resolution theories developed into an interdisciplinary field that moved increasingly toward the constructivist paradigm, drifting away from the binary frames of international relations. Conflict resolution practice, however, was slow to follow. Today constructivist analysis is routinely followed by positivist intervention models that continue to replicate the international relations frames. A few conflict resolution approaches, particularly narrative mediation, made the transition and have been offering constructivist practices particularly when working with interpersonal and family conflict as well as organizational conflicts. These practices, however, struggled to find their application when it comes to violent political conflict.

I start this review with the critical analysis of international relations theories and the dominant trends in the conflict analysis and resolution field that follow the established binary and position themselves as a complement to international relations. I then shift toward alternative trends in conflict analysis and resolution that defy the binary, and on to approaches that view ethnicity and identity as socially constructed categories and that problematize the essentialization of ethnicity and identity in traditional conflict resolution literature. Within the constructivist paradigm, I discuss elicitive and reflective practices that offer conceptually alternative intervention models and postmodernist theories of ethnicity and nationalism that offer alternative language for framing conflict.

Embarking on the journey that would become this book, I was aware that I myself am embedded in the discursive frames that I am planning to critique and find alternatives to. How could I, a person whose identity and worldview was defined by certain structures, see outside of them? In search of methodologies that would facilitate the development of reflective awareness, I was influenced by the structuration theory of Giddens with its rejection of the structure vs. agency dichotomy and argument that while actors are embedded in structures, the structures in turn are reproduced by actors and, therefore, are amenable to transformation. Through structuration, I came to PAR as a corresponding methodology that offers an alternative form of understanding research, questioning the researcher and her worldview, and forging a space where structures were accounted for and the transformation was possible.

Binary frames in conflict resolution

In the international relations field that long was at the forefront of studying conflict, the main division arguably is between the realist and liberal schools of thought. The former typically sees violent conflict as a natural condition of human behavior, with the latter accepting at least the theoretical possibility of sustainable peace. Despite these differences, both realist and liberal schools are based on a similar set of core positivist assumptions that prioritize the state as their main unit of analysis and frame conflict in binary terms. These frames have been accepted also by a number of approaches in the conflict resolution field that position themselves as a complement to international relations and share the umbrella of Track 2 diplomacy.

Realist theories of international relations

Realism has long been the most influential school in international relations. What unites many different schools of thought under the umbrella of realism is their focus on the international systems and their disregard for the internal political structures of the states. Realists believe that the state behavior is influenced mainly by their external environment and not by their internal characteristics. The central postulate of this family of theories is that the international system forces states to maximize their relative power vis à vis the others, because it is the optimal way to maximize their security (Mearsheimer 2003, 17, 21).

There are also disagreements within the different schools of realism. Human nature realism, represented primarily by Morgenthau, advances a Hobbesean argument that human nature is inherently competitive (Hans Joachim Morgenthau 1978). Defensive realism, or structural realism, argues that states aim to survive by maintaining the balance of power (Waltz 2010). Offensive realism has similarities with both, but also has major differences (Mearsheimer 2003). Offensive realism and defensive realism agree that the cause of state competition is the anarchic structure of the international system. This is also the key disagreement of offensive realism with human nature realism that argues that it is the lust for power inherent in states (or their leaders) that causes states to compete. At the same time, offensive realism agrees with human nature realism on goals: states aim to gain as much power as they can, with hegemony as an ultimate goal, in sharp disagreement with defensive realism that maintains that states aim to survive by maintaining the balance of power. Moreover, unlike offensive realism, defensive realism warns against acquiring too much power as it can mobilize others and backfire.

Power and competition, rather than cooperation or negotiation, are seen by realists as avenues for working with conflict. A number of other schools of realism differ from the mentioned three in some aspects, but they share the key principles mentioned above. Relevant to the topic of this research, states are clearly defined in realism as the main actors in conflict. The realist approach, therefore, prevalent in international relations, has the binary opposition of states in its very core and is openly disinterested in evolving intrastate environments and not-well-defined stakeholders. The marginalized populations, as well as any other nonstate actors, are left out in this paradigm.

Liberal theories of international relations

From within the international relations field, the base assumptions of realism are criticized by various liberal schools. Classical liberalism is closely linked with the names of the Enlightenment thinkers such as Locke, Montesquieu, Tocqueville, and Jefferson. Unlike realism, liberalism is very much concerned with the internal characteristics of states and, similar to other positivist schools of thought that have their roots in the Enlightenment, is based on the assumption that reason and knowledge can advance reform, prevent abuse by the state, and resolve conflicts.

The key assumptions of liberalism, which place it in seeming opposition to realism, are that the internal characteristics of states vary considerably, and these differences have profound effects on state behavior (Mearsheimer 2003, 15). As a consequence, some forms of internal political organization, such as democracy, are seen as inherently preferable to others, such as authoritarianism, and are believed to lead to peaceful international relations.

The often-cited liberal theories of international relations argue for the possibility of absolute rather than relative gains. Key arguments of liberal schools include the following:

- high level of economic interdependence among states makes them unlikely to fight each other (see, for example, McMillan 1997);
- the democratic peace hypothesis or that democracies do not go to war with each other (see, for example, Ray 1998), an idea

that originated with Kant's "Perpetual Peace" where he argued that the majority of people would never vote to go to war, unless in self-defense (Kant 2007 [orig. 1795]);
- and international institutions enhance the prospects for cooperation among states and reduce the likelihood of war (see, for example, Keohane 2005).

As liberalism accepts the possibility of absolute and not relative gains, positive-sum conflict resolution models and sustainable peace are seen as attainable. Rational choice models and mediation aimed at finding areas of mutual interest and win-win solutions are some of the main intervention practices associated with these theories.

Similar to realists, liberal theories have states as the main units of analysis, and the focus is primarily on identifying or creating conditions under which states are ready to agree to a negotiated solution. In situations of internal conflict or when the conflict involves nonstate actors, the approach is a push for a negotiated settlement that requires identification of a consolidated enough actor that can serve as a conflict party and who could sit across the table from the state actor.

Today, however, conflicts are rarely an exclusive interstate affair or a struggle for power by well-identified parties within the state. Even in conflicts when two states are involved, such as in the case with Nagorno-Karabakh or the United States and Iraq, various nonstate actors, nonrecognized states, or unaligned groups of populations are often as important to the conflict dynamics as the interstate relations. The negotiation approach might have worked as the primary tool of conflict resolution in the previous two centuries when states were presumed to maintain a monopoly over the use of large-scale violence. However, in today's context the focus on negotiated settlement alone can be detrimental to conflict resolution.

For one, the state actors rarely negotiate with nonstate actors or with nonrecognized states. As of 2017, the cases of Nagorno-Karabakh, Syria, Georgia-South Ossetia, Georgia-Abkhazia, and many others include situations where the recognized state refuses to accept as a negotiating partner any stakeholder that is not an internationally recognized state. In cases where negotiations are ongoing, agreements are very rare, and, whenever reached, are likely to fail due to pressures both from within and outside the societies. Yet the question whether negotiations are the appropriate way to move forward is rarely asked. Instead, all the efforts are directed toward finding or creating actors that could, plausibly, look like a legitimate negotiating partner.

In the next few paragraphs I aim to demonstrate on the example of the Syrian and Nagorno-Karabakh cases how the international relations approaches fail to bring the conflicts closer to solution. In the Nagorno-Karabakh context discussed in more details in Chapters 3 and 5, the leadership of the unrecognized Nagorno-Karabakh Republic, a key actor that is at the center of the conflict, is not allowed to the table and is represented by the government of the Republic of Armenia. The latter, an internationally recognized state, negotiates with the government of the Republic of Azerbaijan with the help of a mediator trio representing the governments of the United States, France, and Russia. The Republic of Armenia certainly should be at the table, as it has its role in the conflict, is in an open confrontation with Azerbaijan, and is likely to participate as a party should there be another war. At the same time, while the Republic of Armenia fully backs the Nagorno-Karabakh leadership militarily and politically, the Republic of Armenia and the unrecognized Nagorno-Karabakh Republic are not the same entity and often have divergent political line. While the Armenian government has been stressing its willingness to find a compromise solution, the authorities in Nagorno-Karabakh have often stated that they would not accept any agreement signed by the government of Armenia that is not to its liking and so far expressed dissatisfaction with all the proposals that were on the table. And indeed, the government of Armenia marred in corruption and allegations of illegal electoral practices has little legitimacy with the Armenian society. As a result, it hardly can afford to sign an agreement, as any possible agreement would be deemed controversial and is likely to lead to active wave of protests and mobilization by nationalist opposition. Neither it has mechanisms for imposing an agreement on Nagorno-Karabakh Armenians against their will. Due to the convention in international relations that prioritizes state actors, we have a situation where a party that is in a position to implement an agreed upon solution (should such an agreement be reached), the authorities of the unrecognized Nagorno-Karabakh Republic, is excluded from the peace process, while a party that has no legitimacy to sign and no leverage to enforce the implementation of an agreement, the government of the recognized Republic of Armenia, is at the table. Not surprisingly, the negotiations are long considered to be a farce by all the societies involved, and no agreement has been signed for over 20 years of negotiations, despite the principled support that the two negotiating governments expressed up to the recent past to various framework documents that outline the presumed eventual deal.

Further, the binary framing of the conflict that allows the governments of the Republics of Armenia and Azerbaijan to monopolize the peace process marginalizes populations that have suffered from this conflict directly. The Nagorno-Karabakh Armenians are left out of the negotiations, yet at least thanks to their affiliation with an unrecognized state of the Nagorno-Karabakh Republic, their presence is partially acknowledged through periodic visits of international mediators and the leadership of the Republic of Armenia, and some consultations with them in regard to the possible settlement. The populations that do not have access to any state or quasi-state entity, on the other hand, such as the Armenians and Azerbaijanis displaced by war or ethnic minorities, are silenced altogether. As a consequence, the solutions discussed take into consideration the interests of those at the table, the governments of the Republics of Azerbaijan and Armenia, and of Russia, the United States, and France, and not of the populations who suffered and still suffer from conflict. Such an approach, I argue, is not only unethical but is also unpractical and it did not bring us closer to any solution.

After over 20 years of failed negotiations and the ongoing exclusion of the affected populations, one would think, ground would be ready for questioning the adequacy of the interstate negotiation format for this conflict. Yet as of 2017, no such questioning has happened. Since the international relations theories have a tight grip on conflict discourses, the analysis of the failures remains within the confines of the negotiations approach and vocabulary. The absence of ripeness or of a mutually hurting stalemate (Zartman and Berman 1982), the absence of will from the political actors, corruption, and other political or economic explanations are used to explain why the presumably adequate format of negotiations would consistently fail. And so immersed are we in the international relations paradigm that we rarely question the negotiations theory itself; we do not even seem to think that there might be alternatives.

I recognize, however, that from the point of view of the international relations field, the Nagorno-Karabakh case, with its relatively well-defined actors, might look like a negotiable case. Maslow comes to mind with his "if all you have is a hammer, everything looks like a nail." At the same time the second case under the scrutiny in this book, the Syrian conflict that started in 2011, must be a negotiator's nightmare. It looks nothing like a nail. One actor, Assad's regime, has been clear and visible. However, from the very first day, there has not been a counterpart. Syria, therefore, could give an even better reason to question the binary framing of conflicts, a reason to contemplate interventions other than the ones that assume binary. And while with time the growing number of actors on the ground forced the analysts of all backgrounds to question the applicability of binary models to Syria, the policy community continued to see the conflict either from a realist perspective as a proxy-war between global and regional powers or from liberal perspective as a need to forge and support a coherent moderate opposition force that can take control of Syria and engage in its eventual liberal-democratic reshaping. To take the Maslow analogy a step further, the international relations approach seemed to be that while the tool is still the hummer, and there is no nail, we will forge a nail.

From the early days of the Syrian conflict, the media and think tanks have been busy with a search of a worthy liberal counterpart to the Assad regime. Could it be the Free Syrian Army? Could it be a coalition of armed groups? Or the Kurds? If there is no one already, how can the pro-western opposition be consolidated to create such a group? In other words, the main question did not seem to be how to make sense of Syria. It was, instead, how to influence the situation in a way that an identifiable and acceptable party could emerge, so that Syria could start looking more like a two-sided conflict we know.

When it comes to Syria, the main articulated alternative to this liberal approach for a long time had been the realist one that saw the conflict as a proxy war where the external powers that are not interested in a negotiated settlement are supporting either the Assad regime or the overthrow of Assad in favor of a government that is to their liking. With all their differences, then, the liberal and the realist approaches have one thing in common: they have "sides," the government and a possible consolidated opposition to the government, as the main units of analysis.

By 2016 and 2017, most everyone seemed to acknowledge that Syria has become a complicated and multifaceted conflict and could not be explained through simple binary terms (Huffington Post 2016; New York Times 2016; International Crisis Group 2017; CNN 2017). But has the Syrian conflict ever been a conflict of a particular opposition group with the government? It started in 2011 as a popular movement of Syrians from all walks of life and all backgrounds for better governance, freedom of expression, and other liberties. No group that has had a claim to be the alternative to the regime, including the Free Syrian Army, other rebels, the Kurds, or lately ISIL, spoke for a broad enough coalition. And if what started in 2011 in Syria were various movements that served as voice of very diverse populations and not a two-party conflict, then why did we invest years of unsuccessful effort into trying to reduce these movements into one identifiable group that could serve as an alternative to Assad? Is our attachment to seeing every conflict as a dichotomy insurmountable?

Reducing the Syrian conflict to the Assad-defined opposition duality for the first few years of the conflict meant empowering the two violent extremes at the expense of everyone else. It meant that the majority of Syrians who were neither Assad nor violent and identifiable opposition lost their voices and were being forced to either take a side with one of the extremes or be silenced. The result was that a great many Christians and Alewites who initially opposed Assad ended up siding with him as they feared opposition groups more. Some others formed their own conflict parties, leading to ongoing formation and reformation of numerous oppositions. Yet many others, arguably the overwhelming majority, who see themselves as Syrians and not as Assad or ISIL or particular opposition group, and who could be the uniting force and the natural peace constituency, are marginalized and voiceless as they do not exist on any known conflict map[2] that takes into consideration only identifiable "parties."

To summarize, the liberal approaches and the win-win negotiation theories they espouse work mainly for the cases with well-defined actors that believe they have a conflict, yet accept each other's legitimacy. When it comes to evolving environments, however, the inherently dualistic negotiation theory tries to make the environment work for itself rather than working with the environment, often creating and sustaining divisions that initially did not exist.

In the shadow of Track 1: interactive problem solving

The international relations field, of course, is not the only one today that studies conflict. The conflict resolution field has been growing as an alternative, bringing with it criticism of the international relations. Within the conflict resolution field itself, however, a number of approaches positioning themselves as complementary to international relations and sharing an umbrella of "Track 2 diplomacy" moved to the forefront of addressing violent conflicts. What is Track 2 diplomacy? It is a term coined in the early 1980s by Montville, a retired US diplomat and academic, who has been advocating for addition of civic and nonformal methods to the arsenal of conflict settlement in addition to official diplomacy or Track 1. The Track 2 approach remains popular in conflict resolution today as evidenced by many ongoing initiatives worldwide using that title. Recent academic works on the topic further point to its contemporary relevance (see, for example, Jones 2015).

Montville's approach is commendable, particularly coming from a former diplomat, in giving voice in conflict resolution to the civil society and not only governmental actors. Yet simultaneously, I see this term to be detrimental to its own stated goal, assuming the goal is some form of sustainable and equitable peace.

---

2   See, for example, the analysis focused on the US, Russia, Assad, ISIL, and a few other major actors by the September 2015 ICG report on Syria at: https://www.crisisgroup.org/middle-east-north-africa/eastern-mediterranean/syria/new-approach-southern-syria. Accessed on April 4, 2017.

First, the track is numbered "2," described also as work with the "pre-influentials," and putting it in a clear subordination to the track numbered "1" or work with "influentials." In other words, the equitable relations within and between the societies are acknowledged, but branded as secondary to the relations between the political elites. This logic led to the subsequent branding of the work with general populations, including youth, marginalized groups, communities affected by war and others, as "Track 3" or "grassroots," something of a tertiary importance.

What makes the Track 2 approaches perhaps most ineffective is the contempt held toward them by the very Track 1 representatives whose work Track 2 aims to complement. In his foreword to the recent book *Track Two Diplomacy: in Theory and Practice*, the former Secretary of State George Shultz writes: "To be honest, I was often somewhat leery of it ... my concern was that it would get in the way of our official diplomatic efforts and confuse others as to where the United States stood on various matters. More than once, I gave instructions to State Department officials to inform a foreign government in no uncertain terms that the US Government had nothing to do with this or that Track Two initiative...." After ending his career as an official, he somewhat softens the attitude by writing: "I now realize that properly done Track Two does not seek to 'get in the way' of Track One diplomacy,... but rather complement it" (Jones 2015, ix). Proponents of Track 2 approaches, therefore, are finding themselves consistently in an uncomfortable position of trying to assist and complement the official efforts, all the while the officials see them as a confusing nuisance that "gets in the way."

The second problem with the term "Track 2 diplomacy" is that named after "Track 1 diplomacy," it has no independent meaning and is doomed to act as a shadow of the latter, constrained by its frames, vocabulary, aims, and methods. Yet Track 1 diplomacy is not necessarily an endeavor that exists to resolve conflicts, but an activity aimed at advancing the interests of a particular state, which might or might not coincide with conflict resolution.

Interactive problem solving

Interactive problem solving also known as problem-solving workshop or PSW represents one key family of Track 2 approaches that aim to assist Track I negotiations in developing political solutions. Initiated by John Burton, the PSW emerged simultaneously as a critique and a complement to international relations. In its early days, the PSW was heavily influenced by psychology in general and Maslow's hierarchy of human needs specifically. John Burton agreed with Maslow that meeting human needs was central to conflict resolution, while at the same time rejecting the notion that needs are hierarchical and arguing that they are all pursued simultaneously (Burton 1990). By moving the human needs to the forefront of conflict resolution, Burton, a disillusioned former diplomat himself, attempted to shift the focus of conflict resolution from states to people.

The PSW originated not as an independent process, but once again, a process that complements official negotiations and was initially led by former diplomats. However, considering the roots of the PSW in psychology, many of the second-generation theorists of it were social-psychologists. Fisher and Keashly, for example, both with PhD in social-psychology and major theorists of problem solving, see Track I mediation (official negotiations) and arbitration as key conflict resolution practices and the PSW, which they also call "consultation," as a complementary mechanism to official negotiations (R. J. Fisher and Keashly 1991, 33).

The vision that PSW should be seen as a process complementary to official negotiations remained central through a few decades of its existence and adaptations. Unlike negotiations, the PSW is not aimed at achieving an immediate resolution to the conflict. It is focused instead on moving away from adversarial positions and analyzing the conflict from the viewpoint of needs, fears, concerns, and hopes of the involved societies, followed by joint explorations of core issues sustaining the conflict and ways of addressing them (Burton 1969; H. Kelman 1972). The PSW is an open-ended analytical process that allows the participants to explore various conflict dynamics, their interrelationship, and the relationship of the participants with these dynamics.

As described by Kelman and Cohen, the format of the PSW is informal: the participants are asked to collaboratively design the agenda of the meeting and the ground rules, thus breaking with a legalistic atmosphere typical for negotiations. The informal atmosphere, they continue, has "the potential for producing changes in the participants' perceptions and attitudes and thus facilitating creative problem solving" (H. C. Kelman and Cohen 1976, 79).

The classic model of the PSW might require major adjustments should it be useful in a conflict like the Syrian one. The PSW, if seen as a process complementary to the official negotiations, has to emulate a negotiation format in many of its characteristics. One of the main PSW theorists, Kelman, puts a major emphasis on the presence of identifiable *sides* in the conflict and their formal leadership. When discussing participant selection, Kelman similarly stresses the belonging of the prospective participants to these conflict *sides*. According to Kelman and Cohen, and supported by other PSW theorists, the PSWs "are intended to give participants the freedom, opportunity, and impetus to move away from the rigid reiteration of official positions and from efforts to justify their own *side* and score points against the other *side*" [emphasis added] (H. C. Kelman and Cohen 1976, 83). Kelman and Cohen continue: "We would argue that the ideal participants [...] would be individuals who are at an intermediate distance from the official leadership" (H. C. Kelman and Cohen 1976, 84). The focus on sides is very central in the writing of other PSW theorists as well, including those who made significant changes to the model (see, for example, Fisher and Keashly 1991; Babbitt and Steiner 2009).

When working on a conflict such as the Syrian one where it is hard to identify clear sides, the PSW approach in its classic form faces a challenge that mirrors the one faced by official negotiations. By having an identifiable conflict "side," recruiting participants based on their position in relation to the leadership of the "sides," and by pursuing an aim of achieving understanding of the "other side," the PSW effectively rewards those who took a side and chose violence even if these groups represent only the small minority of the population, thus empowering the extremes, and producing or reproducing discourses of dichotomy. Conversely, and similar to negotiations, such an approach excludes from the process everyone who does not have a "side," even when they are the clear majority and a ready peace constituency.

At the same time, it is important to stress here that PSW approaches are often flexible, open to exploration and the search for untapped and previously unknown opportunities. As such, PSWs are adaptable and, thus, their elements can be used to work in not well-definable and evolving environments like Syria. To be useful in such an environment, however, a rethinking of many of the base assumptions of the PSW is necessary. Part of the task of the current research is to contribute to such a rethinking.

Alternative to binary frames in conflict resolution

In the 1990s and 2000s, a number of theorists started looking critically at the approaches that closely replicated the international relations frames and started developing alternatives. Among these models a few are discussed below. Diamond's and McDonald's multitrack model that stressed the importance of including in the peace process actors other than governments has become a classic of conflict resolution. Ury's best-sellers popularized conflict resolution and started bringing into the mainstream discourse various alternative methods of approaching conflict. Allen's theory looks into various types of networks, concluding that only inclusive networks contribute to conflict resolution, while exclusive networks serve to sustain conflicts. Galtung's structuralist approach, while not prescribing any resolution methods, questions the primacy of the rational choice approaches in understanding conflict.

Multitrack models of conflict resolution

The multitrack approach to conflict resolution criticizes the notion that states are the only relevant parties to conflict and suggests that it is necessary to work on a variety of levels simultaneously to achieve sustainable peace. The concept of the multitrack diplomacy was developed by Diamond and McDonald as a response to the inefficiency of government mediation. Multitrack diplomacy suggests working on a number of levels, including Government; Nongovernment/Professional; Business; Private Citizen; Research, Training, and Education;

Activism; Religion; Funding; and Communications and the Media tracks (Diamond 1996).

The multitrack approach suggests parallel work with every possible institution, group and constituency one can think of. Multitrack diplomacy interventions, therefore, are more likely to contribute to the resolution of a complex conflict such as the one over Nagorno-Karabakh or in Syria than Track 1 negotiations alone.

The multitrack approach, however, is still bound by the format of two "sides," having these as an overarching point of reference for involving actors of various levels. Further, multitrack diplomacy in its current format resembles a "kitchen sink" approach that offers to address every thinkable actor, factor, and dynamic simultaneously. And while the approach is likely to bring results if implemented, given the scarcity of resources available for conflict resolution, addressing even a few of the tracks is a complex task, and addressing all of them together and in a coordinated manner is not very practical.

Meta-conflict resolution is a similar approach, which suggests that many of the existing conflict resolution methods taken alone are not enough to adequately explain or address conflicts and a comprehensive multilevel approach is needed. Different from a multitrack approach, however, it does not predetermine what are the set number of "tracks" where the work has to be done, and advocates instead for a facilitated process where the stakeholders can agree on the major facets of a particular conflict that will need to be addressed. This agreement can be followed up by development of a comprehensive intervention that addresses the identified needs which can include structural dynamics, such as political, legal, and economic, as well as psycho-cultural dynamics, such as attitudes, relationships, and divided histories (Fitzduff and INCORE 2002).

Network theory

Allen's and her colleagues' work on social networks advocates for the need for coordination among nongovernmental actors involved in conflict resolution on the ground, putting a big emphasis on questions of inclusion and exclusion. Allen sees a qualitative difference between networks that support conflict and networks that support peace efforts: the former are exclusive in nature, and the latter are inclusive. She writes that in exclusive networks the social capital "can fuel conflict by exacerbating conflict dividing lines." At the same time, inclusive networks can "support conflict resolution by creating cross-cutting ties engaging in constructive conflict resolution processes." Allen continues, suggesting that "networks which include both intra-group ties and inter-group cross-cutting ties are those which support peacebuilding" (Allen Nan 2008, 173).

In their article-reflection on six years of action research, Garb and Allen discuss how Georgian-Abkhazian peacebuilders developed a "coordination network based on cooperative working relationships between themselves, their organizations, their citizen peacebuilding initiatives, and the official actors." Coordination here refers to "negotiations that are aimed at increasing the efficacy of separate or related efforts." Building networks, in turn, is seen by them as a way of strengthening the capacity of peacebuilders and enhancing the peace process. The process of building coordinating networks among organizations working on the Georgian-Abkhazian conflict did not come without the consideration of potential challenges, including but not limited to "competition for funding and prestige, differences in conflict resolution approaches, difficulties of regular communication among conflict interveners living in different parts of the world, and unwillingness on the part of the outside interveners to give up autonomy." Garb and Allen conclude that several factors make inclusive networks effective: complete inclusivity and transparency, in-person meetings, lack of a formal organizational structure, autonomy of each member, an integrative agreement focus, and a culture of coordination, where rather than seeing each other as competitors, the participants create partnerships that strengthen the whole peacebuilding community (Garb and Allen Nan 2006, 7, 10, 18, 32).

While the framing of the conflict itself remains binary in Allen's writing, she advocates strongly for the development of inclusive relationships and close coordination between international and local actors involved—all qualities that I in this book also identified as indispensable for transformative and ethical conflict resolution efforts.

The third side

In his bestseller *The Third Side*, William Ury, as many before him, frames conflicts in binary terms, "it takes two sides to fight, but a third to stop" (Ury and Ury 2000). The book, however, acknowledges the need to involve the entire community and not only those on the two extremes into the conflict resolution process. By referring to everyone not in direct confrontation, be they insiders or outsiders, as the "third side," he outlines ten roles that the "third side" can play in helping the sides to resolve their conflict, including mediator, arbiter, equalizer, teacher, healer, and others. The approach has been popular and along with Ury's earlier co-authored bestseller *Getting to Yes* (R. Fisher, Ury, and Patton 1991) has often been used in practice.

In the South Caucasus, Ury's approach was adapted by MercyCorps/CM Partners based in Cambridge, Massachusetts, for a capacity-building initiative called "The Momentum Program." The program lasted from 2001 to 2008 and aimed at bringing negotiation and leadership skills to young professionals from Armenia and Georgia. As I interned with this program during my MA studies in Boston in 2005, I witnessed its focus on building the capacity of the civil society and community leaders in acting as the "third side." The trainings, in practice, came down to teaching participants negotiation skills, so they can act as mediators, once again, between two *sides*.

Implicitly, "The Third Side" made a step toward inclusiveness and advocated for the need of involving the entire community in a conflict resolution process, searching for roles in the process for various actors. Explicitly, however, even by the very virtue of its name, the "third side" reinforced the discourse of conflict as an affair of *two* principal *sides* and of solution as a form of negotiation between them mediated by a third one.

Constructivist trends in conflict analysis

Narrowly understood as a process to reach a secession of violence and political agreement, practice-oriented conflict resolution theories are typically limited in scope and confined to work with two sides.[3] Theories that help us conceptualize violent conflict, at the same time, have a much broader scope. Numerous paradigms are used today in helping us understand conflict ranging from rational choice approaches to post-positivist, structural, post-structural, postmodern approaches and more. Mapping all of these is outside the scope of this book, but even the brief overview of a few often-cited authors will show that not all approaches to conceptualizing conflict are preoccupied with the notion of "sides." Moreover, conflict analysis and resolution field, similar to most other social science disciplines, is an arena for epistemological struggles of positivist and constructivist paradigms.

Until the early 1990s violent conflicts were understood and addressed primarily through various positivist approaches and the international relations field in particular. The interstate wars and super-power confrontations such as World War II and the Cold War were the primary focus of conflict studies generating respective responses in the form of negotiations and nuclear arms control. The "smaller" conflicts were seen as proxies of super-power rivalry (Demmers 2012, 8). Many of the pioneers of the conflict resolution field, particularly in the United States, opted initially to be intelligible for realists, adopted the understanding of violent conflict as inherently unsolvable and focused on the management of conflicts rather than their resolution in the international arena. A direction of conflict resolution known as Alternative Dispute Resolution or ADR developed in courts as a form of mediation aimed at resolving conflict directly between the parties without bringing them to litigation. It was criticized from outside the field as a practice aimed at pacifying the less powerful party. Avruch and Black summarized these objections to ADR "as an instrument of social control, not social change" (Avruch and Black 1996, 52).

---

[3] Approaches to conflict resolution practice understood in broader sense as aimed at achieving social justice can transcend the notion of sides. Nonviolent action—a practice of achieving social justice by civil disobedience, protests, and economic non-cooperation—is perhaps the best-known example with Martin Luther King, Nelson Mandela, and Mahatma Gandhi as its standard-bearers on various continents. The discourse of nonviolent action is inclusive; it appeals to the humanity of everyone involved transcending the "us vs. them" binary.

In immediate post-Cold War era of domination of the liberal order the focus shifted toward Transitional Justice and other win-win scenarios. The aim was to move the world toward the democratic peace scenario through the transition of the societies from violence to peace and from authoritarianism to democracy, promoting free market and economic interdependence. With time, however, it became clear that the liberal, or rather neo-liberal, order did not abolish violence and its tenets such as human rights regime and free market economy were criticized for upholding existing hegemonies and supporting neo-colonialism (Shaw, Waldorf, and Hazan 2010).

In the early twenty-first century proponents of constructivist approaches based on the epistemological stance that considers knowledge inherently subjective and socially mediated started challenging the primacy of positivist methods of understanding conflict. In one of the most spirited debates between proponents of positivist and constructivist assumptions in conflict analysis, Jabri engages one of the founders of the field Christopher Mitchell:

> Mitchell makes the assumption that social kinds (agents, groups, communities, institutions, relationships) have an existence that is independent of the discursive frames that render them meaningful. Parties to a conflict, their conflict situation, behaviour and attitudes are rendered an objective existence independent of the discursive framing that the conflict analyst, as well as others on the ground, so to speak, give such constructs substance.... However, when we recognise that analysis is itself implicated in the construction of the world, we begin to recognise that analysis is part and parcel of the signifying practices that come to constitute the discursive frames that confer content to a seemingly contentless classifying process. Parties to a conflict, in this sense, can never simply be parties to a conflict, but are sovereign states, factions in government, clandestine organisations, terrorist groups, criminal gangs, teenage thugs, and so on. Each in turn is imbued with meaning, each contested, each differently situated within global, as well as local, structural continuities (for the full debate between Mitchell and Jabri, see Mitchell 2005a, b; Jabri 2006).

Constructivist approaches, which feature prominently in contemporary conflict analysis literature, treat identities as socially constructed categories and their interrelationships as transformable. The implication of an approach to analysis that sees identities as constructed, one would assume, should be the absence in it of "sides" as an identifiable analytic category. Antithetically, however, as exposed by Brubaker, "one often finds constructivist and groupist[4] language casually conjoined" (Brubaker 2004, 3). In other words, the proclaimed constructivism often cohabits with the essentialized treatment of groups as actors. Having said that, the constructivist paradigm that I also espouse if applied consistently allows for rethinking and reframing of conflict as not limited to interaction between identifiable sides.

Starting from the late 1990s and especially in the early 2000s, the post-positivist and then constructivist trends in conflict analysis started affecting the conflict resolution literature. Narrative analysis and narrative mediation, as well as discourse analytic approaches and particularly Critical Discourse Analysis (CDA), tried to create bridges between the constructivist paradigm and conflict resolution practice. Many individual case studies, particularly those that espoused ethnographic approaches, distanced themselves from grand theories and defied the conventional binary frames presenting more complex pictures of a particular context. The rich and evolving literature on nationalism and ethnicity complexified the concept of identity and suggested new possibilities for working with identity conflicts. Finally, the discourse analytic and participatory approaches opened the door for merging analysis with intervention and working with people as they gain awareness and transform structures they are embedded in.

Perhaps best known in conflict resolution openly constructivist theory is the narrative analysis. Its approach to identity and conflict can be summarized in the phrase "we are the stories we tell" (Cobb 2003). Cobb, one of the main theorists of the approach, attempts not only to explain the influence of narratives on identity construction and on the reproduction of violent conflict but also to develop a theoretical framework and practical tools to reduce violence. Cobb, following Ricœur, sees "plot" as central to narrative. Further, she builds on Feldman's idea of the "origin myths," which are "stories that justify the violence in the present and in the future as they preserve and embellish the story of the origin of violence, which is never the function of the storyteller, the narrator, but always a result of acts of the other"

---

4   Brubaker defines groupism as "the tendency to take bounded groups as fundamental units of analysis and basic constituents of the social world" (Brubaker 2004, 2).

(Cobb 2004, 294-95). Cobb, as well as her colleagues Winslade and Monk, applies the learning from narrative analysis to propose narrative mediation as a form of conflict resolution practice. Central to narrative mediation is the notion that the stories that construct our reality are never neutral. Conflict resolution, consequently, is an attempt to transform the conflict story into a story of peace (Winslade and Monk 2000). In practice, the method has been primarily applied in family mediation or other individual disputes and struggles in finding application in political conflicts. In theory, however, narrative mediation, which does not presuppose a particular number of sides and sees their relationships as socially constructed, is a major step forward compared to the conflict resolution's traditional emphasis on work with predetermined "sides." Moreover, its scholars have been contemplating about the adaptation of the method to transform collective narratives (Cobb 2013).

Reflective and elicitive practice

The reflective and elicitive practices get closer than many others to the type of adaptive workshop design that I advocate for in this book. Reflective practice is empowering, self-critical and open not to pass any prior judgment on who are the sides to the conflict or what are the dynamics in play. Schon advocates for a move from technical rationality, which we have seen in abundance in most approaches discussed above, toward reflection-in-action (Schon 1984, 21-76). Critical of the limits of rational knowledge, open to constant self-questioning, adjustability, and in a lookout for emerging opportunities, reflection in one form or another has long been practiced by facilitators and other conflict resolution practitioners as a method of improving their own learning, questioning their own assumptions, and developing interventions.

Yet the use of reflection does not have to be limited to facilitators. Reflection in action with populations affected by conflict can be a powerful conflict resolution intervention that empowers the marginalized to gain awareness of the context and their place in it and to regain voice.

Lederach in his approach of the "integrated framework" does just that. He opposes to each other the "prescriptive model" of trainings built around the specialized knowledge of the professional that has a claim to be transferable and universal and the "elicitive model" that sees training as a process that emerges from the local knowledge and where participants are encouraged to take the lead in the creation of the process and to take ownership of it (Lederach 2008).

Learning from Lederach's work had been key to this research. I share his commitment to empowerment that emerges from promoting participation. Different from Lederach, however, I do not necessarily privilege indigenous knowledge over academic knowledge. Coming from a conflict zone where I was brought up on the ideology of nationalism that resembles closely its European counterparts, I would argue that no "indigenous knowledge" is free of the legacy of colonialism and resulting power structures. Both conceptual academic knowledge and indigenous knowledge, therefore, can be useful in devising alternative and inclusive methods of addressing conflicts, and yet both of them need to be treated critically.

Theories of ethnicity and nationalism

Despite the growing shift in social sciences toward constructivism, including in studies of ethnicity (see most notably Hobsbawm and Ranger 2012), the conflict resolution practice continues to routinely frame many conflicts as "ethnic" or taking place "between ethnic groups" (the framing is often evident from the very title of conflict resolution-oriented works, such as the influential "Ethnic Groups in Conflict" by Horowitz 2000). The framing of conflicts as "Armenian-Azerbaijani," "Israeli-Palestinian," and so on implies that these ethnic groups are homogenous entities and are in a totalizing conflict with one another, reinforcing the binary framing and treating ethnic groups as units of analysis.

The disconnect between such essentializing treatment of ethnicity in conflict resolution practice and the increasingly constructivist understanding of the term in conflict scholarship has been noted by Brubaker. As mentioned above, Brubaker criticizes the tendency of many authors to casually combine self-proclaimed constructivism with "groupist" language (Brubaker 2004, 8). Ethnicity, argues Brubaker, "is what we need to explain, not what we need to explain *with*," moving away from equating ethnically framed conflicts as conflicts between ethnic groups, same as we would not equate a racially framed conflict as conflicts between races. He calls the colleagues in academia to stop "reifying" and thus "constituting" ethnicity as a bounded group, treating it instead as a performative category, analyzing it in relational, processual, dynamic, and eventful terms (Brubaker 2004, 9–12).

In the chapter "Myths and Misconceptions in the Study of Nationalism," Brubaker criticizes the frames used by five trends of literature on nationalism, looking into postcommunist conflicts as examples (Brubaker 1998). The first set of perspectives that he criticizes is what he calls the "architectonic illusion," the belief that one needs to discover the correct way of analyzing the conflict, get the "grand architecture right," and as a result devise a just and sustainable solution that satisfies competing nationalist demands. Without dismissing the need to conduct systematic analysis, Brubaker shows that the attempt to get the grand architecture of any conflict right is not practical and contains many internal contradictions. The meaning of ethnicity varies from one case to another. Ethno-national groups cannot be considered monolithic and bounded entities distinctly separated from neighbors. The national-self-determination concept is a contradiction in itself as it presupposes a prior determination of the unit—the nation, while that very determination of the boundaries of the unit is understood to be a result of recognition by others. He calls the second set of perspectives the "seething cauldron." It is effectively an orientalist view that the nationalisms of the "eastern" kind are ethnic and more violent than their "western" and "civic" counterparts: the former are irrational, based on passion making the conflicts unsolvable. Brubaker shows that, conceptually, "eastern" and "western" nationalisms are not that different, and that the imagery of a particularly violent "east" that we might have is the result of a selection bias by a broadly defined "western" reporters and others who frame these conflicts. The third perspective he criticizes are the theories of the "return of the repressed" and of the "ancient hatreds," which suggest that the post-

Soviet and Yugoslav conflicts and the consciousness of nations involved in them were "frozen" by the repressive communist regimes and "re-emerged" with the fall of the latter. This perspective gets things almost backwards, I agree with Brubaker, as the Soviet and Yugoslav regimes were supportive of the formation of distinct "nations," and had respective nationality policies that in effect institutionalized various ethno-nations that today constitute the sides to the conflicts. The groups and the relationships as we have them today, therefore, are hardly "ancient" and are the legacy of the communist, yet also ethno-national, institutions and policies. The fourth problematic perspective on nationalism that Brubaker criticizes is the "elite manipulation" argument that assumes that stirring nationalist mobilization and violence pays off as a political strategy that consolidates power of social entrepreneurs and therefore is a rational. This rational choice argument ignores the politics of identity and that politicians are a product of the same institutional and cultural frameworks that shape populations and thus driven by and not only the drivers of nationalist discourse. Further, Brubaker shows that elite-mobilization happened in all the postcommunist regions, yet only in a few did it lead to violence. This approach alone, therefore, cannot explain violence or the intractability of conflicts (Brubaker 2004, 274–92).

Finally, the fifth perspective, particularly relevant for this book, is as I mentioned above what Brubaker calls "groupism" that is prevalent in most studies of ethnicity. Authors across disciplines routinely write about ethnic groups as actors, despite many trends within the same disciplines that have shown in theory that groups cannot be treated as real entities or units of analysis. Yet, even in literature that claims to be constructivist, references to "the Azerbaijanis," "the Armenians," "the Serbs," and other ethnic groups as actors remain commonplace. Literature on the diversity within a society or on multiculturalism, similarly, employs groupist language referring to subentities within an entity, such as the US population is composed of African-Americans, Native Americans, Caucasian Americans, and so on. The problematic groupist language not only is prevalent in academia but also informs policymaking on various levels, leading to the institutionalization of groups (Brubaker 2004, 292–98). One explicit example of such institutionalization was the Soviet Nationalities Policy that divided the Soviet territory into distinct partly autonomous ethno-national units and fixed each individual's ethno-nationality in their passports. This created a hierarchy of "titular" ethno-nations attached to ethno-territorial units, titular minority groups within them, as well as groups that received a status of a nation yet no territory. All the violence and territorial conflicts in the post-Soviet space emerged as mutually exclusive claims over ownership of territories by one or the other titular group, accompanied by ethnic cleansing of "the other" from these territories. The present-day conflicts in the South Caucasus, therefore, are the first and foremost the legacy of the Soviet Nationalities Policy and exhibit many dynamics characteristic of postcolonial conflicts. Yet with the ethnic frames dominating, the lens of postcolonial critique is rarely if ever applied to understand these.

Brubaker points to a visible contradiction within many disciplines, from rational choice theory with its focus on individuals to constructivism with its focus on the constructed nature of social categories, where the conceptual treatment of groups as nonsuitable units of analysis exists side by side with the casual use of groupist language when explaining conflicts. In his *Ethnicity without Groups*, he offers alternatives to groupist language of identity and ethnicity. Depending on the context, he suggests terms that indicate a process or performance, such as "identification" or "categorization," that do not reify ethnicity. While "identification" describes relation to others, he offers "self-identification" as a term suitable for describing oneself. Relational terms such as "commonality," "connectedness," and "groupness" can describe the emotional sense of belonging, shared attributes, and relations that tie people (Brubaker 2004, 41–48).

Rethinking conflicts from ethnic to ethnically framed and taking the *concepts* of ethnicity, race, religion, rather than the *group* as the unit of analysis helps greatly in my endeavor of not only in problematizing binary frames such as "Armenian-Azerbaijani" or "Assad-opposition" but also in looking for alternative and inclusive practices.

Critical theory

Critical Discourse Analysis or CDA advanced is relevant for conflict resolution practice as an analytic and descriptive method, and also as a normative and an activist one. According to Fairclough, one of those who developed the concept, CDA is concerned with "what is wrong with a society ... and how 'wrongs' can be 'righted.'" He continues that CDA "assesses what exists, what might exist, and what should exist on the basis of a coherent set of values" (Fairclough 2010, 7). CDA, as a methodology, calls us to make our values explicit and assess our work against these values, identify where we fail, where we can improve, particularly when it comes to power relations and inequalities.

To better understand the relevance of CDA for transforming conflict resolution work, it is important to consider the meaning of the term itself. "Critical," clarifies Candlin in his introduction to "Critical Discourse Analysis," is not a reference to criticism. Instead, it is "means of explaining data in a context of social, political and institutional analysis, and in terms of critiquing the ideologically invested modes of explaining and interpreting, but always with the sights set on positively motivated change" (in Fairclough 2010, ix). CDA, therefore, is a call for developing a critical outlook at our own modes of explaining with an aim of transforming and improving them.

As discourse is relational, Fairclough suggests refocusing from "critique of structures to critique of strategies" (Fairclough 2010, 15, 17). Further, he argues that the problematic of language and power in any particular discipline, the conflict resolution discipline in our case, cannot be isolated from the same problematic in the society in general and those subject to domination, therefore, need to take these up as political issues, as feminists have done in regard to language and gender. Some struggles against domination are more successful than others; he continues, "[O]ne factor in success is the theoretical and analytical resources an opposition has access to." Fairclough suggests then that educational practices as well as the media constitute an important domain of linguistic and discursive power. He stresses the importance, consequently, of developing a "critical tradition within language studies and discourse analysis," followed by the "development of critical language awareness work within schools and other educational organizations." Different from "language awareness" that often overlooks relations of power, he concludes, the *"critical* language awareness work can lead to reflective analysis of practices of domination implicit in transmission and learning of academic discourse, and the engagement of learners in the struggle to contest and change such practices" (Fairclough 2010, 531–32).

The patterns of marginalization and exclusion produced by conflict resolution work that I discuss in this book, of course, are also intimately related to questions of power and powerlessness. Yet "power," certainly, is one of the most contested terms in social science. It defies an easy definition and in light of the availability of extensive literature on the subject will not be discussed here in great detail. As noted by Avruch after surveying many approaches, power "may thus appear simultaneously the central concept in all the social science (Russell 1962 [orig. 1938]), vague and better discarded than kept (McClelland 1971), or an essentially contested concept—though indispensable for all that (Lukes 2004)" (Avruch 2012, 145).

I agree with Lukes' version and also look at the notion of power from the social constructivist lens, as a contested category. Therefore, I see marginalization and exclusion of affected populations from conflict resolution process as relational and performative and therefore avoidable offenses that contradict the aims of social justice and fulfilling human needs advanced by conflict resolution field.

I use the word "marginalization" to denote relations and structures that disempower individuals or groups or deprive them of voice. The notion of power, therefore, is relevant to conflict resolution as it proclaims contributing to sustainable peace through social justice as one of its main aims, which in turn requires actively addressing marginalization and empowering the powerless. Yet in addition to failing to address marginalization created by external structures, as I will show later in this book, the conflict resolution practice itself produces arenas for power struggles over the control of the conflict discourses and results in marginalization. In some instances, the struggle is subtle, while in others it is open and intentional. The power struggles producing marginalization are easily visible in conflict resolution initiatives that have an explicit claim to influence policy. But even in endeavors that work with youth or culture, the power struggles over discourse creation are often located right below the surface.

In this book, I discuss power as a set of relationships constructed and expressed through language that contribute to the domination of some people by others. As an example of a structure that produces relationships of power and domination, Faiclough cites medicine, where, by virtue of her diploma, the doctor has the power to determine what could be done with another individual, while that very individual loses control over their own body (Fairclough 2001, 2). Illich takes these examples further and suggests that the discourses of "professions," including medicine and education, are effectively taking away the ability of people to fulfil their own needs. The professionals first legislate the needs for the society, and then fulfil them often possessing the ability to restrain the person who chooses to reject the prescribed need (Illich 1987).

In this book, I suggest to approach professionalization of conflict resolution with caution, without, however, arguing against the professionalization of conflict resolution altogether. As war-making and nationalism have been systematized, institutionalized, and professionalized, a certain degree of professionalization of some approaches to peacebuilding and conflict resolution is necessary to systemically counter the influence of the former. However, we should be careful not to equate peacebuilding in general with professional conflict resolution and welcome many nonprofessional approaches, local and traditional conflict resolution mechanisms and other measures that bring entire populations and not only a few university graduates into the process. Moreover, as my research shows, we should be mindful of the implications of Fairclough's and Illich's critique for conflict resolution as a profession and work on developing awareness of the language we produce and the effects it can have. Similar to medicine, we run the risk of turning those affected by conflicts into our clients, giving ourselves power to frame both the problem and its solution in the process marginalizing entire communities who become little more than "subjects" of conflict resolution practice.

Structuration theory: segue into participatory research design

For a number of decades, the conflict resolution field has been struggling with the structure vs. agency debate. The theories that use the rational choice argument, from international relations and negotiation to micro-economic theories (Collier 2001) that equate ethnic grievances and rebellions with organized crime, either implicitly or explicitly have assumed that individuals and other actors have the deliberate ability to start and resolve conflicts, as well as influence the structures that sustain them.

At the same time, structural theories have argued about the limits of agency that are inevitably embedded in the structures, defined by them, and serve the function of perpetuating them. Today's structural approaches are rooted in Marxian and Durkheimian sociological traditions. Marxism is an economic theory and sees capitalism as an inherently oppressive structure where those who control the means of production are in an inevitable conflict with workers. At the same time Durkheimian approach looks into social structures such as shared belief systems that hold the society together and the shaking of which can lead to weaker ties and to conflict. Closer to conflict resolution itself, Galtung's structural violence became one of the canons of the theory that explains conflict not as a relationship between rational actors but as a consequence of unjust institutions, laws, and social structures that prevent people from reaching their full potential (Galtung 1969; Galtung 1990, 292).

Both the agency-based and the structural approaches, however, have rigid frames and limitations if taken in isolation. Advocating for cross-disciplinary dialogue and integration of approaches, Giddens criticizes the concept of structure understood in the Durkheimian way as external to social actors and fixed. While he agrees that actors often draw upon external rules, he also argues that just as often they distance themselves from these rules in order to challenge and transform them. Put simply, the structuration theory states that, on the one hand, the actions of individuals are limited by language, institutions, and other social structures in which they are embedded, and on the other, these very structures are reproduced by agents who have a certain degree of control over their actions, and so they constantly are reshaping or transforming these structures. As neither agency nor structure can be understood in isolation from the other, it is their relationship that shapes them both (Giddens 1993).

A key term in Giddens's approach is the duality of structure. According to Stones, Giddens sees structures as both internal, embedded within agents in their memory, and external, such as institutions and manifestation of social actions (Stones 2005). Similarly, social structures contain agents and/or are the product of past actions of agents (Giddens 1986). The concept would be easier to grasp, I would agree with McLennan here, if instead of "duality of structure" it was called "the duality of structure and agency" since both aspects are involved in using and producing social actions (McLennan 1997).

I am in agreement with the structuration theory of Giddens, which upholds the notion that studying either structures or agency is not enough, and that it is the interplay of both that can best explain social phenomena (Giddens 1993, 4). The methodological approach of this book, therefore, is focused on the interplay of the two. Giddens himself, however, did not link any research method to the structuration theory. Despite that, structuration theory has clear implications for research. Building on Giddens's work in suggesting appropriate approaches to research, Coenen and Khonraad see the place of the researchers "not above but among people as social actors, and not outside the way in which they understand social reality." They continue that the researcher "must be aware that the problems posed by the researched parties can only be understood on the basis of knowledge available to them, and on the basis of knowledge of social structures" (2003, 440).

The above considerations lead my inquiry to segue into a participatory research design. It proceeds with the assumption that the structures in which we are embedded heavily influence our views, choices, as well as learning and reflection patterns. At the same time, we are able to influence and change these structures, but only if we gain awareness of them and their influence on us. The research design has a few cycles of action and reflection, each cycle of reflection aimed at uncovering new layers of structures, and each action aimed at influencing and when needed transforming these structures.

The research method that I find most appropriate for such an aim is PAR complemented with individual and collective auto-ethnography, which allows me to engage in self-criticism and self-reflection, as well as ethnographic observations that will give a richer context to the work of the other participants of this study. More importantly, PAR allows me to engage in this research other practitioners as co-creators of knowledge.

To briefly summarize the chapter, conflict analysis and resolution emerged as a critique of international relations, yet initially stayed in the latter's shadow reduced to its binary frames and the "us vs. them" discourse of conflict "sides." With time, and under the influence of the constructivist paradigm, we saw a shift, particularly in conceptual approaches. Alternatives emerged that broke with the binary frames and positivism in general, drew on structuralist, post-structuralist, and later postmodernist thinking, and offered reframing of the concepts of identity and conflict. The research conducted for this book and detailed in the next chapter aims to integrate this conceptual shift into conflict resolution practice.

Chapter 2

Methodology

The research questions that drive this inquiry aim to (a) identify patterns of conflict resolution practice that (re)produce frames that sustain conflict or that contribute to exclusion from the peace processes of populations affected by conflict and marginalization of peace constituencies; (b) rethink conflict and conflict resolution; and (c) transform the language through which we analyze conflict developing inclusive conflict resolution practices.

As the focus of this book is on the development of methods of conflict resolution practice that do not marginalize, or better yet, bring in marginalized voices, I find it necessary to ensure that my own research methods do not marginalize either.

Participatory action research

PAR that I chose for this inquiry is a relatively new design; it takes various forms depending on the field it is used in and can vary even within the same field. All action research, at the same time, has the following in common, as an "inquiry that is done by or with insiders to an organization or community, but never *to* or *on* them. It is a reflective process, but is different from isolated, spontaneous reflection in that it is deliberately and systematically undertaken and generally requires that some form of evidence be presented to support assertions" (Herr and Anderson 2015, 3).

The methods and tools that PAR uses are not necessarily unconventional. Researchers can rely on a variety of better-known qualitative and quantitative approaches such as interviews or focus groups. What distinguishes PAR from other research is not the toolkit, but the relationship of the researcher and the researched. If in the positivist research tradition, people in conflict, their attitudes, narratives, and emotions are treated as objects of research, in PAR, they are both the decision maker and the beneficiary. Park sees PAR as a "self-conscious way of empowering people to take effective action toward improving conditions in their lives" (Park 1993, 1).

According to Reason and Bradbury in action research, "the distinction between researchers and subjects may become quite blurred in the course of what is usually a lengthy, collaborative relationship." Research and action are also interconnected and often inseparable. A compelling action research would follow three pathways at once: the focus of the first-person action research is on the reflective approach to the researcher's own life and work; the focus of the second-person action research is the joint inquiry together with others on issues of mutual concern; and the third-person action research involves extending the learning from the first two into the wider community of inquiry (Handbook of Action Research 2006, xxv–xxvi).

In this research, I follow these three pathways: I start with first-person auto-ethnographic inquiry reflecting on my life and career in the conflict resolution field as well as my work at the Imagine Center for Conflict Transformation (Imagine Center) where I am a co-founder and as of this writing, serve as the director of programs; I follow with second-person action research of joint inquiry together with colleagues who work in the Imagine Center, as well as with colleagues not engaged with the Imagine Center but who work in the same conflict contexts as the Imagine Center; and finally I engage in the third-person action research by bringing the learning from the first two into facilitation practice and sharing it with a wider community that I work with through the publication of this book.

The research design that I developed involved the following specific procedures, some of which were interlinked:

- auto-ethnographic reflection on my own life and career;
- first-person action research in the context of my work in the Syrian and the Nagorno-Karabakh conflicts;
- second-person action research involving over 20 colleagues who work in the Syrian and Nagorno-Karabakh contexts. Ten or so colleagues involved participated in the reflection and action mainly in the early stages of the research and were less involved at the later stages, some due to extreme busyness

and others because they stopped working in the Syrian or Nagorno-Karabakh contexts. Five more colleagues participated in the PAR process continually, but not extensively. And six other colleagues remained involved with the PAR closely through the entire life of the research, participating actively in the reflection and action cycle.
- Third-person action research that involves consultations with an extended group of colleagues working in Syria, Nagorno-Karabakh, and in other contexts, as well the eventual publishing and dissemination of this book.

In line with the PAR methodology, I try to use the term "colleagues" when possible as I find it to be more inclusive, replacing the terms such as "research subjects" or "project participants" that can produce hierarchy where there does not need to be one. In some cases, however, I find it necessary to use the terminology of "practitioners" and "participants" to preserve the language and logic of the particular initiatives that I discuss.

By referring to many of those involved in the study as colleagues, however, I would like to warn against an impression that I involved in this PAR professionals and affected populations equally. Most of my work for this research has been done with colleagues who are engaged in conflict resolution practice professionally, primarily because of the cyclical structure of PAR that requires continuous engagement of colleagues through the life of my research. This made it impractical for those uninterested in the topic professionally to commit considerable time to this book. I consider this discrepancy in the numbers and only occasional involvement in this research of individuals who did not practice conflict resolution professionally as a limitation of the current research. Future research is necessary to involve the marginalized populations affected by the conflicts more centrally into the process of assessing the current or alternative conflict resolution practices and their effects, or absence of thereof, on the daily lives of these populations.

Further difficulty with action research is that to date, it is used primarily in practice and its "research" component is often questioned in academia. When I was considering changing my initial research design and adopting action research as a methodology, I was confronted by an influential professor at my university who questioned whether action research qualifies as research, telling me bluntly that it was not a category he understands. I have been lucky, however, to be encouraged by the members of my dissertation committee and other colleagues who saw the value in developing participatory research methods. I accept that the research design that I built was experiential and continues to remain work in progress. I hope also that the work I have done with the continuous critical support of my colleagues would embolden others to challenge the boundaries of research and practice taking participatory methods to the next level and contributing to qualitative change in conflict resolution.

Case selection

As my aim was the identification of patterns in conflict resolution practice that contribute to marginalization and the development of interventions and facilitation approaches that are inclusive, I was looking for cases that would represent a spectrum: one of them would have an evolving environment and an acknowledged presence of multiplicity of identities and conflict parties; and the second would be commonly seen as a classic case of a binary "ethnic" conflict. The first case, where parties are not well-defined and the binary framing of the conflict itself is not strongly pronounced, was likely to prompt practitioners to either adopt a nonbinary approach or intentionally exclude many prospective participants to create an artificial binary. As a consequence, the questions related to binary framing, exclusion, marginalization, and the need for developing nonbinary inclusive approaches would be close to the surface and would be easy to identify. At the same time, in the case that is commonly presumed to be a binary ethnic conflict, the marginalization of populations who fall outside this binary would not be readily seen as problematic by practitioners. This would help me evaluate if the binary frames that replicate the international relations approach are in certain contexts appropriate and if the marginalization of those who fall outside the binary is justified by the considerations of effectiveness or expediency.

Because part of my methodology is auto-ethnographic, another criterion was to choose among the cases that are located in the contexts where I was involved as a practitioner. The conflicts I worked in by the start of this research included the Syrian case, the Turkish-Armenian case, the Nagorno-Karabakh case, and the Georgian-South Ossetian case. Out of these four, I found the Syrian and the Nagorno-Karabakh cases to be the most disparate on the evolving multiparty vs. classic two-party continuum. If Syria has clearly been an evolving environment with a multiplicity of identities and with many Syrians not accepting their belonging to any known conflict side, in the Nagorno-Karabakh case the ethnic identities and the dividing lines seemed to be well consolidated, and it has been routinely discussed as an "ethnic" or "Armenian-Azerbaijani" conflict.

The Armenian-Turkish and the Georgian-South Ossetian cases fall somewhere in between, despite the binary and ethnic naming that I used here following the convention. Unlike in the Nagorno-Karabakh case, the dichotomy is easy to question once examining either of these cases. In the Turkish-Armenian context, one of the central issues is the struggle for the recognition of the Armenian genocide, and taking it as an example of an ethnically framed binary conflict would show an obvious disregard to many Turkish human rights activists, academics, and others who also struggle for the recognition. To paraphrase Brubaker, this is a conflict *about* the historical memories of Turks and Armenians, and visibly not a conflict *between* the two monolithic groups or their memories. The Georgian-South Ossetian case also routinely carries an ethnic framing; at the same time, the conflict is widely acknowledged to be multilayered and having third parties immediately involved, which makes the ethnic frame "one of the" rather than the only focus of analysis and interventions.

Also, while the Nagorno-Karabakh and the Syrian contexts are the two main case studies of this book, when appropriate I also bring in a few experiences from the Turkish-Armenian and the Georgian-South Ossetian contexts.

Auto-ethnography

Auto-ethnography, which is where I start my research, is described as a method of social research that explores the researcher's personal experience and connects the autobiographical story to wider cultural, political, and social meanings and understandings (Allen-Collinson and Hockey 2008; Ellis, Adams, and Bochner 2010). White stresses that this approach can "open up for debate previously unquestioned aspects of practice," and building on that refers to Gould who, writing about the character of the reflexivity necessary for an auto-ethnographic analysis, describes it as a process of looking inward and thinking about how our own life experiences or significant events may have impacted our thinking, the research, or the assessment (White 2001, 100–101). In other words, by problematizing and destabilizing the taken-for-granted knowledge, we raise our own awareness not only about our agency but also about structures in which we are embedded, which is one of the objectives of this book.

First-person action research and collective auto-ethnography

I next follow the PAR procedure described by Heron and Reason as a four-phased action research process. For Phase 1, I invited dozens of colleagues to engage in a preliminary exploration of the topic, asked questions about their practices and the assumptions behind them (Heron and Reason 2006, 145–46). Not all colleagues were receptive or interested to continue. With those who shared the concerns I was raising and who agreed to participate, we agreed on data collection and analysis procedures that we all would engage in during our practices. Phase 2 happened when I and my colleagues engaged in practices, adding to them an ongoing documented reflection. As some colleagues were more diligent in documenting their reflections than others, I relied also on periodic interviews, focus groups, and reflective practice sessions for data collection. Phase 3 involved making changes to the practices based on the learning from Phases 1 and 2. I and my colleagues, at the same time, continued building awareness and reflexivity in regard to our work. Phase 4, which took place a few months later, involved sharing our practical and experiential data and findings and considering our original ideas in the light of it. As a result, many of us reframed our ideas and posed new questions, after which we repeated the reflection and action cycle.

Choosing PAR as a methodology and asking colleagues to engage in reflection and questioning of their work and base assumptions, I found it necessary to start the process with my own work and opening myself and my practice up to criticism by others. At the same time, I am not alone at the Imagine Center, and we work as a team—which leads in the direction that Herr and Anderson described as research "in which insiders, either alone or in collaboration with other insiders, are researching their own practice and/or practice setting" and falls into the "insider in collaboration with other insiders" PAR category as different from its other forms such as the "outsider in collaboration with insiders" or others. The "insider in collaboration with insiders" was complemented with "insider in collaboration with outsiders" approach as in some cases I invited outside facilitators to lead the reflection sessions for the Imagine Center's team and contribute with advice (Herr and Anderson 2015, 31–33).

When starting this research, I faced a dilemma on whether I should write the entire book about my work at the Imagine Center as an individual auto-ethnography or if I should focus mainly on writing about colleagues engaged in action research, while acknowledging my own role in it. In the process, I ended up combining the two, forging a modest methodological innovation—collective auto-ethnography. The method involved an auto-ethnographic reflection in action conducted by a team rather than an individual and the learning contributed to the ongoing development of the Imagine Center's work. And while the big part of the credit for the insights developed is shared with all members of our team, the responsibility for any misrepresentation or mistake in the written product presented here, of course, lies with me as the author of the book.

I should acknowledge here that questioning the taken-for-granted knowledge has not been simple. More than once, for example, our team planned to observe and reflect on the dynamics of marginalization in an ongoing project that we were leading. Yet once we were in the meeting itself and the old binary routines of conflict resolution practice as an exercise between two sides took hold, we would get consumed by the familiar dynamics of the binary conflict and forget all about the questioning. And only later, reflecting on the workshops, we would realize that we have that "blind spot" and once in the meeting, we time and again miss blatant cases of marginalization that were taking place right in front of our eyes or were perpetuated by us.

Aware of the difficulty of seeing past our own frames and noticing our own blind spots, I invited a number of colleagues with whom I work at the Imagine Center to join me in a cycle of reflection and action where we would question the basis of our knowledge and approaches to facilitation in focus group discussions, followed by a documented reflection of our facilitation and further cycles of reflection and action. Some of our focus group discussions were facilitated by the group members themselves and others by outside facilitators, to allow for more than one way of questioning. That debriefings and reflection were already a regular practice for the Imagine team helped greatly in making the procedure acceptable and relatively painless.

The questions asked during the formal focus group discussions with the Imagine Center's team centered around: how did we understand conflict and conflict resolution? How did that influence the design of our interventions? Against that background, what was working, what was not working and could be improved? What were the benefits and downsides of the innovations we were experimenting with in the action part of the reflection and action cycle? What further changes and improvements had to be made? Which innovations did not work and had to be dropped? If there were new patterns of conflict perpetuation or marginalization that we noticed, how these could be conceptualized and addressed? And more.

These internally facilitated formal focus-groups and informal debriefing sessions were important, but also did not seem enough as we realized that this group had already worked together for a long time and in addition to individual "blind spots" had developed also collective ones. In some cases, therefore, it was hard for us to think outside of our usual patterns of reflection. Two colleagues and fellow students from the GMU, Matthew Graville and Jacquelyn Greiff, came to help. Outsiders to the Imagine Center's work, they had their own and alternative to Imagine Center's debriefing models, and they led a series of reflection sessions helping us reassess our procedures.

Jacquelyn and Matthew each adopted different approaches, based on their own professional interests. Jacquelyn joined some of the projects of the Imagine Center as a developmental evaluator and at times as a guest facilitator and led the reflection sessions during the work, while keeping herself positioned as an outsider to the Imagine Center's team. In contrast, Matthew never joined any of the projects and remained throughout an outside debriefer who would meet with us before and after the projects.

These three concurrent models of reflection, internal and led by the team itself (Gamaghelyan and Littlefield 2012); mixed method led by Jacquelyn as external facilitator who was present at the program; and an external one led by Matthew (for the latter two see Greiff et al. 2015, 5–6), complemented each other, exposing what was hard to see using one method only.

I engaged with colleagues at the Imagine Center and beyond in ongoing reflections on these topics in the context of multiple programs with diverse target populations and methods of work. The programs during which the reflection and action cycle was implemented included:

- workshops for Armenian and Azerbaijani, as well as Georgian and South Ossetian historians held through 2013 and 2014;
- a conflict sensitive coverage program for journalists in the South Caucasus implemented in 2014 and 2015;
- a series of analytic initiatives for quasi-political actors and analysts organized in the context of the conflicts in South Caucasus in 2013–2015;
- a dialogue program for Syrian peace activists held in 2013;
- and a number of summer and winter schools in conflict transformation in Syrian and Nagorno-Karabakh conflict contexts in 2013–2015.

Before incorporating parts of our reflection into this book, particularly the insights generated during the ad hoc or nonrecorded conversations, I shared all the drafts with the colleagues who were part of PAR and incorporated their feedback. The anonymity of the people who participated in the focus groups was guarded, unless they explicitly chose to be identified.

The questions of initial inquiry discussed in preparation for, during, and after a variety of programs led by the Imagine Center in late 2013 and in early 2014 focused around the themes of the existing facilitation processes and adaptations to changing dynamics. In parallel, I started posing similar questions to colleagues not engaged with the Imagine Center yet who also worked in the conflict contexts of Nagorno-Karabakh and Syria. The topics discussed concerned conflict and conflict resolution practices as concepts and included but were not limited to the following:

How did we define conflict? How did this definition influence the conception and design of our interventions? What did we try to achieve? Were our frames or workshop designs contributing to exclusion and marginalization? If so, how? How did we decide what to do and when? How do we know what we know? What past experiences informed our aspirations and our daily choices when we engaged in conflict resolution practice? What other past experiences could have had an influence? How did we increase our awareness regarding our role in marginalization?

The second round of reflection that again involved the Imagine Center's team and other colleagues took place again in late 2013 and throughout 2014 and focused on the questions of framing and voice in the specific Syrian and the Nagorno-Karabakh conflicts.

How did we frame the Syrian and the Nagorno-Karabakh conflicts? How did we frame our interventions in these contexts? Were our framings binary or otherwise exclusive? How did the framing influence our approach to recruitment, facilitation, and follow up? Did we, through our work, marginalize and exclude potential peace constituencies or other groups affected by conflict and empower the violent extremes or did we manage to give voice to the marginalized? Were we rigid in our approaches or were we open to emerging opportunities? How did we decide what are the opportunities?

Following this exploration of our own awareness and framing patterns, we turned to the final series of questions of this research. What could we learn from this reflection? How could our increased awareness inform our approach while facilitating dialogues in the

Syrian and Nagorno-Karabakh contexts and beyond? And, centrally, how could conflict resolution intervention designs be adapted to become inclusive and empowering? What alternative designs are possible?

Many of the reflection sessions continued for hours; three initial group reflection sessions by the Imagine Center's team were done formally and on-record, and dozens more ad hoc and without formal recording, uncovering layers of information and relationships. In this process, many of the involved colleagues, as well as myself, continued practicing and leading programs gradually incorporating the new learning into our work and posing new questions. The reflection and action cycles were done repeatedly through the life of the project, and the questions of the later reflections incorporated the findings from the previous reflections.

The recorded reflection sessions and for informal sessions, we adapted an open-ended process that involved setting the agenda collaboratively, sharing the results of reflection in action, and comparing the new insights with the insights from the previous sessions and reflecting on the learning. When the sessions were not audio recorded, I took extensive handwritten notes during the conversation. In some cases, when the project required my close involvement, and I could not resort to extensive note-taking without taking time away from the project, the notes were made immediately after the project and checked with others present. In other cases, the needs of a particular program took priority, and we did not record our reflections. Therefore, they did not make it into these pages explicitly, but they contributed to our learning and improved practices.

In addition, many program-specific debriefing sessions, as well as conversations over dinner or lunch, generated important insights that were later tried in practice, reflected upon, and incorporated into the findings.

Second-person action research

In parallel with the collective auto-ethnography conducted with the team of the Imagine Center, I worked also with other colleagues engaged in the Syrian and the Nagorno-Karabakh contexts. One key challenge that I faced here that I did not face when working with the colleagues from the Imagine Center was the absence of ongoing face-to-face access to people. In the Nagorno-Karabakh case, I had more access as I spend considerable time in the South Caucasus. In the Syrian case, however, I had difficulty meeting my colleagues enough times to go through the full reflection-action-reflection cycle. Given this limitation, I conducted most of the work with these practitioners over Skype, yet this made the interaction considerably more limited compared to the one I had with the colleagues in the South Caucasus. The reflections shared with the colleagues working in Syria were not any less insightful.

My initial outreach to colleagues working in the Syrian context showed two seemingly contradictory trends. On the one hand, the colleagues all confessed that they also find themselves questioning the applicability of the traditional conflict resolution practices in the current Syrian context and might appreciate an opportunity to engage in deep reflection and learning in order to develop new methods. At the same time, the physical and emotional intensity that comes with working in the situation of ongoing mass violence left little energy or time for many of them to commit to a prolonged reflection and action cycle. Considering these difficulties, I had to eventually limit the number of colleagues in this group to three people with whom I had more than one interaction, as conducting in-depth longitudinal work with more practitioners working in Syria did not seem feasible.

Following the four-phase approach to action research outlined in the previous section, I started by scheduling three face-to-face conversations with three facilitators working in the Syrian context. We discussed the aims and procedures of the study, as well as the long-term commitment necessary if they decide to engage. As one of those who I interviewed initially decided not to engage in PAR beyond a few initial interviews, I continued contacting other practitioners until I had three commitments. Even then, only two of them stayed in touch regularly and the third practitioner was responsive only occasionally.

In Phase 1 of second-person action research, we engaged in a preliminary exploration of the topic of conflict framing, our own identity and memory, and the influence of framing and our identity on facilitation in the Syrian context. I worked with each of the three colleagues separately as they were not connected and we had no opportunity to meet as a group. With each of them, we discussed our practices and assumptions behind them; we agreed on the topic of further inquiry, on data collection and analysis procedures that we would engage during our practices. We discussed the role of everyone as colleagues with shared interest rather than participants of this research. Most importantly, we agreed that their work with Syrians should be of the priority, and they will engage in action research only and when it is possible without creating any additional safety concerns for themselves or participants.

The initial interviews with these colleagues evolved around the following themes. What was the context in which they have worked? How did they frame the conflict? How did their framing influence their work? How did they work with other individuals who do not see the conflict in terms of binary opposites or who do not align with any known party to the conflict?

From that point on, the research continued in one of the two directions. In one case, the facilitator's framing of the context was not dualistic and the colleague was open to participants setting their own agenda. As this practitioner had experience involving participants not belonging to either the Assad or opposition "side" into dialogue, our conversation focused on learning from practice and developing further procedures for documented reflection and introspection during their ongoing work.

Other facilitators framed the conflict in binary terms and saw their role in supporting those in opposition to Assad through capacity-building. The interviews then continued with developing documented reflection procedures where the facilitator would pay attention to possible patterns of exclusion as a result of their own framing and methodology.

In Phase 2, as the colleagues further engaged in their practice at their own time and place in late 2013, the entire 2014 and early 2015, we talked again, mostly over Skype, and I acted as a debriefer. These debriefing sessions served a dual purpose of a data gathering mechanism for me, while helping the colleagues to reflect on and improve their practice. In Phase 3, we discussed possible changes to the practice of the colleagues based on the learning from the previous conversations. Two of the colleagues agreed to try to implement some of these changes, but only when they found them beneficial to the populations they work with. Phase 4 took place a few months later, at different times with different practitioners, to allow for a deeper reflection process. During this final phase, the colleagues shared their practical and experiential data and findings, and considered reframing their original approaches in the light of new learning.

The conversations with the colleagues working in the Syrian context generated great insights both in terms of patterns of exclusion and marginalization and in terms of possible alternative approaches to conflict resolution. Unlike the Nagorno-Karabakh case, however, within the framework and life of this research, we did not manage to apply any considerable changes to the work of my colleagues working in Syria. This was due to the stressful environment in which they worked, the preference to carry on with the tested methods in an environment that posed physical and emotional dangers to everyone involved, and the absence of time and space that would be needed to coordinate any major changes with other colleagues and donors.

In the Nagorno-Karabakh case, I spent considerable time in the South Caucasus and was able to continuously meet with my colleagues in person. Most of the interviews and focus groups were conducted face to face in the summer of 2013 and the spring and summer of 2014, as well as in the winter of 2014–2015. Here I started from interviewing 19 people engaged in conflict resolution activities in various forms: I talked to practitioners, participants as well as individuals displaced by the conflict. The initial focus of the inquiry was similar to the one I had in the Syrian context: my colleagues reflected on their framing and its influence on their work, their experience of engaging with participants of mixed heritage or others whose identities did not align with the conflict parties.

While the questions were similar, the outcome was very different. The framing of the conflict when working with practitioners engaged with Nagorno-Karabakh was almost invariably binary, and they acknowledged that such a frame excludes many people affected by the conflict. Yet most colleagues actively justified this choice, a position that I will discuss in greater detail in the following chapters.

Only a few of the initial interviewees agreed immediately that such exclusion was problematic, with most others expressing willingness to discuss these questions further and to explore alternative frames. As we addressed the possibility of engaging in action research and discussed in detail the degree of openness to challenge and change and the vulnerability that it assumes, nine colleagues declined the offer, some citing the need not to expose "trade secrets," such as quote, "names of participant and methodologies to competitors," others citing safety concerns if the names of the participants were exposed in politically sensitive environments. Another group of five colleagues expressed interest, and contributed to the research occasionally, but not extensively. Finally, five other colleagues expressed a strong degree of willingness to engage in action research and remained involved throughout.

In light of this development, I restructured my initial research design and the new approach assumed longitudinal study that involves six colleagues giving permanent input, another six giving continual but not extensive input, and a dozen more giving occasional input. I continued interviewing the bigger group of over 20 colleagues until I discussed in depth over 30 cases of conflict resolution practices, mainly in the contexts of Nagorno-Karabakh and Syria and in a few cases in the contexts of Georgian-South Ossetian and Armenian-Turkish relations. In these interviews, I primarily focused on the understanding of what patterns of exclusion and marginalization emerge in conflict resolution work, and whether these patterns were justified or contributed to perpetuation of conflicts or violence, whether direct or structural. From there on, I continued communicating with those colleagues who expressed interest in engaging in action research either extensively or occasionally. With the colleagues who stayed involved, we continued with the four-step process of action research outlined above, identified the topics of common concern related to conflict resolution interventions and engaged in ongoing discussion as they experimented with the reflection and action cycle incorporating changes into the design of their initiatives.

A further change to the methodology of this research emerged at this point. According to the initial plan, the auto-ethnography and the first-person action research conducted with the team of the Imagine

Center were to serve as the prelude to the main research conducted in collaboration with other colleagues. Time constraints and the protocols of the organizations where they worked sometimes limited the degree to which colleagues not working for the Imagine Center could disclose their designs and programs, thus making the data collection spotty. Some great insights emerged in our conversations, but later I was asked not to mention many of these in writing in order to not affect the ongoing programs of colleagues or their relationships with others. This was not the first time I encountered the tension between publishing on practice and the needs of the practice. A number of my colleagues I interacted with prior to this research also felt the need to refrain from writing about their own work in order to not harm the work itself or the people involved.

As I was struggling with the conflicting needs of presenting in-depth case studies in the pages of this research and of restricting the information I could disclose about the work of my colleagues to the information they were comfortable sharing publicly, the action research within the Imagine Center's team was moving forward full force. And when I started drafting this book, it became increasingly clear that my supposed prelude with its thick and vivid descriptions, unrestricted input of the Imagine Center's colleagues, and ongoing experimentation with reflection and action cycle had evolved into the main piece. The findings from the dozens of cases that did not involve the Imagine Center and that were initially meant to be the main research, conversely, served to triangulate my findings and provide additional insights into the patterns of exclusion and marginalization and into the possible alternative ways forward.

Ethical considerations and limitations

As this book is based on my dissertation, following the established institutional procedures and obtaining a decision from the Human Subjects Review Board (HSRB) was the first and required step in ensuring that my research was ethical. As stipulated by the document I signed with the board, I discussed with each colleague with whom I would work the aims of the research, the procedures involved, the issue of confidentiality, and risks. After they agreed to participate, we signed an informed consent form. I discussed the procedure again with everyone whom I interviewed the second or third time, and each time I asked to give consent to be interviewed or recorded.

I find, however, procedural ethics necessary but not sufficient when working with people and I subscribe to the view of ethics as a relational category. Rossman and Rallis write, and I concur, that, "the public discourse [...] focuses on getting the procedural matters right, rather than on getting the ethical matters right. However, the ethical matters that arise in the everyday conduct of research demand deep engagement with how we relate to the persons who participate in a study" (Rossman and Rallis 2010, 380). Procedural ethics, they insist, are not enough to address the moral challenges that any research involving people can pose, and it is certainly the case with my research where I already had prior relationships with some of the colleague who joined my study.

The difference between procedural and relational ethics has been relevant for each step of this PAR process, starting from the need to obtain informed consent. Procedurally, it required the participants to sign the relevant document. Relationally, however, the picture has been more complicated. As I had a working relationship with many colleagues involved, they were willing to sign the consent form without reading it, because I asked them to. I saw it as my responsibility, therefore, not to be satisfied with their automatic agreement and to thoroughly discuss the possible implications of research with each potential participant before signing the form. I informed them also that my default approach is to preserve the confidentiality of my colleagues. The only instances where I mention names are when acknowledgment is due and where the colleague does not carry responsibility for the content of these pages.

Further, I was requesting those who I approached to join my research as colleagues who co-create knowledge rather than respondents. I had to further explain that the research might have an impact on their work, as it assumed asking them to question their own assumptions and their own work and contemplate changes to established procedures and practices. As new insights would be gained through the life of the project, the meaning of the participation in the research itself would change as well, and so would the meaning of the consent form they had signed. I saw the ethical approach to informed consent, in this case, as having an ongoing reflection/conversation about where everyone is, how they feel about the process, its purpose, and the risks involved. Were they comfortable continuing. or would they prefer to adjust the process, or would they even prefer to withdraw? As I discussed above, some of the colleagues chose indeed to withdraw at one stage of the process or another or asked me not to put in writing certain information they shared.

The decision to make the study of the Imagine Center, where I work, central to this book warranted additional ethical considerations. The approach had advantages and carried potential risks. Herr and Anderson, in their discussion of action research dissertation, suggest that "insider researchers often collaborate with other insiders as a way to do research that not only might have a greater impact on the setting, but is also more democratic." At the same time, they continue "[…] power relations in a setting operate even when insiders think they are being collaborative. […] their action research might benefit them at the expense of the powerless" (Herr and Anderson 2015, 36). This warning was more than relevant for my circumstances as I am one of the founders and was the acting executive director of the Imagine Center at the time when I started this research. To address this concern, prior to starting the action research with my teammates, we abolished the position of the executive director. I became instead the director of programs of the organization, responsible for the design of new initiatives and for the methodology of the ongoing work. I would contribute in other areas also, but as one of the members of the team with an equal voice to the others, not as the main voice. My "demotion" was not the only step we undertook. All the permanent members of Imagine Center's team simultaneously assumed responsibilities for other key areas of our work. The positions included: the developmental director responsible for fundraising and donor relations, country directors responsible for all operations in their home countries, financial and administrative director, methodological coordinator. Each core team member was agreed to have equal voice to all others, yet carry primary responsibility for their particular area of work. The implications of such a change went, of course, far beyond the frames of this research as discussed in Chapter 8.

The power relations, however, are conditioned not only by the organizational position of individuals but also by gender, age, experience, and more. I encountered compelling critiques of PAR when working with feminist colleagues, and this was in line with the critique of the "gender-blind politics" of PAR (see, for example, van der Meulen 2011). This critique is particularly relevant when working in openly patriarchal cultures, as it is the case with my research, where the male voices are likely to dominate and simply including women in the group might not be enough. My own male gender then in this context was an additional ethical challenge and a limitation. The way I tried to address this dilemma was through inviting experienced feminists research with whom I have long-lasting and trusting relationships to join in as colleagues in PAR, lead some of the interviews and the focus groups, and keep me in check by continuously challenging me and my procedures. I am very indebted to my colleagues who tirelessly worked with me, criticizing the approaches I took and helping to ensure that the gender-related power dynamics are accounted for in the findings. Moreover, these conversations prompted me to start working on a follow up article devoted to the discussion of gender in conflict resolution practice.

As studying marginalization and exclusion perpetuated by the conflict resolution field was part of the research, a big question followed, flagged by a colleague: how to ensure that the research itself does not contribute to marginalization? How to avoid turning this into a self-serving exercise that projects claims by conflict practitioners about the realities of others who are presumed to be marginalized, without learning the opinion of those directly excluded? Further, as the number of those who I could engage as colleagues was to be limited, what about the voices excluded by my research design itself?

I worked to address these by asking my colleagues, as well as myself, to pay special attention to those we marginalize during the "action" part of PAR, by questioning the influence of every step of the process and asking for feedback from those not included and those in the process who did not have much voice. As we had established during the initial round of interviews, marginalization can be happening at every stage of conflict resolution practice starting from the project naming and design, to the choice of methodology, and in the program itself. During the second and third round of interviews the colleagues who shared the concerns raised by this research were asked to reflect on these questions. Further, as through the process we were identifying patterns of marginalization, I started involving further colleagues who were marginalized or excluded by our initial framing of this research. These included junior members of facilitation teams, feminists, LGBTI activists, people of mixed heritage, representatives of minority groups, and those who hold unconventional for their societies' views. As these colleagues helped to identify further patterns of marginalization, I did my best to involve into the conversation the views of others who could be marginalized by these new patterns.

And of course, despite these efforts, and considering the limitations of time and resources and my focus on conflict resolution practitioners, voices of many groups still remained outside of the scope of this book. Among others this applies to those who are typically excluded from conflict resolution processes and whose reflections could greatly enhance the learning in this book. Further research would be necessary focusing intentionally on those typically excluded, to uncover additional patterns of exclusion that perpetuate social injustice and conflict. The main value of this research, in this respect, is the awareness developed by the practitioners involved regarding marginalization patterns in their own practice, rather than marginalization in conflict resolution work in general.

Adopting a PAR approach led me to a number of additional limitations that come with this method. I had to recognize that I myself am embedded in many discourses and relationships, and my ability to develop awareness of them and of my own taken-for-granted frames is limited. Such "blind spots," inevitably, mean that conclusions I reach in this book are incomplete and open to further challenge and transformation. I consider all I write here, therefore, consistent with all constructivist work, not a final verdict on any given topic but instead an invitation to an on-going dialogue.

The inherent subjectivity of PAR leads me also to address the trustworthiness of this research. "Trustworthiness" itself is a term that in qualitative science often serves as the equivalent of the validity and reliability of the quantitative methods. It was first used by Lincoln and

Guba and developed further ever since (Lincoln and Guba 1985). Borrowing from Marshall and Rossman, the key questions I aimed to answer to ensure that this research is trustworthy were: on what ground can we judge that the claims of this research are credible? What evidence is put forward to support these claims? Are these claims useful for the problems we are trying to address? (Marshall and Rossman 2011, 40). Creswell and Miller suggest a list of procedures that can help us answer these questions. These include: triangulation, search for disconfirming evidence, engaging in reflexivity, member checking, prolonged engagement in the field, collaboration, developing an audit trail, and peer debriefing (Creswell and Miller 2000).

I incorporated all of these procedures into my work to the best of my ability. The auto-ethnographic and PAR approaches themselves helped me address some of these points. Reflexivity, of course, is at the very core of PAR. Member checking, collaboration, and peer debriefing were also all parts of my methodology. Alternating reflections sessions internal to the team with debriefing sessions led by outside facilitators and evaluators, working with two different conflicts in the context of over 30 interventions, and comparing the insights developed by the Imagine Center's team with those of other colleagues were all triangulation procedures. Finally, our focus on continuously problematizing the very basis of our knowledge through the life of this research helped us with the search for disconfirming evidence.

Some of the biggest dilemmas in this research were created by the need to maintain the confidentiality or even anonymity of many of the respondents and the initiatives, while making public enough data to make the findings of the book credible. In some of the initiatives, particularly those in the Syrian context where the violence has been ongoing through the entire time of this research and the peace activists were in danger, maintaining the anonymity and not disclosing any details of the programs that could help identify them had been explicitly requested by some of the colleagues. While complying with this request unquestionably was my priority, this conflicted with the trustworthiness of the methods I had chosen that relied heavily on detailed description.

In addressing this dilemma, the priority was always given to the safety and anonymity of the colleagues and others whose identities this book could expose. The identities of everyone who did not explicitly agree to be a co-creator of knowledge yet whose work is mentioned in some form were very carefully concealed or anonymized; and when it comes to the participating colleagues, every section of the research that concerned them has been shared, feedback sought, and the requests to remove a section that could identify them incorporated prior to finalizing this research. The details and descriptions that could help identify were not used, including in cases when this would prevent me from articulating a critical finding. In one of the case studies where I have been involved as a facilitator and where maintaining the anonymity was necessary and identifying my presence in the program could in itself compromise it, I base my ethnographic description and findings on the interviews with other facilitators without mentioning my own involvement.

The methodology of the research that resulted in this book, as expected from PAR, has been in a process of continuous evolution. Adapting PAR as a methodology has been a challenging yet rewarding experience that led me to question everything I knew about conflict and conflict resolution, to see my own role in perpetuating exclusion, marginalization, and reproduction of conflict frames. The insights generated through the alternation of reflection and action, the ongoing critique by dozens of colleagues working in active conflict contexts of my and their own work led me to fundamentally rethink and reshape the meaning of conflict and conflict resolution practice and the relationships between the conflict resolution practitioner and those whom she works with, as well as the relationships between conflict resolution practitioners themselves.

Chapter 3

Auto-ethnographic sketch

Part II of this book presents a reflection on my work in the Syrian and Nagorno-Karabakh contexts. Prior to presenting you my work, however, I find it necessary to briefly discuss my background, my experiences that are relevant for understanding this research and their influence on the resulting perspective.

My background, the resulting perspective and subjectivity, and their role in this research

I was born in the Soviet Socialist Republic (SSR) of Armenia, at that time part of the Soviet Union. I grew up in a family of apolitical Tbilisi-born musicians from my mother's side, and a rather nationalist academic grandfather from my father's side. My paternal grandmother was a doctor who also stayed away from politics. The always present latent conflicts between my primarily Russian-speaking cosmopolitan maternal and my primarily Armenian-speaking and proud of national traditions paternal homes were a microcosm of the deep social cleavage that divided the Soviet Armenia, as well as most other Soviet republics, mainly along language lines. My mother was a teacher of French. And my father was a member of the communist party, I would think more out of convenience than conviction, and during the Soviet years worked at the Ministry of Culture, an institution that perhaps more than any other is the poster child of Hobsbawm's invention of tradition (Hobsbawm and Ranger 2012). By 1989 my father was among great many former party members who renounced communism and passionately joined the independence campaign.

My teenage years coincided with Gorbachev's Perestroika, resulting in the opening of the political space, followed by the development of social movements in Armenia: starting from the ecological one, followed by the movement for the unification of the predominantly Armenian-populated Nagorno-Karabakh Autonomous Oblast (NKAO) of the Azerbaijani SSR with the Armenian SSR, and ending in the movement and referendum for Armenia's independence from the Soviet Union. That period was characterized with the rise and development of nationalist ideology as an alternative to communism, and as most of my friends, I turned into a passionate nationalist myself. As a socially active young person, between 1988 and 1991, I was at the forefront of organizing anti-Soviet strikes in the secondary school where I studied, and a regular participant of various marches, sit-in protests, and demonstrations.

As Armenia and Azerbaijan gained their independence in 1991, their developing conflict over Nagorno-Karabakh turned into an open war that was halted by a Russian-mediated cease-fire agreement in 1994. The war left 25,000–30,000 people dead, hundreds of thousands displaced and the economies collapsed. A quarter of a century later, the conflict has not been resolved, the status of the disputed territories has never been agreed upon, the displaced have never returned, and the negotiations are stagnant. According to Carnegie Endowment's expert on the Caucasus de Waal and others, as of this writing, the conflict has a realistic chance of escalating into a new war (De Waal 2015).

The narrative of the conflict I held at the time of the war in early 1990s, mediated by books and articles of the mushrooming field of Armenian nationalist intellectuals, was one of aggressive and bloodthirsty Azerbaijanis who for decades had discriminated the Armenian population of Nagorno-Karabakh and were now engaged in a campaign of complete annihilation of the Armenians. As we commonly referred to the Azerbaijanis as "Turks," the narrative of the Nagorno-Karabakh war for many of us was part of the master-narrative of the memory of the Armenian genocide, one of the pillars of the contemporary Armenian identity. The anti-Armenian pogroms in Sumgait in 1988 and in Baku in 1990, extensively covered in the Armenian media with detailed descriptions of rape and execution, rechanneled my activism in the direction of the war effort, up to an attempt to volunteer as a soldier.

I never went to the war. Luckily for me, then a 16-year-old, I was deemed to be too young for the front line and sent home.

A few months later, as my friends and acquaintances started returning from the war, I was exposed to first-hand accounts of violence.

The violence that in my narrative was the function of the Other had now been committed by the side I considered mine.

This was the turning point that transformed a nationalist teenager into a peace activist and set on the path of becoming a conflict resolution practitioner. When I first became aware of the violence committed by "my side," I tried to deny the reality, justify it as necessary and noncharacteristic of the Armenians, but gradually came to accept that I never fully realized what exactly going to the war meant: what actions I would have to perform were I to end up on the front line.

This turning point influenced my later career choice. I realized that I had been incredibly lucky; that I had put myself very close to a position where I would have had to engage in violence, including possible violence against civilians; that it was only the accident of my date of birth that made me ineligible for the war, which I otherwise was ready to jump into; and that this accident did not free me from the responsibility for the violence committed and lives destroyed. Having been close to becoming a fighter by choice helped me later in life to also understand and appreciate the sentiments that drive others to take arms, not out of some sadistic instinct, but, perhaps misguided, yet sincere urge to stand up to perceived injustice. A fan of Sartre, when volunteering for war I had thought of myself as engaging in violence of the oppressed, performing resistance. Now I had to accept that the violence I almost engaged in was the violence of some of the oppressed against the others equally oppressed, neither able to identify nor confront the larger structures of oppression (Sartre 2004).

In 1992–1997, having made a commitment to myself to engage in conflict resolution work, I gave up the chance to go to medical school, and instead worked on my BA/MA degree in political science and French at what was then the Institute of Foreign Languages after Valeri Brusov[5] as I understood conflict resolution to be a subset of international relations. To say that political sciences in Armenia at the time were underdeveloped would be an understatement. Armenia gained

---

5   Later the Institute was renamed into Yerevan State Linguistic University after Valeri Brusov and recently yet into Yerevan Brusov State University of Languages and Social Sciences.

independence only a year prior, and 1992 was the first year that a political science degree was offered at my university. We had no textbooks, only limited literature available on political theory and, perhaps most critically, no professors with respective education. To complete the picture, these were the years of war and complete economic collapse, when all the commodities we were used to disappeared in the middle of the winter. The natural gas flow to residences and schools was cut off; the electricity was present from half an hour to a few hours a day. There was a shortage of food, the kind when a "good" week would mean acquiring a loaf or two of low-quality bread for a family without much else to supplement it with. The improvised handmade stoves that would burn the already rare forests were the main source of heat, later replaced by smoky kerosene lamps.

Against this background, once again I was incredibly lucky as we had a dedicated professional, Irina Anatolievna Kuznetsova, as our professor of political science. Having taught Scientific Communism in her Soviet-era career, she was now committed to giving us the best possible education under the circumstances, while also contributing to the development of the field of political science in Armenia. Part of our studies were devoted to identifying existing literature in Russian on political theory in various libraries, as well as to translating the works of major thinkers from French, English, and German (the three languages that students in her class minored or majored in). It was in her classes that I first encountered the enlightenment theories of Kant, Montesquieu, Tocqueville, Locke, Jefferson, as well as the works of the realist ideologues such as Kissinger and Brzezinski. A parallel important influence on my thinking about conflicts were the classes on philosophy, a rather well-developed field in Soviet and early post-Soviet academia, where the competing ideas of various schools from topologists to empiricists, from existentialists to Frankfurt School made me consider alternative approaches to social relationships. My BA/MA thesis was a comparative study of the ideologies of liberalism/neoliberalism and conservatism/neo-conservatism. In my undergraduate years, I learned more about conflict resolution or more precisely "conflictology." Yet at the time, I was not able to obtain much literature on the topic or meet professionals in the field.[6]

In 1997, my intention to study political science or if possible conflict resolution at a doctoral level, either at home or abroad, was put on hold by the mandatory service in the army where I served as a tank commander on the Armenian-Azerbaijani border, now at a cease-fire time. Soon after my discharge from the army, Zara and I got married. Zara is a ceramic artist-turned-designer. We have been in love and together ever since we met in our early undergraduate years, dated all through college, and survived the long-distance relationship during my army service.

In another major development, by the time of my discharge in late 1998 my parents had emigrated to France, and the need to sustain myself and our newly born family led me to the business sector. For a few years, I collaborated with a childhood friend in establishing and running an eclectic set of business ventures ranging from one of the first insurance companies in Armenia to a vacuum packaging machines production, telecommunication, and export of Armenian wine, beer, and dry fruit to Europe. Despite a relative success in business, as the time went by, I found myself increasingly questioning my career choice. I had to continuously compete in a predatory environment of a shadow economy where the laws and institutions of the newly independent Armenia were slow to develop, often having to resort to practices that I considered unethical, and that did not fit well with the way I hoped to live my life.

In the late 1990s, confronted with a question posed by my grandmother about the meaning of my life, I engaged in extensive reading of philosophical literature. My grandmother's question was of an existential nature. I had a difficult relationship with my parents and grandparents in the preceding years that had led for a short period to my homelessness. Looking back, I understand that they all had difficulty coping with the collapse of a country, of the one value and economic system they knew. Overnight we were not living anymore in a

---

6   In 1996, the Center for Regional Integration and Conflict Resolution was founded at the Yerevan State University with support from the GMU. Later, an MA degree program was also instituted, as a concentration basis in the sociology department.

communist country where everyone was economically equal, where education and basic needs such as home and healthcare were free, and the concept of unemployment did not exist. The country, of course, was also politically repressive which led many of us into the streets demanding freedom, independence, and, implicitly, capitalism. But we knew nothing about capitalism, as it turned out, and those in my family who were socialized in the communist system had an extreme difficulty finding themselves in this new value system ravaged by war, extreme corruption, and private enterprise. Some resorted to heavy drinking, others emigrated, and yet others severed relationships with the rest of the family, which was probably their way of adapting to the change but which I, as an impressionable teenager, interpreted as betrayal. When, soon after the discharge from the army and despite not having a place to live, I succeeded in business and became the main breadwinner for my grandparents, I rather arrogantly assumed to soon be elevated in the family to a position of respect. Instead, my grandmother questioned the meaning of my life as it was devoted exclusively to moneymaking and was void of ideals or of anything spiritual.

On the surface defiant, deep inside I knew that she was right. It led me to philosophy, if in a chaotic manner. I was jumping from ancient Indian Upanishads to St. Augustine to enlightenment thinkers and to anarchist and Marxists. Camus, and particularly Sartre, fascinated me most. They were forcing me to question this alternative-to-communism nationalist and capitalist system that I had been idealizing and fighting for ever since my childhood. By the 2000s, I was ready to pursue my long-term interest in learning about conflict resolution and continuing my graduate education. In parallel to running a business, I started learning English, volunteering in civil society organizations; I became part of various youth activist groups.

By 2004, I was living in Boston working on my MA degree in conflict resolution at Brandeis University. While at Brandeis, I started noticing students of Turkish and Armenian background engage in confrontations during public events on whether the World War I-time massacres of Armenians in the Ottoman Empire constituted a genocide or a civil war. Determined to question my own stereotypes and assumption, in late 2005, I joined forces with a Turkish graduate student from Brandeis University, and we co-established the Turkish-Armenian Dialogue Group of Boston that united students from the Boston area universities interested in Armenian-Turkish relations.

I started the dialogue as a co-facilitator, but soon had to ask the group to help me find another facilitator, so that I can become a participant. I had thought of myself as open-minded enough to be able to facilitate that dialogue as in the summer of 2005, I had worked at Seeds of Peace,[7] an organization devoted to Arab-Israeli dialogue, coordinating a group of Israeli, Palestinian, Jordanian, Egyptian, Afghani, and other educators. Working with "my own" conflict, however, proved to be much harder than I thought. I was ready to remain calm and facilitate were the Turkish participants unaware of or even denying the Armenian genocide. As I learned, however, I was not ready to hear a Turkish participant accept that a mass murder of Armenians had happened, and that it was justified. My extreme reaction showed to me that I was not ready to facilitate and had to go through a dialogue myself. We invited an external facilitator to lead the group, while the Turkish co-facilitator and I became participants.

Although the conflict over the interpretation of history plays a central role in the Armenian-Turkish context, as we started that dialogue, we tried to avoid discussing history and focused on the present-day relations between these societies. History, however, would come up continuously leading to confrontations and not allowing us to move forward. Gradually we accepted the need to talk about history. With most of the participants studying international relations or law, however, we did not know how. We spent months in heated debates that brought us close to abandoning the dialogue. Eventually one of the participants, Ceren Ergenc, a Turkish PhD student whose research was on collective memory in China, introduced us to constructivist approaches to understanding history, allowing us to look at it as a subjective narrative that can be analyzed and retaught, and not a battle of truths.

The reflection sessions that followed, with time, helped us process our own emotions and stereotypes. We analyzed each instance

---

7   http://www.seedsofpeace.org. Accessed on April 17, 2017.

and phrase that triggered one of us or the other, causing emotional outbreak.

A few months into the dialogue, we made a decision to proceed without the external facilitator. The facilitator had been our safety net that had allowed us to start the dialogue, but she was also the net that was helping us avoid taking responsibility for the process. We agreed that breaking the vicious cycle and having a true breakthrough required us to develop our own ability to communicate directly without help from a "third party."

As we learned to listen, reflect, self-facilitate, the conversations became increasingly constructive. The curiosity to learn from one another became more important than proving a point. We started seeing how differently the Turks and the Armenians construct the past and how unfamiliar we were with what the "other side" saw as key in our relationship. No topic remained taboo from that point on, including the most sensitive ones. We shared some very personal family stories—stories that had had a very strong impact on every one of us.

A day prior to April 24, 2006,[8] the Turkish members of the group contacted the Armenians asking if they could join the commemoration. By that time, some among the Turkish participants referred to the event as genocide, and others did not, stressing, however, that irrespective of the term they consider it a colossal tragedy, and the memory of the victims had to be honored.

On the 24th, walking all together toward the commemoration venue, we recalled stories we read about Jews and Germans jointly visiting Auschwitz, and how hard the experience was for the Germans. And that this commemoration might be similarly hard for our Turkish friends. What followed was unexpected. The event was less of a commemoration ritual as I imagined it and more of a series of ultra-nationalist and anti-Turkish speeches. Some 30 minutes into the event, a renowned American-Armenian journalist told the following story (reproduced in my words): "…recently I forced myself finally to visit that terrible country—Turkey. The first thing I noticed on my way to the hotel from the airport were two kinds of houses: some had big and large windows, and the others small and narrow. And I knew

---

[8] April 24 is the day when the Armenian genocide is commemorated.

immediately that the houses with large windows used to belong to Armenians as they are open to the world and full of light, just as the Armenian hearts are. And the houses with small windows always belonged to the Turks. They are small and dark as Turkish souls...."

Hearing these words, all the Armenian participants left the event. We came in thinking that it will be hard for our Turkish friends to be present at the genocide commemoration, yet it was us, Armenians, who left ashamed. The next dialogue session turned out to be the last one for the group. There was nothing left to say. The Turks in the group had understood what it meant to be an Armenian, to carry the memory of the genocide and face the official Turkish denial and participated in the commemoration event. The Armenians in the group understood what it was to be a Turk who starts by not knowing anything about the genocide, and once she tries to learn, she is confronted by a discourse of a "small and dark Turkish soul" that is predisposed to commit genocides.[9]

This dialogue led me to collaboration with Ceren Ergenc in developing a dialogue methodology for "mediating history" that could be applied in other conflict contexts as well. As a result, when in 2007 I co-founded the Imagine Center for Conflict Transformation together with Christopher Littlefield and Jale Sultanli, it was this same methodology that was at the core of our work. Between 2007 and 2009, we used the methodology to facilitate a number of successful dialogues, mainly in the Nagorno-Karabakh conflict context for Armenian and Azerbaijani graduate students.

At first, improving the "mediating history" methodology and leading dialogues that change the perception of the participants was in itself the motivation for my work. By 2009, as we settled into the methodology, I stated asking myself "what next." How can our practice influence not only the individuals who take part in our dialogues but the conflict discourses on the level of the societies?

This question led me to undertake PhD studies at S-CAR, GMU in 2010. The years at S-CAR helped me further explore constructivist

---

9 For a more detailed analysis of the work of the Turkish-Armenian Dialogue Group of Boston, see Gamaghelyan (2017).

and critical approaches to conflict resolution. With my thinking gradually evolving, I currently find my approach to conflict is closest to postmodernism and discourse analysis and more specifically CDA.

These academic explorations influenced and were paralleled by developments in my practice. From 2011, we reached an agreement in the growing team of the Imagine Center that our methodology is guided by a constructivist paradigm and aims to question and help transform the conflict-sustaining discourses. We worked primarily in the South Caucasus, open to collaborations internationally. To my surprise, I soon discovered that we occupied a unique niche, at least in the South Caucasus, where most conflict work is done either from a positivist positions or without an explicitly articulated methodology. Our constructivist approach allowed us to tackle issues, such as history, that had been seen as unresolvable: we started actively working with discourse creating professionals, such as journalists, analysts, educators, and historians, in areas where the previous experiences had not been particularly successful as the interventions stayed on course with trying to establish the truth, historical or otherwise, finding themselves instead in deep disagreements with each other's narratives.

The exposure and deconstruction of discourses and narratives became central to the methodology of the Imagine Center. When working with youth or journalists from conflict zones, we start our efforts from a dialogue focused on the analysis and deconstruction of conflict narratives. The approach helps them build a shared understanding of the context and basis for future collaboration. With historians, we start from establishing a common methodological basis. In the South Caucasus context, our initial efforts resulted in the co-authorship of a "Methodological Manual on Principles of Historiography and History Education" by Armenian, Azerbaijani, Georgian, and South Ossetian historians, espousing an explicitly constructivist approach. After agreeing on the methodological principles and publishing the manual, the historians engaged in writing alternative educational texts.

As of this writing, having the backing of a few dozens of colleagues from all parts of the South Caucasus, Turkey, Ukraine, and Russia, the Imagine Center is engaged in the efforts to institutionalize a Conflict Studies Center for Eastern Europe and Turkey. It is envisioned to be a transnational think tank and postgraduate education space that espouses a constructivist and even postmodernist philosophy and is engaged in development and advocacy for a new progressive and transformative vision for the post-Soviet societies and Turkey where we all originate from.

Part II

There have been many initiatives in which I was involved that deserve to be retold in detail, both as an acknowledgement of the incredible effort and, often, risks of the people who participated in them and as case studies that could benefit this book. No to abuse my reader's attention, however, I limit the description to two cases, one from the Syrian and one from the Nagorno-Karabakh contexts presented in Part II of this book.

Chapter 4
On ethical and methodological challenges of leading a Syrian dialogue program in the middle of a civil war: from exclusion to inclusion

This chapter is focused on an initiative that took place in the context of the Syrian conflict in early 2013. I chose this case to be discussed in detail because it demonstrates clearly the harm that can be caused by well-meaning conflict resolution practices that unreflectively follow the binary international relations frames in understanding conflicts as a disagreement between well-defined sides and attempt to create dialogue between them. In the Syrian context, that in 2013 was commonly seen to be a confrontation between the Assad-regime and the organized opposition, framing the workshop as a dialogue between them served to construct and reinforce conflict discourses that empowered the supporters of these two extremes, marginalizing the majority of the participates who did not align with either. Having recognized the problem, the facilitators and the participants worked together to find new inclusive frames. The case, therefore, is instructive for my research as it exposes the problem of adopting the binary conflict frames customary for international relations in conflict resolution practice. The case also describes the attempt to engage the entire group into the evolving design in search of an inclusive alternative to this problematic, albeit well-established approach.

This very case, I should note, is the inspiration for this book. The primary sources of data used in this chapter are interviews, reflections, and focus group discussions with colleagues who were involved with these projects either as facilitators or as participants. My own reflections were conducted with help from colleagues who acted as interviewers or focus group facilitators.

The next few pages were initially drafted in the airplane, on the way back home from perhaps the most challenging yet inspiring program that I have had an opportunity to co-facilitate. Ethically, this is a difficult program to discuss. It took place in the middle of the raging civil war, with participants coming from all across Syria, a few of them jailed by the Syrian regime both prior and following the program; some have lost family members to war, including children; other participants' towns got massacred and they barely escaped. Many live under the imminent threat of violence or are experiencing violence as of this writing, and exposing their cooperation might further endanger them. Considering this, I have to exercise care in ensuring their anonymity. I will be referring simply to the "Syrian dialogue" and "participants" here, removing any markers that can help identify the program or those involved. Further, I was hired as an external facilitator in this program, and the organization that invited me and two of my colleagues continues to work in Syria. Any breach of confidentiality could damage their work also. In this text, therefore, they will be referred to as the "organizers."

The program took place in a neighboring country and brought together young activists from Syria, including pro-regime, pro-revolutionary, and unaligned. We had seven full days to train the activists in conflict resolution skills, so they can work more effectively in their communities. The challenges started piling up from the start. As the activists were from various parts of Syria, many had to cross the entire country to reach the program location, driving through zones of active fighting. This meant that some participants arrived early, while others half a day later extremely tired, stressed, and weary. The second challenge was in the numbers: we were expecting 20–22 participants, yet as everyone arrived, we counted 35. The reason, as we learned, was that having previous experience of mass cancelations because of security risks, the organizers invited more people than listed in the project documents, as they were not sure that everyone would make it to the program location. Yet this time everyone did, and we had only 11 double rooms to accommodate 35 people. Without any additional budget, we had to ask the participants to have three to four people in each room, sharing this tight space with those they considered enemies. The facilitators were not living in luxury conditions either, one of the colleagues and myself moving into the living room couches to free up a bedroom. I will leave out here the story of negotiating with the hotel for additional meals without additional payment, although this and other administrative matters took a big chunk of our time and added an incredible amount of stress. I will let the logistical struggles remain one of the untold stories of the daily life of a facilitator.

Yet the biggest challenges were yet to come. Only a few hours into our training, we realized that not everyone in the group was emotionally ready to engage in skill-building, something that was the proclaimed goal of the program. Some in the group were professional trainers and ready indeed to learn technical skills. The majority, however, were people from various fields—teachers, doctors, musicians, lawyers, and even a banker—whose life was suddenly interrupted by violence and who had a strong desire to contribute to peace. But they were also, in their own words, hurt, scared, mistrusting or even hating the others. They communicated a clear need to discuss the conflict, to share and to hear from those in other communities against whom by now they had built up an enemy image and stereotypes, to reconcile, before they could work on skills. And considering how fresh and immediate the pain was, this was not an easy or short conversation to have.

After some intense reflection within the facilitation team, which we refer to as facilitator co-debriefing[10] (Gamaghelyan and Littlefield 2012), we decided to consult the group in changing the agenda and strengthening the dialogue component of the program. We argued also that dialogue and skills were not mutually exclusive. The ability to go through one's own dialogue with "the other," to find processes that allow one to handle the conflict within are critical skills that any facilitator or trainer should have. The rest, various toolkits, are useful, but technical. The participants were all supportive.

We adapted the general framework of the Imagine Center's dialogue program design and methodology tested for a number of years in other conflict contexts. Our methodology has been based on a combination of mediating history and PSW methodologies. The first one, as discussed in the previous chapter, helps develop reflective abilities of the participants and guides them through an open and constructive

---

10   Facilitator co-debriefings are ongoing reflection sessions aimed at continuous improvements in the program. They can take place prior to, during, and after the program, involve the entire program team, and are co-facilitated by the team members themselves, thus "co-debriefing."

discussion of the conflict narratives and memories. The second shifts the discussion from the positions of the conflict sides toward the present-day needs, fears, concerns, and hopes and looking for ways of addressing and satisfying them.[11] Our methodology also puts a strong emphasis onto trust- and team-building, as well as training and skill-building, all of which aim to develop the participants' ability to express themselves freely, constructively, and self-critically; listen and empathize with others even when they disagree[12]; put oneself into the other's shoes and see the situation with their eyes; go through intense dialogue, periodically stepping back and reflecting on what can be learned from the experience both emotionally and intellectually; leave the program ready for collaborations across the conflict divide.

Adapting our methodology tested in other conflict contexts to the Syrian case was not easy. Many aspects of the conflict and the program set-up were different from the workshops we had conducted previously.

One difference was striking, and became the basis for this very research: in all the other conflict contexts we worked in (Arab-Israeli, Turkish-Armenian, Armenian-Azerbaijani, and more) the dichotomous nature of the actors seemed to be well preestablished. A later look, as I accept now and discuss in the following chapters, revealed that adopting a binary frame in the other conflicts, similar to Syria, led us to exclude many groups who did not neatly "fit" the binary frame. But the Syrian case presented a new challenge altogether: who were the sides to the conflict? When recruiting, the organizers assumed that the conflict "sides" were those who support the government and those who oppose it. However, was the entire population divided along these lines? Or at least, were our participants?

Next, in 2013, and still as of this writing, Syria was in the middle of a civil war. In the past, we had worked with conflicts that are not resolved, such as the Armenian-Azerbaijani case, and where the slow-burning violence is ongoing, and the resumption of large-scale war

---

11   The PSW methodology was discussed in the introduction and the review of conflict resolution theories chapters refereeing to H. Kelman (1972), Babbitt and Steiner (2009), and others.
12   For discussion of empathy (not to be confused with sympathy), see Halpern and Weinstein (2004).

possible. But in none of the conflicts we had worked in, the large-scale mass violence was occurring as the dialogue was taking place. For the Syrian participants, even traveling to the workshop venue was not safe.

We had a number of other visible challenges as well: the group was mainly Arabic-speaking, with only four or five participants fluent in English, while only one of the three facilitators who was from Lebanon spoke Arabic. The second facilitator was US-born, and I was the third one, born in Armenia and living in the United States, both of us having to rely on English and work through simultaneous interpreters during the day and through voluntary translation by the English-speaking participants after 5pm.

Our perceived national and ethnic identities posed an additional challenge: the United States was at the time of this workshop considering a military intervention in Syria; Lebanon has had its own uneasy relationship with Syria and mirrors its ethno-religious divides; and Armenians are one of the main Christian minority groups in Syria and were considered to be largely pro-regime. We had to work extra hard, therefore, to establish trust and position ourselves as complex individuals and comrades in looking for ways out of violence, rather than a Lebanese, an American, and an Armenian who are there to teach Syrian participant some lessons.

Further, in many programs we had a team of insider and outsider facilitators: for example, all our Armenian-Azerbaijani dialogues have been run by a team that consists of one Azerbaijani, one Armenian, and one or two external facilitators. The insiders have been closely involved with the recruitment of the participants, and co-facilitated most of the dialogue sessions that touch on the content of the conflict and actively cooperate with participants in follow up work; and the outside facilitators have been working on team-building and creating a safe space. Yet in this initiative, we had no Syrian facilitator and found ourselves in a position of leading a dialogue among Syrians, while being outsiders. Moreover, as meeting in Syria was not possible for safety reasons, we had to ask the group to travel to a neighboring country (one having its own stake in the conflict), where they would have to meet and discuss internal Syrian matters.

Finally, this group involved 35 participants, which was almost double the size of the biggest group we had worked with previously, making it challenging to create a space where everyone is heard and has the opportunity to reflect and learn. Leading a skill-building workshop with all these limitations seemed challenging, but doable. Leading a dialogue with these limitations was a challenge of a different magnitude.

When the idea of transforming the training into a dialogue came up and we articulated all these difficulties within the facilitation team, to say that we felt intimidated and questioned our ability to facilitate such dialogue would be an understatement. We had to step back and ask ourselves if we were ready: if we were the right fit for this case and whether we were certain that we could contribute positively rather than doing harm; whether our motives for getting involved were ethical or not. The answer could have been different, were we not already in the program location. But we were already there, with the group. The best we could do at the time, we felt, was to move forward with full transparency and close consultation with the participants.

The program design and implementation

The program design we adopted by Day 2, not aware that framing the conflict we were facing as dichotomous could be problematic, was focused on stepping away from structured skill-building and moving toward dialogue between Assad and opposition supporters. The design was to be semi-structured: some sessions—on history, PSWs and future planning—would be preestablished, while the rest would be open and invite the participants to develop their own process.

What we left to the group to decide included:

- developing their own vision and specific objectives, expectations and hopes that they had for the program, with an understanding that we, the facilitators, would then work on helping them meet these goals;
- outlining the concerns that they had with the program and developing ground rules that would prevent their concerns from materializing;

- collaboratively developing their own historical narratives, and lists of needs, fears, concerns, and hopes;
- outlining a vision for the future and specific commitments they could or could not make to each other in staying involved in peacebuilding.

What the facilitators would bring to the table was:

- creating a safe space within which the above-mentioned conversations could happen;
- helping to build trust, understanding, and empathy among the group members;
- building skills that would help the group have hard conversations constructively, while also taking these skills with them back to their society;
- fostering a collaborative and creative process so that all the voices are included and heard;
- providing guidance when necessary and facilitating hardest sessions, while stepping back as much as possible and allowing the participants to take control over their own process;
- leading regular reflective sessions when the group steps back from the dialogue and engages in active intellectual and emotional learning;
- bringing in theoretical and practical knowledge from the Imagine Center's past experiences to offer possible frameworks of communication;
- helping the group to have fun along with their hard work.

Considering the objectives, we understood that the dialogue process was not going to look like a straight line that goes from a departure point A to a destination point B. Instead we expected our journey graph to look like a messy zigzag of great progress and inspiring moments; alternated with intense conflicts, disorientation, and a feeling that the program was failing; followed by learning from these moments, shifting conversations from intellectual to emotional or vice versa; and doing that with the group's outlined objectives as a guide and ensuring that even in the inevitable moments when we feel like we are failing, we could recalibrate and design a new path toward our target.

Based on the above considerations we redesigned the program during Day 2 to look as follows:

Day 1 (already completed at the time of redesign):

The trainers and the participants arrived; initial introductions and icebreakers were held. The participants were asked to roommate with others of the same sex but from different regions of Syria. We moved into two big villas—one for all the female participants and one for all the male participants. This living arrangement would allow the participants from different regions and viewpoints to create a human connection and friendships.

Day 2 (partially completed by the time of redesign):

Before lunch: deeper introductions and getting to know each other; team-building exercises; outlining the vision and specific expectations and concerns for the program; coming up with ground rules; skill-building including discussion of active listening and other practical tools. By this point, we learned that the group prefers to engage in dialogue and not only skill-building. The rest of the activities were gradually redesigned.

After lunch, the group would be offered to discuss and decide what is the main fault line of the Syrian conflict: what are the sides? After deciding this, the group would break into two sides and develop historical narratives of the conflict for each of these sides.

After dinner, we would plan a light activity that would bring the participants together and help build relationships. We would start an activity called "Color Games" borrowed from Seeds of Peace where both the American facilitator and I had worked in the past. The ongoing activity would involve breaking the group into three "color" teams—blue, yellow, and green—of mixed gender, regional, and political affiliation and leading it through a competition built around fun exercises such as putting together a fashion show from limited materials available in the room or a dance performance, creating a short video on some silly topic. This should help the group to have a lot of fun every evening after a hard day of dialogue and would also redraw the fault lines in a nonthreatening way, preventing the participants from breaking into factions or subgroups that replicate the conflict divide.

Day 3:
This entire day would be devoted to discussing the narratives of each of the two conflicting sides. The skill-building in the morning would be focused on handling difficult conversations, with a message that understanding does not equal agreeing, that our aim for this session is not to establish one truth, but instead to understand the stories that drive each of the sides of the conflict. We would offer exercises that illustrate how the stories that one disagrees with are the ones that one knows the least and could benefit the most from understanding.

This day we expected to be one of the hardest and likely to bring the conflict into the open, therefore, we also planned an intense evening activity within the framework of the Color Games.

Day 4:
In the morning, we would ask the group to take a step back, reflect on the experience, reengage in relationship building and learning. We would start the morning from discussing the idea of reflective practice (Schon 1984), an ability to observe oneself from aside. We also planned to discuss the overall concept of dialogue and the possibility that the positions of people might not change, but that an overarching and inclusive (in this case, an all-Syrian one) frame can be built that is shared by everyone, which has space in it for all positions, even if they seem mutually exclusive. We would conduct further skill-building exercises.

After lunch, we would switch from analytical to personal and discuss how this conflict affected each personally. This session, which had emerged spontaneously in our work in the Nagorno-Karabakh context and has been held during most of our previous dialogue workshops, allows for each individual participant to share their pain and for the group to bond on a very deep and personal level.

Day 5:
Having discussed the narratives and what had led to the conflict according to conflict sides, it would now be time to focus on what sustains the conflict at present. For this session, we would use an adaptation of the PSW methodology discussed in the Introduction and Chapter 1.

As a theoretical introduction, we planned to discuss Maslow's hierarchy of needs (Maslow 1943) followed by Burton's instrumentalization of Maslow's theory for conflict resolution (Burton 1990).

As the next step, we would ask the group to break back into two conflict sides again, each outlining the needs, fears, concerns, and hopes of the respective part of the society. The subgroups would then reunite and present the lists of their needs, fears, concerns, and hopes in the joint session.

Day 6:

By this time of the dialogue, the discussion of the conflict itself should be completed, and it would be time again to step back and reflect on the entire experience, from the moment of applying to the program through the latest PSW session. What did we learn? What did this mean for each one of us? What does this mean for our role as peacebuilders? What can we take from this into our future work?

This would also be the time to work on personal relations, resolving any outstanding conflicts, misunderstandings, sharing acknowledgments and thanks.

In the afternoon of Day 6, we planned a break from the program: traveling to a nearby city or hiking in the mountains.

Day 7:

This was to be the last day of the program. Chances were that by this point the agenda would be considerably altered compared to what was planned. For now, we planned to start this day from a symbolic exercise of transitioning from thinking about the past and the present into developing a vision of a shared future. The morning would be devoted to a presentation by the organizers and the donors of the project, inviting the participants to join their peacebuilding efforts in Syria. We then planned to follow with a discussion of how the participants can integrate and further their own peace efforts. We would also hold a reentry conversation (H. Kelman 1972), preparing the participants to face emotional challenges as they return home and to the conflict context. We would develop agreements regarding confidentiality, photo sharing in social media, and discuss other safety concerns.

The final competition in Color Games would identify the winning team, and every group would receive a prize. As a final activity, the participants would be asked (in advance) to design and lead their own closing session.

On paper, our design was completed. Now it was time to implement it.

Program design vs. program reality

We had chosen a remote and isolated location for the program not far from the Syrian border. The group started arriving from the morning. As already mentioned, we had 35 participants instead of the expected 22. Moreover, according to the program design, the participants had to share rooms with someone from another region, often a person they would see as representing an enemy group. We had considered whether asking them to roommate with an "enemy" was safe and ethical, and had decided in favor. First, the organizers had assured us that every person was carefully vetted and there was little to no chance of violent behavior. Second, one of the aims of the program was to help participants to get to know and understand the others and what better way is there to do that than by sharing a room? Finally, the alternative to cross-regional room-mating was to pair participants with others from their own town, most likely of a similar background and views. In our experience, this would facilitate their staying "in a box," communicating mainly with someone they already know, possibly turning the rooms into "headquarters" for one conflict side or the other, a division that would be prevented by the absence of a single-group space in the context of cross-town room-mating.

As one can imagine, asking the participants to share rooms with people they consider enemies was not easy and generated anxiety and resistance, particularly among men. Later on, as the program progressed, our insistence was vindicated as the room-mating arrangements received a lot of acknowledgments from all the participants.

On Day 2, the group communicated a strong need for a dialogue prior to skill-building leading us to redesign the program from primarily a training into primarily a dialogue with elements of training. As we engaged in dialogue, however, many dynamics emerged that made us question the concept of "sides" that had been so axiomatic to our conflict resolution practice. Days 2 and 3, according to our redesign, were devoted to team-building followed by sharing and analysis of the narratives of the conflict sides. The exercise, as done in the past, assumed the presence of distinct sides, whose representatives hold collective memories. The initial question we asked, therefore, was what were the main "sides" to the Syrian conflict. The participants all agreed that the sides were the Assad regime and the opposition groups. Up to this point, therefore, not only the facilitators but also the participants shared the binary frame for understanding the conflict. As the next step, we asked the participants to self-identify as supporters of one or the other side, separate into single-party groups and work on the development of a historical timeline of the conflict from that side's perspective.

What happened next was disorienting: three people self-identified as pro-Assad and five as pro-opposition with one or two more hesitating whether to join a group or not. The rest—more than 25—could not self-identify. Still stuck in the binary mindset, the facilitators assumed that people had sides and did not self-identify because of safety concerns. We voiced this assumption, calling a coffee break to consult the participants in private with an intention of finding an alternative way forward. The ensuing consultations revealed an interesting picture: yes, a number of participants confirmed that people worry to self-identify as either pro-Assad or pro-opposition fearing others in the room who they just met. But that was not the majority's concern. Almost every person from those who did not already self-identify said that they intensely disliked both Assad and any known opposition. In other words, the overwhelming majority, 27 out of the 35 participants, did not see themselves as part of any known conflict side. We later learned that if not asked to choose between only two options, a number of those who initially self-identified as one or the other would also join the unaligned, leaving only four to five people who strongly identified with either Assad or opposition.

We were faced with an apparent paradox: a group from a conflict zone eager to engage in dialogue but not representing clear conflict sides. How were we to lead a dialogue, without sides?

This revelation certainly warranted soul searching for facilitators, which we had to postpone at the moment as we were in the middle of the work-day and the events were unfolding rapidly. This was only our second day together and the mistrust among the participants was still present: as if to deepen it, we had an unexpected guest.

Intermission

As we were trying to break into conflict sides, a man walked into the conference room, asked if this was the "peace conference" and if he could join. As no one seemed to know him, we called a coffee break to talk to him.

The man presented himself as a rebel, who had heard about the "peace conference" and had decided to cross the border, join us, and give peace a chance. We, as facilitators, expressed our admiration to him, offered coffee, and conferred facing an impossible dilemma: on the one hand, we could not invite him to join. Each participant was carefully vetted, had a history of peace activism, and no violent background. And even then, people were visibly scared of each other. Suddenly we had a self-identified rebel, who had not applied to the program and had not been selected, while we had three open Assad supporters in the room, one of them a known journalist, who was now following me everywhere telling I was his only protection since the rebels (he had assumed there would be more rebels outside) had come after him.

The alternative—asking the guest to leave—did not look appealing either: our conference room was in the basement of an isolated hotel in the mountains, very close to the Syrian border. We did not know if our guest was armed, or if he was alone. Asking him to leave meant keeping the group trapped in the basement from where we would have to emerge eventually, unprotected and not sure who would be meeting us outside.

After a rather long break, we ended up choosing to invite our guest to stay. The calculation was simple: we had no safe option, but asking a potentially armed rebel to leave thus angering him and facing him later was riskier than having him as a participant with us in the room, engaged in dialogue.

We also tried to devise an "escape plan." Over the break, I secretly arranged a car. I then told those who had self-identified as pro-Assad (two women and one man) that a car was ready and they could leave during a break quietly, get into the car, cross the border, and return home. This was the safest option we could offer under the circumstances. Were they to stay, this would be their choice and a shared responsibility.

To convey how unsafe the situation felt, I will describe my own reaction: when I called home that evening and Zara, my wife, asked me how I was and if things were safe, I could not find an answer. I thought that considering the proximity and the porousness of the border, that we had a mixed group and our program location was apparently known to at least some rebels one of whom was now with us, there was a chance that I would not be coming out of the workshop alive. And if so, this might have been the time to say good-bye. Had I raised this concern, of course, and in the event of nothing violent happening, I would have given my family an unfounded reason for a "heart attack." I did not share my worry, perhaps predictably, but the hesitation was there.

The pro-Assad folks decided to stay. And I am glad they did. Everything turned out well, in the end, though it looked not certain at the time.

Back to dialogue

The initial adjustment we made was rather cosmetic: instead of breaking into real "conflict sides," we decided to role-play them. The participants randomly separated into pro-Assad and opposition teams and each tried to present the narrative of the conflict from that perspective. Later we reversed the roles.

The discussion of narratives took a day and a half and was followed by a reflection session where the group analyzed what they had learned about each side, its needs, identity; what they had discovered about themselves; how the two stories compared; what their own feelings associated with these narratives were; what we could learn about the emotions and identities of the sides.

It was a warm day, with clear blue skies and trees blossoming, and the reflection was taking place outdoors. A few minutes into the conversation, an explosion was followed by a cloud of smoke going off across the hill, from what we thought was the Syrian side of the border. The facilitators jumped. None of the participants even turned her head. When I asked whether they felt safe and would consider going inside, a few people shook their head, two or three grinned semi-sarcastically, the rest continued reflecting without paying much attention to the explosion or my question. Soon another explosion went off; the conversation continued quietly. We found out later that these were mining activities in Lebanon, not bombs in Syria.

Methodological agony

At night, the facilitators co-debriefing did not seem to have an end. All we knew was that nothing from what we knew was working. We knew well how to work with conflict sides, help them understand each other, step back from their positions, speak of interests and needs, share emotions, look at the conflict as a joint problem to be resolved cooperatively, work with trauma, reconcile. We were comfortable with open conflict *between sides*: we had experience working with the pain of the sides, with emotions. We thought we had the whole array of conflict resolution methods, that is of conflict resolution *between sides*. But we had no sides. We had a conflict, but not identifiable sides.

We recalled every experience, called a number of colleagues, revisited any article we could find on topics of dialogue and problem-solving program design: they all assumed sides.

Our time was running out as we had to return in the morning to the dialogue room and facilitate the discussion of the present-day dynamics of the conflict. We considered the option of engaging in another role-play, trying to understand the present-day needs of the Assad supporters and opposition. But we deemed that approach unethical. We did a role-play with conflict narratives when we were only beginning to gain awareness of the problem of "sides" and did not fully grasp it yet. But role-playing for the second time, with the full awareness that most of the participants in the room had no sides, would be a conscious, calculated, and desperate move. And the more we talked, the deeper we understood the discursive repercussions of such a move: in our work, we aim to move the "sides" away from their positions in order to see the problem as a common one, to help transform or even expand their understanding of identities as a concept that can be inclusive and not exclusive. And this group already had such an overarching and inclusive identity—the Syrian one that united them. Moreover, they already saw the conflict as a common problem. We would have to try to help them develop a common vision for a future; and they had it also, shared and articulated as a dream of a multicultural, inclusive, peaceful Syria. Had they all indeed been Assad or opposition supporters, we would be trying to have them see themselves also as doctors, lawyers, women, men, and so on, and not only as conflict sides; but they were already doctors, lawyers, women and men. Asking them to further role-play Assad and opposition supporters would mean to give priority to these two identities only, identities adopted by just a few people in the room, and ignore the 27 others. We would effectively ask them to perform a dichotomy that did not exist in the room, and then perform a solution.

Was this really what we were doing for the last few years? Did we, consciously or not, in one context or another, repeatedly invite to dialogue only those who took a side leaving out the rest? I knew now that we did exactly that: we did that as we assumed that those who are at the two binary ends were the majority, the mainstream, the ones who were in conflict; in other words, or rather without words, those who "really mattered." But was it possible that those left out from our binary framing because of our fascination with "sides" were not marginal and not a minority? What if in other contexts too, we overlooked 27 out of every 35. And then, what if the nonaligned were indeed a minority: if they were 8 out of every 35 or even 1 out of every 35? Why would we employ processes that leave them out by design, depriving them of voice? Simply because we did not know what to do with them; because they did not fit our neat frames? Were our frames all that important or even relevant in the violent contexts the participants lived in?

Not having "sides" in the room did not mean yet that there was no conflict to resolve. The violent conflict was there in full force. It was real, making it hard not to see that conflict is not always what international relations and other positivist theories made it to be: a confrontation or a disagreement between defined sides. To do conflict resolution now meant to rethink the concept of conflict itself. And conflict resolution work was needed, even expected. That's why these 35 people came to meet us and demanded something from us: something relevant, something that they would take back with them to their communities.

We still had to walk into the conference room ready to discuss the present-day dynamics of the conflict in Syria. That did not change. Just the means we had, the tools we thought to work with, were not adequate.

Reframing

We went to bed without a solution. In the morning, we decided to do with the group what we typically do in our facilitation team: we shared with the group the method we used for our own reflective process already mentioned and that we call "facilitators co-debriefing" (Gamaghelyan and Littlefield 2012). We designed co-debriefing through our practice as a process in which the facilitators allocate a specific time prior, during, and after the program they facilitated to engage in reflective practice (Schon 1984) and continuously adjust and develop their process. Co-debriefing is led by the facilitators themselves who debrief each other (thus "co-" in "co-debriefing") and not by an outside debriefer or evaluator. It has a number of aims: it helps to improve the process by identifying and attending to any hidden dynamics that can hinder the progress of the group they are working with; it helps to create synergy within the facilitation team; and it also contributes to personal development of individual facilitators. In addition to the dynamics within the group, and most relevant for the current situation, co-debriefing also provides a format for an ongoing assessment of the progress and adjustment of the program, maximizing the effectiveness of the process—all goals associated with formative evaluation (Bamberger, Rugh, and Mabry 2012). The co-debriefing is an opportunity for the facilitators to develop awareness and consensus, adjust the process moving forward, and be transparent about it with each other.

The co-debriefing can be conducted pre-program, in-program, and post-program with different aims. The pre-program co-debriefing is key for creating harmonious relationships between and among facilitators. The post-program co-debriefings are important for discussing the achievements of the program, for giving and receiving positive feedback and constructive criticism, for discussing personal growth, and sharing acknowledgements, for making future plans. Most relevant here, still, is the in-program co-debriefings aimed at attending to the ongoing dynamics among and between the participants, and for providing a forum for the assessment of the dialogue process and the discussion of the needed and possible adjustments to the process or structure. The facilitators decide together what is important to discuss at a particular point, how much time to spend on each topic, and in what format (Gamaghelyan and Littlefield 2012). This is a highly flexible, creative, transparent, and open-ended process, and in my experience, also an extremely effective one.

We walked into the conference room the next morning, and confessed to the group that we do not have any ready process for them: that the frameworks we had been using previously are binary and not adequate in their context; that we do appreciate their diversity and do not want to tame it, but instead find a way to foster it; and that we need their help in finding a way forward.

An initial chaos ensued, with the participants having to relinquish the sense of safety created by the presence of presumed "know-it-all" facilitators. Then gradually some participants stepped up, offering leadership, supporting the new process. The group also agreed that up to this point they were not ready to "be real," preferring to hide behind role plays and put the responsibility for the process and content on facilitators. This was the time to take responsibility, to open up and have a real and not simulated discussion. They realized that we are all leaving the program in three to four days and this was one chance to have that open conversation that they came here for. But how? The group then asked us to continue facilitating this now open process, granting us back our legitimacy, now based on the shared sense of responsibility.

We posed the open-ended question regarding how to discuss the present-day dynamics and gradually consensus emerged that the Syrian conflict has many actors and not two, and they are not clearly delineated. We suggested to try conflict mapping. As a first round, the group proceeded to identify the international actors who influence the Syrian conflict. We ended up with a list of over 30 players, including every possible big power one can think of such as the United States, Russia, Turkey, China, Iran, the EU, the Gulf States, oil corporations, the Arab League, and many others. We used the floor of the conference room for the mapping and the visual was overwhelming, with Syria in the middle of a densely populated map, with every possible influential actor surrounding it with the web of competing interests. And while others are playing geo-politics, Syrians day by day intensify the divisions among themselves, making the conflict increasingly intractable, violence unbearable and the future dependent on the interests of third parties. If we do not stop, take a step back and unite, the participants agreed, our future will not be ours to decide. This map created a sense of solidarity and a further unity around the common Syrian identity, common Syrian future: the divisions were proclaimed secondary.

We then proceeded to create a map of the relevant actors within Syria. The list kept growing, surpassing 40: many military groups and subgroups, religious groups, movements, youth groups. The internal list was as overwhelming as the external one, but now showing the extent of the divisions. As the aim for the next session was to try and understand the needs and concerns of the actors, we were faced with an impossible prospect: first, the participants represented some, but certainly not all the groups listed; second, even if we had the people, it would be logistically very hard, to say the least, to represent views of the 40 actors in the context of a week-long program.

By this time, frustration started to grow within the group toward the facilitators. We accepted the criticism, suggesting in return for the participants to step up: there is only so much that we, as outsiders, know or can do. If we all were here for technical skill-building, then great: we would have had only trainings during the process and the goal would have been achieved. And we could have stopped at that. If they wanted to go further, this was their chance. Neither us, nor them, nor anyone outside of this group was able to explain or solve this conflict as of that day; there were no ready schemes. This was our chance, their chance, to try to make sense of the conflict for themselves, as they were in the presence of many other bright people from across Syria ready to talk, share, explore, and create. They agreed and came back asking for a few process suggestions.

We discussed a number of processes we, as facilitators, used in the past, and agreed on the following one: we would leave for discussion only those actors whose views the participants present in the room could represent. We agreed that there are no criteria or particular frame for the choice of the actors to be represented: it did not have to be political affiliation, religion, ethnicity, or gender or any other predetermined category or it could be any of these; we are not looking for a uniform structure, we want the process to determine what are the identity groups relevant to these particular participants. Each of the participants would choose the actors that they felt connected to and could represent. The actors that no participant picked were eliminated. We ended up with actors representing categories as diverse as government, Syrian Army, oppositional Free Syrian Army, intellectuals, civil society, Palestinian minority, minorities in general, Alewite minority, communists, anarchists, and a few others, well over a dozen in all.

This was deemed too broad still, and the participants agreed to further consolidate the categories into the following:

- Intellectuals;
- Civil society;
- Youth;
- The Assad government and the Alewite minority;
- Syrian Army;
- Unarmed opposition/protesters;
- Minorities.

We acknowledged that each person had multiple affiliations and identities and could potentially represent a number of groups. But in this exercise, each person would pick only one actor from the list whose views they would then represent. Contestation, realignment, and further consolidation started to take place as the participants started to sign up to these categories: the "intellectuals" and "youth" decided to join the "civil society," a group that already united those who initially self-identified as representatives of NGOs, communists, anarchists, and others who did not categorize themselves in ethno-religious terms. This group was the most numerous.

After some time, a number of those who self-identified as Alewites decided to leave the coalition with the government and joined the "minorities" group. Those who self-identified as opposition decided that it would not be right to overlook the position of the armed rebels and renamed their group, previously called "unarmed opposition," into "rebels/revolutionaries." With the "government," we had another limitation: everyone agreed that this actor should be represented, yet we did not have any official in the room to do that. We renamed the group into "government supporters or sympathizers." This shifted five people back into that group.

Through an unstructured, and frankly messy, process we arrived into a place where the participants were divided into four distinct categories. These categories were not predetermined and were painstakingly crafted by the group itself, thus making the picture both complete and representative, as seen by this particular group of 35.

We now have:

- the government supporters;
- the armed rebels and political opposition;
- minorities;
- and a large segment of a civil society.

We ended the day with the Color Games, and a distinct feeling that the conversation is now "getting real."

Getting real

Getting real comes with a price. A day before, they were all Syrians, united against outside forces and violence, ready to advance a common and inclusive future. Now again they were different: a repressive regime and a violent opposition, persecuted minorities who fear them both, and a civil society trying to piece it all together.

While the relationship seemed perfect just a day ago, we were now having a real conflict. People got into the identity groups they subscribed to and went at each other full force. To facilitate the conversation, we resorted to the PSW process, asking them to step back from positions and think of the conflict from the point of view of the needs, fears, concerns, and hopes that drive the actions of the subgroup they crafted and chose to represent. We gave each group time to work on their presentations. As we had four groups and only three facilitators, we asked one of the participants, a Kurdish woman experienced in conflict resolution work, to facilitate the conversation in the "minorities" subgroup.

When the subgroups started working, we could see the conflict gaining human flesh, mind, and spirit. All those who for the past few days timidly and separately mentioned minority rights —Kurds, Alewites, Palestinians, and Christians—were now united and clearly empowered. All those who till now only uncomfortably expressed support for the Assad regime now felt emboldened to present the needs and fears of the supporters of the regime. The subgroup of mostly religious men and a sole woman who were vocally anti-government all along, but felt uneasy about exposing their religious side in a group that had many strong secular voices, now went praying all together. And the majority, a collection of people from many walks of life who refused to align with any ethnic, religious, or political group were now the "civil society."

I was assigned to facilitate the government supporters group, and the discomfort within this group was growing: the participants knew well the position of and sympathized with the government supporters. But other than one or two, they had chosen in their real life to be in opposition to the regime and did not want to look as if associated with it. Then we found a creative solution: to resort to art. The group would not be representing themselves. Instead, they would stage a performance enacting the government supporters, the real ones: their own families, neighbors, and friends.

As the pro-government subgroup decided to change the process, we informed the other subgroups asking about their comfort with receiving a performance rather than a presentation from the "Assad supporters." The reaction was surprising and inspiring: all the subgroup decided to turn to art. The "minorities" built a colorful poster session. The "revolutionaries" started their presentation with a dramatic song about the war that opened the floodgates for tears and became the symbol of the dialogue. The "civil society," that learned about the turn to art later as they were working in a separate building, had to improvise, creating in my view the most powerful display of all (discussed later).

It is hard to write further about this session without giving up the specifics of the dialogue content, which was private to the group. I will be brief, therefore, and mention the highlights only.

The government supporters performed the following key message. We did not all start as Assad supporters. Many of us are democratically minded; we joined the initial demonstrations and demanded change. We still want change. But then the conflict turned violent. We are mainly Alewites, Christians, or seculars. The rebel groups are mostly religious and see us as a threat and kidnap, rape, burn, torture and kill us, our families, our communities. We do not like Assad, but the alternative is terrifying. Should Assad fall, most of us will die with the survivors condemned to a repressed minority status in an Islamist state.

The rebels started with a song—not a revolutionary song or a militant one, at least that's not how it sounded to me, but a song mourning Syria and Syrians, the social fabric that was disintegrating. The song communicated the losses of the Syrians and the loss of hope—profound hopelessness. I learned this through translation (not sure how accurate), and even then, it was an incredibly moving song. As the song went on, one by one, the participants started crying: man, woman, Alewite, Kurd, Sunni, Marxist, everyone. We cried for at least half an hour in silence. Then the rebel spoke: the one who walked into the dialogue on Day 2, who had scared many of us. He was a doctor, had two little kids. Then one was killed by the government forces. As he spoke, we stared at the picture of his slain son, on display, on the chair, barely two years of age. I do not want to fight, he said. But I have another child. Still alive. What should I do? He asked. What could he do?

I was sure he would go back fighting. But for now, he chose to be at a "peace conference."

I have two children. "Still alive" are not the words, I dream, I would ever have to utter or even consider uttering about them. Ever. No one should.

The "minorities" had posters, colorful, in the shape of flowers and butterflies with pictures and words full of hope and terror. Their story was similar to that of the government sympathizers: they hoped for change, but were terrorized. Yet there was a major difference too: unlike the government supporters, the minorities could rely on no one. For decades discriminated against by the regime, they were now an easy target for the government and rebel groups alike. They had no side: they could not have a side. They were excluded from the conflict, from the peace process and quietly brutalized. Yet they stood there: Kurds, Alewites, Christians, and a Palestinian, mostly women, strong, diverse, united, embodying the civic solidarity and as a clear display of the solution this conflict could have.

And these were the people who would be once again marginalized, now by conflict resolution practice, had we chosen to continue with the Assad-opposition binary.

The civil society went last: assertive, well spoken, diverse; their needs were the verbalization of the inclusive future that the minority group silently embodied.

As they did not preplan their presentation as art, they started improvising: as they spoke, in the back of the room one of the subgroup members started amassing a house from little colorful building blocks that we used in team-building exercises. As the group articulated its vision, the house of blocks grew colorful, wide, and tall. Then the conversation took a turn toward the conflict of the competing exclusivist visions of Assad and opposition supporters. Rather spontaneously, the performer leveled the brick house he was building and went back to his chair. As the conversation took a visionary turn again, another member of the group stood up, attempting to rebuild the house. As the Assad-opposition dichotomy started dominating the room again, he destroyed the house once more, this time intentionally, and went back to his chair. By this time, the entire group stared catching up with the improvised symbolism of the performance. As the conversation went on, taking visionary and destructive turns, one after another the participants rose, built, and destroyed their creation. That building was now Syria.

The performance gradually and dramatically changed the conversation: with each destruction, more and more voices started to speak of inclusivity and civic solidarity and against competing visions. The sole performer at the back stage was joined by two, three, thirty comrades: soon all of us surrounded the table with little blocks. The initiator was now back, building the house again. No one else would dare to touch it, but everyone knew that the fate of the building depended on each of them and their unity. The artist built masterfully when the common vision was voiced and destroyed ruthlessly at each sound of conflict. He carried this Sisyphus' curse tirelessly: we all knew he will not stop, not until we have unity.

They built the house. Together. Not across the hill yet, not where the explosions continue to go off. But they built one in our bubble.

As he added the last brick to the structure, the room went silent. No one said anything anymore. There was nothing left to say. It was well past midnight.

Closure

The last two days were devoted to reflection, to the reentry conversation, a very critical one with this group that had built hope and was returning to destruction, and to the discussion of possibilities for future engagement with peace activism and joining the ranks of the organizing institution.

The reflection that followed the performances showed that a deep level of understanding was built among the participants. If the Assad regime was still seen as the enemy by many, the plights of Assad supporters and of minorities who were threatened was acknowledged. The rebels were not seen as inherently violent, but people driven to take arms as a result of repressions and many injustices and crimes committed against them and their families. The civil society group stood as a group that offered unity, in terms of both vision and process. Many participants agreed to collaborate across sectarian lines on peacebuilding activities. This was particularly true for the "civil society," "minorities," and "Assad supporters." The "revolutionaries" had perhaps the hardest road ahead of them in deciding where to go from the dialogue.

As the program moved toward its end, the nights became longer. From about Day 4, more and more people started staying up, trying to maximize the time together. By Day 6 or 7, as the departure neared, the sleep time shrank further, the nights passed in singing, playing, chatting.

For some prior commitment, I had to leave the program a day before it ended. I left toward the morning before the last day started and as most of the participants had just gone to bed. Around 6am, a dedicated group of eight still awake, men and women, decided to take a hike down a mountain to a waterfall they had spotted previously. One of the two remaining facilitators who were also up, a white American male, tried to convince them of the need to take care of their health, to sleep, and not to risk a dangerous hike when they were clearly tired. As the rest looked at him in silence, his eyes opened, "it just hit me now what reality you folks are going back to tomorrow," and broke into tears. Many participants who had managed to fight back tears for all these days could not hold any longer. The clear and inhumane image of the near future invoked by this phrase did not allow. One of the religious male participants in the group, who had proclaimed mistrust toward the American facilitator all along, sat next to him, then hugged him in tears. He said that he trusted him now.

They hiked. And the entire group hiked with them the next and last morning. That last hike turned into a long acknowledgement session: the personal stories that had remained not shared came out; many were heartbreaking stories of bombs in their universities, of lost friends, of jailed families. Lots of tears were shed.

Right after the program, the organizers demanded from the facilitators to cut any contact with the group out of safety concerns. We complied, though it was not easy as many of the participants were now our friends. Some of the participants objected. We reached a compromise that the facilitators would not initiate any contact but could stay in touch individually with those participants who reach out to us themselves.

Since then, from what I learned, three participants were jailed by the Assad regime, one in Damascus, one in Homs, and one in Aleppo; two got married to each other; the town of two others was massacred by a rebel group, and they somehow escaped to refugee camps, with one of them later making her way to Europe and the second detained as of this writing. A number of others are now working in their communities as trainers and educators.

Implications of the Syrian dialogue for this research: toward inclusive frames that do not privilege the violent extremes

The reflection on this program helped me in starting to identify possible changes that can be made in conflict resolution practice to foster inclusion: the key was to avoid bringing ready and rigid methodologies to the initiatives, and instead be ready to continuously evolve the design starting from approaches to selection, moving to changes in program designs and implementation. The constant questioning, rethinking, and adjusting of practice both conceptually and practically within the framework of a particular initiative seemed necessary. In the Syrian dialogue discussed above, following conventional approaches would lead us to augment the voice of Assad and opposition supporters and painting a dichotomous picture of the conflict, while marginalizing the majority. At the very least, the conflict resolution practitioners should work on gaining awareness about possible harm their own approach can bring and go out of their way not to contribute to further marginalization and exclusion.

But how? Seeing outside of the discourses in which we are embedded is a daunting task, not least because our discourses are also stories about our own identity. Questioning them and looking at them from outside often means questioning not only what we do but who we are: our own identity as conflict practitioners. It is disorienting and requires belief in the evolving designs and that the developing a better approach is always possible and attainable.

This program demonstrated both the problem of always framing conflicts in binary terms and the possible ways forward. The program also demonstrated, however, the immense difficulty, if not impossibility, of building a fully inclusive design. Despite tireless efforts by the participants and the facilitators to establish an inclusive process, new forms of marginalization and exclusion, even though more subtle ones, continued to surface.

This program had profound implications for my understanding of conflict resolution practice. From that point on, bringing two sides together to resolve the breakdown of their relations without questioning the implications of such framing became impossible for me. I am not suggesting that binary frames are inherently harmful or not useful or that I do not see a value in working with two sides who are in open conflict: I do. In many circumstances, when two particular groups or individuals choose to put themselves in the opposite sides of a conflict, working on improving their relationship presents a value. I myself continue working with such groups. What I think is harmful, therefore, is not any and all binary framing, but having the binary as the default framing for all situations. While designing a workshop as binary or otherwise, I suggest we ask ourselves: Why are we choosing this particular frame? Who are we leaving out of the process? Who are we depriving of voice? Are we pushing the participants to perform preconceived roles of conflicting actors, stripping them of their diverse identities? With our framing, are we transforming the structures that support the conflict or are we perpetuating them?

Facilitating this program with the Syrian participants led me to question many assumptions that my colleagues and I held in understanding conflict and conflict resolution and gave rise to this book. It also helped me find preliminary answers to some of the core questions guiding this inquiry. What started as a program where our binary frames almost forced the participants to adapt to dichotomy ended up as an open and multidimensional process where the diversity of the group was openly expressed, and an attempt to build a vision for inclusive future was made.

Yet this awareness alone did not provide any ready solutions or directions for designing more inclusive programs. My subsequent work, now informed by the active interest in identifying and confronting marginalization, showed how difficult breaking the existing frames is. Perhaps precisely because the Syrian program was taking place in the midst of ongoing violence, with the identities and conflict discourses in flux, was it possible to develop a relatively inclusive frame without facing strong resistance. In contrast, as the next chapter indicates, in a conflict with solidified structures, adjusting conflict resolution processes and questioning the existing frames is not an easy task.

Chapter 5

On methodological challenges of leading an analytic initiative in the context of the long-lasting Nagorno-Karabakh conflict: from inclusion to exclusion

The Nagorno-Karabakh case presented here followed the reverse trajectory of the Syrian one discussed in the previous chapter. In the Syrian case, the initial facilitation design with its binary frame set the stage for marginalization, yet the group worked hard to be inclusive. The Nagorno-Karabakh case started as a Track 1.5 initiative, to the contrary, aimed to include all possible voices, yet demonstrated many forms of exclusion and marginalization as it progressed.

The primary sources of data from this project, called here NK (Nagorno-Karabakh) Analytic Initiative, similar to the case before, are interviews, reflections, and focus group discussions with colleagues who were involved with this project. Here, too, my personal reflections were often facilitated by colleagues who were acting as interviewers questioning my assumptions and analysis.

The Nagorno-Karabakh Analytic Initiative

The initiative that I present here, that took place in the context of the Nagorno-Karabakh conflict, is a project that explicitly aimed to build an inclusive format, yet demonstrated abundant patterns of exclusion and marginalization. The Syrian dialogue discussed in Chapter 4 was an example of a conflict resolution intervention that takes place in an evolving conflict where the frames are still contested. It demonstrated how the binary frames of international relations applied to a complex situation could empower the violent extremes, pushing out and marginalizing the majority who refused to take sides in the conflict and who could serve as the peace constituency. The initiative discussed in Chapter 5 examines an intervention that takes place in a conflict that is longer-lasting and in which the binary ethnic frames have prevailed as of this writing and have pushed out all alternative explanations.

The analysis of the initiative in the Nagorno-Karabakh context demonstrates the difficulty of bringing about change and transformation in a conflict with such well-established frames. Despite proclaiming the commitment to inclusion and devoting the NK Analytic Initiative to expanding the understanding of the Nagorno-Karabakh conflict, the participants and the organizers alike continually defaulted to the binary ethnic frames marginalizing all but those who claimed to represent the two nationalist extremes. The NK Analytic Initiative, therefore, is an example of how the discourse of international relations, when adopted by conflict resolution practitioners to frame a project, serves to perpetuate the conflict, making it very hard for those involved to see or act outside of it.

Unlike the Syrian dialogue described in Chapter 4, some of the meetings of the NK Analytic Initiative were public and present fewer challenges related to ensuring confidentiality. Nevertheless, as the analysis presented here is critical and might affect colleagues who continue working in the field, I will refrain from naming the initiative or the individuals involved. Further, as most of the meetings of the initiative were held under Chatham House rules, I follow the respective procedures, making public the information received, but keeping the identity and the affiliation of the speaker and the participants confidential.[13]

The Nagorno-Karabakh conflict had started in the late 1980s as a dispute between the Armenian SSR and the Azerbaijani SSR about the belonging of the NKAO. In 1918–1920, prior to the sovietization of the South Caucasus, Armenia and Azerbaijan had fought a war over this territory, as well as over the neighboring regions of Zangezur and Nakhichevan. Under the Soviet rule, Nagorno-Karabakh was awarded an Autonomous Oblast within the Azerbaijani SSR, substantiated by its economic integration with Azerbaijan and absence of convenient land connection with population centers in Armenia. The decision led to periodically voiced discontent by NKAO's majority-Armenian population. After a series of unsuccessful petitions to the Soviet leadership

---

13 http://www.chathamhouse.org/about/chatham-house-rule#sthash.2L8Dog3h.dpuf. Accessed on April 4, 2017.

in the 1960s and 1970s, the movement to unite NKAO with the Armenian SSR gathered pace during Gorbachev's Perestroika culminating in mass demonstrations in NKAO's capital Stepanakert and in Yerevan and counter-demonstrations in Baku, rise of nationalist rhetoric, ethnic violence, and ethnic cleansings of hundreds of thousands of Azerbaijanis from Armenia and hundreds of thousands of Armenians from Azerbaijan. Immediately after gaining independence in 1991, Armenia and Nagorno-Karabakh on one side and Azerbaijan on the other engaged in a full-scale war that ended with a Russian-brokered ceasefire agreement in 1994, leaving the Armenian forces in control of NKAO and surrounding Azerbaijani territories, all of them ethnically cleansed during the war. The war resulted in well over 20,000 dead and over a million displaced (for a detailed analysis of the Nagorno-Karabakh conflict, see Abasov and Khachatrian 2004; Gamaghelyan 2005; ICG 2009; Hopmann and Zartman 2010; Conciliation Resources 2012; De Waal 2013).

The official negotiating body for the conflict, the OSCE Minsk Group, was created in 1992 by the Conference on Security and Cooperation in Europe (CSCE, now Organization for Security and Cooperation in Europe (OSCE)) and has been cochaired by the United States, Russia, and France.[14] The decades of negotiations, however, did not yield any results and as of the publication of this book in 2017, the violence is on the rise and a new full-scale war seems likely.

Starting from the late 1990s, in both formal and informal platforms, the Azerbaijani government aimed to frame the Nagorno-Karabakh conflict as an aggression of Armenia against Azerbaijani territory and insisted on direct negotiations with the Armenian government. As a consequence, it attempted to sideline the Armenian population of Nagorno-Karabakh and silence their expression of grievances. And to the contrary, the Armenian government aimed to portray the conflict as a struggle for liberation by the Armenian population of Nagorno-Karabakh oppressed by the Azerbaijani authorities and insisted on inclusion in the peace process of Nagorno-Karabakh Armenians. Further, it attempted to exclude from the peace process

---

14   http://www.osce.org/mg. Accessed on April 4, 2017.

the displaced Nagorno-Karabakh Azerbaijanis to silence their expression of grievances.

The first meeting

Late in 2007, an Azerbaijani graduate student in the United States approached me with a suggestion to set up a joint panel during an academic conference with three Azerbaijani and three Armenian graduate students coming together to discuss the Nagorno-Karabakh conflict. We agreed to approach the conflict as a joint problem to be resolved constructively, by developing a common analytic framework for understanding it and outlining a strategy for a way out of it. With certain modifications, these remained the guiding principles of the NK Analytic Initiative for a number of years. As a first meeting of its kind, the 2008 panel was an attempt at establishing a common framework for understanding the Nagorno-Karabakh conflict; the participants were self-selected; and the meeting did not exhibit any signs of active exclusion.

In an atmosphere where the Nagorno-Karabakh conflict was commonly discussed confrontationally from the Armenian and Azerbaijani positions, often aggressively, the panel created a precedent when a group of participants originating from the two countries were speaking of the conflict as a shared problem. This constructive attitude was received well by many in the audience. It also triggered those in the audience who represented the Armenian and the Azerbaijani well-organized groups of nationalists and diasporan organizations who roam Nagorno-Karabakh-focused events to confront each other and the speakers. As the panel was not typical and the speakers agreed with each other more than usual, the challenges from the nationalist members of the audience were directed toward the speakers from their own country, questioning their patriotism and calling to conform with the official line. Despite the challenge, the collaboration among the panelists continued following the event, and an agreement was reached to set up a symposium devoted entirely to the Nagorno-Karabakh conflict.

The first full symposium

The symposium devoted entirely to the Nagorno-Karabakh conflict took place in 2009. It had two components. The first was an open-door conference on the Nagorno-Karabakh conflict with the participation of eight Armenian and eight Azerbaijani diplomats, academics, and analysts. The second was a closed-door meeting based on the PSW methodology. During the closed-door meeting, the topics for the next round of discussions were outlined. A series of joint or parallel publications focused on the analysis and of the Nagorno-Karabakh conflict and the peace process was launched as a result.

The meeting was successful in terms of delivering concrete outcomes and generating a constructive debate. The questions of exclusion, however, were now becoming central. The initial aim of the conference was to have an academic event devoted to the constructive analysis of the Nagorno-Karabakh conflict. As the event was taking shape, however, the organizers that included Armenian and Azerbaijani young professionals, as well as professors from a high-ranking US university specializing in conflict resolution and negotiations, opted to invite Armenian and Azerbaijani diplomats as keynote speakers. When the university, which was acting as the convener, sent out the invitations to the Azerbaijani and Armenian diplomats, the Azerbaijanis replied that they would accept the invitation if the organizers could guarantee that the list of the speakers does not include any officials from the unrecognized Nagorno-Karabakh Republic. Ironically, the initial list of the invitees did not contain any official from Nagorno-Karabakh as the conference was low budget, did not provide any travel funds, and meant to have an academic focus. The participants were invited from among those already in the United States and based on their expertise and not political affiliation. This might have worked, but the decision to invite Armenian and Azerbaijani officials as keynote speakers turned the event political.

The request by the Azerbaijani representatives was followed by a mirror request from the Armenian representatives to include also representatives of the Nagorno-Karabakh Republic into the conversation. As this latter request came very late, and close to the start day of the conference, the event moved forward with the original list of the invitees, which included officials from Armenia and Azerbaijan, but not from Nagorno-Karabakh—a format that became contentious and itself a central part of the discussion during the conference.

While not among the speakers, the representative of Nagorno-Karabakh to the United States was in the audience and was invited by the organizers to take the front row sit. The speech of the Azerbaijani official and the following questions and answers session turned into the contestation of who should have a voice in this conflict and who not.

The Azerbaijani official's position was that Nagorno-Karabakh is a conflict between the Armenian and Azerbaijani states, and only those two should have voice; the Armenian and the Nagorno-Karabakh officials' joint position was that this is a conflict between Azerbaijan and Nagorno-Karabakh, with Armenia acting as a supporter and a security guarantor of Nagorno-Karabakh. Other attendees were demanding the inclusion of the Azerbaijani population of Nagorno-Karabakh, currently displaced, in the conversation, and a few were discussing the need for a fully inclusive process.

The conference covered other topics also, and here the conversation was constructive. All the panels included voices of speakers originating from Armenia and Azerbaijan, and discussed the geo-politics surrounding the Nagorno-Karabakh conflict in the aftermath of the August 2008 war in neighboring South Ossetia, questions of historical memory construction, and the need for an increased role for the civil society in the Nagorno-Karabakh peace process. The conversation built on the work started in 2008 and expanded the network of professionals ready to engage constructively.

During the closed-door meeting that took place a day after the open-door conference, the question of exclusion was raised by many; the Armenian officials argued for the need to include Nagorno-Karabakh Armenians into the peace process on both ethical and practical grounds, as without them the Armenian government could not legitimately sign any agreement; and the Azerbaijani officials argued for the need of inclusion of the Azerbaijanis from Nagorno-Karabakh. It was agreed that the peace process, particularly on the unofficial level, needs to be inclusive, and that we should not intentionally exclude anyone affected by the conflict. As everyone seemed to support the need for inclusion in principle, but not yet ready to agree on the specifics of the inclusive format, we discussed the possibility of making the question of participation of the Nagorno-Karabakh populations in the peace process and search for an appropriate format as one of the main topics of the next round of meetings.

The second full symposium

The third meeting of the series and the second full symposium took place in Washington, DC, in 2011 and was co-hosted by three organizations, including the Imagine Center that I had co-founded by this time jointly with Azerbaijani colleagues, a different US university, and a Washington, DC-based think tank. As the international attention towards the NK Analytic Initiative kept growing, the organizers invited representatives of the Armenian and the Azerbaijani foreign ministries, the OSCE, the US, and the UK governments, as well as a number of Armenian and Azerbaijani conflict resolution experts and civil society representatives to take part in the symposium.

Unlike in the first full symposium, where the organizers tried to avoid addressing the questions of representation and exclusion through packaging the conversation as an academic one where the political identities of speakers were of no importance, this time the organizers decided to acknowledge the so-called "problem of the format" and try to find a proactive solution. The "problem of the format" in the context of the Nagorno-Karabakh conflict is a veiled reference to who can and cannot be included in the peace process, with the Armenian government preferring a three-party format or talks between the officials from Armenia, Azerbaijan, and the breakaway Nagorno-Karabakh Republic. At the same time, the Azerbaijani government prefers either a two-party or a four-party format: talks between officials from the Republics of Armenia and Azerbaijan, or talks between these two as well as the Armenian and the Azerbaijani communities of Nagorno-Karabakh.

When planning the symposium, the initial plan was to make the format "all-inclusive." Yet the puzzle seemed unsolvable. The Armenian officials saw the "all-inclusive" format resemble closely the four-party format and made it clear that they would boycott the meeting should we invite any representative of the Azerbaijani community of Nagorno-Karabakh; at the same time, they were insisting on having an official from Nagorno-Karabakh to be among the speakers. The Azerbaijani officials, in turn, made it clear that they would boycott the meeting should there be any official from Nagorno-Karabakh among the speakers.

As a solution, the organizers decided to break the symposium into a series of events and put forward a number of formats, rather than having one, trying through the combination of these formats to ensure maximum inclusivity. We planned a series of three-day events: the first would be an academic conference focused on the Nagorno-Karabakh conflict with the participation of scholars-practitioners, including nonofficial speakers from Nagorno-Karabakh, and with keynote speeches from officials from the Republics of Armenia and Azerbaijan; the second day would be a closed-door meeting with an alternative format; and the third would be an all-inclusive open-door roundtable. As agreed during the previous meeting, one of the main topics would be the discussion of the need and possibilities for the inclusion of the Nagorno-Karabakh population into the peace process. In other words, while accepting the partially exclusive format of some of the sessions in the short term, we rationalized that we are doing this as part of a working process aimed at finding an inclusive option for the next meeting. To get the buy in of various possible stakeholders in line with the PSW methodology (H. Kelman 1972), we met with them separately and discussed this strategy of a step-by-step move toward an inclusive process. We also communicated to all the involved parties our determination to use this meeting as a platform for finding solutions to the "format" dilemma.

We attempted to find creative solutions during these series of events also. We planned our third-day session as an open-door roundtable, thus making it fully inclusive and not restricting anyone's participation. To minimize the hierarchy, during the open-door session we decided against having any formal speakers: opening words would be said by the organizing committee members, followed by an open roundtable discussion.

Not everyone was happy with our approach. When prior to the conference, we met the representatives of the Nagorno-Karabakh authorities, they expressed disbelief that their inclusion was our long-term aim, despite our assurances that there will be no further meetings that are exclusive. The Azerbaijani authorities also were not satisfied with the absence of representatives of the Azerbaijani community of Nagorno-Karabakh among speakers. These behind-the-scenes battles and satisfactions expressed when a party was excluded were a strong indication that we were not succeeding in organizing an all-inclusive event.

At the symposium, constructive sessions alternated with confrontational ones, depending on the topic and the speakers. The academics, analysts, and civil society representatives did their best to keep the conversation collaborative. At the same time, those closer to the authorities, influenced by the presence of media and international actors, resorted to the official talking points. The audience in Washington, DC, has also been peculiar consisting, in addition to international actors, also of Armenian and Azerbaijani embassy representatives and lobby groups used to public confrontations. The constant interruptions and provocations from the audience, therefore, were an additional dynamic that was disrupting the collaborative tone that a number of speakers were trying to strike. One of the final speakers, reflecting on the day, praised the constructive voices and urged the rest to refrain in the future from turning such efforts into a "Ping-Pong match," a reference to the continuous exchange of clichés and talking points that we have all heard numerously and that would prevent the development of a dialogue.

During the evening co-debriefing of the organizers, we discussed how to transform the conversation and maximize its constrictive potential, while minimizing the "Ping-Pong." The following day we held a closed-door session in an informal setting, at a pristine location outside of Washington, DC, overseeing a bay. The lead facilitator, an American university professor with many years of experience in the South Caucasus, came to the meeting with unexpected gear—a bag of Ping-Pong balls and a bag of chocolates. As we started the discussion, every time a participant would make a constructive point, the facilitator would hand them a chocolate; and every time someone would resort to confrontation, she would hand them a Ping-Pong ball. The intervention was accepted with enthusiasm, both as it discharged the atmosphere by bringing a light element into an otherwise hard conversation and because it gave a symbolic tool for the participants tired from the overly politicized public event of the day prior to call out any sabotage and encourage a constructive conversation. The facilitator soon passed the bag to the group, and anyone could now hand others a chocolate of praise or a Ping-Pong ball of shame. I am still amazed by wonders that creative facilitation and skillful work with symbols can bring.

Thanks to the efforts of the facilitator, as well as to the informal atmosphere and the absence of an audience and media, the conversation quickly took a constructive turn. The participants agreed on the need to continue the meetings, as this was a rare platform for analytic collaboration. Moreover, they discussed the possibility of making the meetings more regular and frequent, aiming to positively influence the peace process. By the end of the meeting, we reached an agreement to develop the program in two directions—analytic and practical. The analytic direction would bring together Azerbaijani and Armenian experts in conflict resolution providing them with an opportunity to engage in a constructive dialogue targeting the conflict in a comprehensive analysis. It would allow for the generation of a vision in the form of an innovative yet realistic strategic joint platform toward the peaceful future of the societies building on academic research as well as practice of conflict resolution. It would work in coordination with the OSCE Minsk Group mediators, the official negotiating body cochaired by the United States, France, and Russia, and other international actors engaged with the conflict. The new practical direction would contribute to the improved effectiveness of the Nagorno-Karabakh peace process through increased informal coordination between Track 1 and Track 2 levels, including between governmental representatives acting in their personal capacity, representatives of governmental think tanks, conflict resolution experts, civil society actors, and representatives of the international community. This direction would contribute to the peace process through the development of a strategic approach to confidence-building that can complement and strengthen the official process.

Overall, the second full symposium received positive feedback, particularly from the part of the international actors; it generated interest and attention in Azerbaijan and Armenia; helped with the coordination between official and unofficial efforts and among various unofficial efforts. It also received criticism, particularly from the officials from Armenia and Azerbaijan, for not following their preferred format of discussions.

Working group

During the second symposium, a number of participants agreed to make the meetings more frequent and support the work of official mediators. By late 2011, however, the official peace process was entering an obvious deadlock, and we agreed on the need of developing proactive unofficial efforts aimed at bringing fresh energy to the peace process. In early 2012, we, at the Imagine Center and with support of partner organizations, started a series of private consultations with various stakeholders to find an acceptable yet inclusive format for moving forward.

The year 2012 was a difficult one for the Nagorno-Karabakh peace process: a three-year-long active push for a solution led by the then Russian president Medvedev and supported by the US president Obama had just failed, with the presidents of Armenia and Azerbaijan unable to reach an agreement. Putin had returned to presidency in Russia, clearly indicating that the era of the Russian interest in resolving that conflict was over, and quickly moved to reassert the Russian influence over Armenia. The tensions on the border and the line of contact started escalating; in August 2012, the Azerbaijani authorities negotiated the extradition home of Ramil Safarov, an Azerbaijani officer who was serving a sentence in Hungary for brutally murdering an Armenian officer during the North Atlantic Treaty Organization's (NATO) Partnership for Peace training. Right after the extradition, Safarov was released and received a hero's welcome by the Azerbaijani authorities, leading to a new cycle of escalation and crisis on the official level, and also cancelation of many unofficial initiatives.

We continued the work in this tense atmosphere, by gathering feedback in late 2012 and early 2013 in Azerbaijan, Armenia, and Nagorno-Karabakh as to what was possible and meaningful and how to move forward with the analytic and practical work. We were able to mobilize enough support to continue. We agreed to hold a series of four meetings in 2013 focused on the practical end of the process, developing recommendations for strategic confidence-building measures, and to continue fostering coordination between official and unofficial tracks.

The next step again was to find possibilities for making the format inclusive. We were determined not to exclude anyone intentionally and due to political pressures. With Azerbaijani officials, we focused on ensuring support for the inclusion of Armenians from Nagorno-Karabakh. We were able to reach this agreement with certain conditions: the meetings were not to be public any longer, and we could be more flexible with who is present in the room. We accepted these conditions, as our thinking on the topic of the open-door meeting was similar: by now, we had seen that the presence of media was forcing the participants to retreat to hardline positions rather than engage in an open exploration of new possibilities. We therefore agreed that the workshops would be conducted with Chatham House rules in a closed-door format to minimize the outside pressures on the participants. Another condition was that the participants from Nagorno-Karabakh would not have any official positions. As we were determined not to agree on marginalization of any of the voices, one of the organizers offered a compromise where none of the sides would have officials in the room and not only Nagorno-Karabakh. This move, however, was hard to reconcile with the aim of the NK Analytic Initiative of ensuring Tracks 1 and 2 coordination. The solution we found was to invite individuals close to the governments, such as in advisory positions and from governmental think tanks, including from Nagorno-Karabakh. This way the connection with the authorities would be ensured, yet no one in the room would be an official—not from Nagorno-Karabakh, nor from anywhere else.

It was not easy, however, to persuade potential participants from Nagorno-Karabakh to take part in the initiative at this stage. Having been excluded from the previous meetings, they had little trust toward the organizers or the NK Analytic Initiative. Thanks to recommendations from a few partners, colleagues from Nagorno-Karabakh eventually joined the initiative, but with a number of conditions on their own. Initially they requested to exclude any participation of the Azerbaijanis from Nagorno-Karabakh. We explained our aim to be inclusive, and they also agreed that in principle, no one should be excluded from the peace process and softened their position by accepting the presence of the Azerbaijanis from Nagorno-Karabakh, with new conditions: while present in the room, the Azerbaijanis from Nagorno-Karabakh should not be representing a distinct conflict side. Aiming to further depoliticize the "format" question, we again offered an alternative: no one would be representing any side in the room at all. As customary for PSW meetings, everyone would represent only themselves and act in personal capacity. The second condition was to have a coordinator in Nagorno-Karabakh, along with coordinators in Yerevan and Baku. With the consent from the Azerbaijani coordinator, we were able to accept this condition also. The agreement was that the work for advancing confidence-building measures and creating ground for a solution to the conflict had to be conducted in the entire region of the Nagorno-Karabakh conflict and the local coordinators were to be chosen based on the location where the work was to be done, which included Nagorno-Karabakh, and without regard to their ethnicity or nationality.

Another early achievement of the process was the decision to work through consensus; and in addition to sharing the recommendations developed by the group with policymakers, to also publicize them in the media to affect the public discourse. We understood that working through consensus might make it harder to reach a decision, yet agreed that the recommendations developed in this manner would have greater legitimacy and impact.

Having agreed on what we saw as a relatively inclusive composition of the group, we scheduled a series of meetings during which various topics pertinent to the conflict would be discussed and policy recommendations jointly developed. The topics themselves were discussed and devised during the first meeting that took place in January 2013 and included:

- Recommendations for Confidence-Building Measures in the Region of the Nagorno-Karabakh Conflict;
- Recommendations for Donors and Other Interested Parties and Organizations Concerned with the Resolution of the Nagorno-Karabakh Conflict;
- Recommendations on the Format of Dialogue Platforms;
- Recommendations on Questions of Security in the Region of the Nagorno-Karabakh Conflict.
- Glossary of Conflict Sensitive Terms.

While all the topics touched upon dynamics critical for conflict resolution in the region, two sets of recommendations are of particular importance for this research. The Glossary of Conflict Sensitive Terms was an attempt to develop a language of speaking and writing about the Nagorno-Karabakh conflict that would help to transform rather than sustain the conflict. The Glossary was important not only for the outside world but for the group itself, as we desperately needed a common language of speaking and writing about the conflict to use in our joint recommendations.

This direction took long and hard efforts from the group. We started by identifying the categories of vocabulary that contained politically sensitive terms, such as toponymy, naming of the conflict sides, naming of actors and heroes, of massacres and others. We then established a working group consisting of journalists and linguists who would develop a list of possible inclusive terms. These terms then would be tested in focus groups in Armenia, Azerbaijan, and Nagorno-Karabakh, and the results discussed during the following meeting. Many of the terms developed and agreed upon were indeed used in the recommendations developed by the NK Analytic Initiative. A number of us who took part in the initiative continue using these terms in our other work as well. One such example is the reference to the "region of the Nagorno-Karabakh conflict" (in reference to Armenia, Azerbaijan, and Nagorno-Karabakh together) or "zone of the Nagorno-Karabakh conflict" (in lieu of the more customary yet divisive "Nagorno-Karabakh Republic" or the "occupied territory of Nagorno-Karabakh"). This was the only topic, still, on which the group was never able to develop full consensus or make the document public, highlighting the difficulty of developing a common vocabulary and the importance of language that sustains conflicts. Even the name of the Nagorno-Karabakh conflict has been hotly contested, with any possible term used seen as favoring one side or the other.

Another document relevant for this research was the Recommendations on the Format of Dialogue Platforms, intending to discuss the topic of exclusion and the need for inclusive approaches to the peace process. The discussion was important not only for the NK Analytic Initiative itself but for most other efforts in the Nagorno-Karabakh conflict context, as we knew that initiative after initiative would fail or have a limited scope because of the mutual requests to exclude groups of populations. The group accepted the following guidelines:

- all parties involved in the settlement of the Nagorno-Karabakh conflict need to increase openness and transparency of the negotiation process;
- all dialogue platforms on the civil society level need to be depoliticized and inclusively developed;
- all government authorities need to initiate dialogue with their former residents;
- the format of dialogue platforms needs to expand to involve representatives of parliaments, governments, religious leaders, diaspora, and so on.

The text was focused on fostering inclusivity, yet that very inclusivity was missing in the initiative that developed the text and where the ongoing struggle aimed at preserving each side's or individual's preferred format of the peace process led to many instances of exclusion and marginalization, culminating in the monopoly on voice by the government advisers. Next, I explore how such an extreme exclusion and marginalization patterns surfaced in the NK Analytic Initiative despite the stated agreement to be inclusive.

First to come under attack were the team of organizers and facilitators, the holders of the symbolic power, despite our explicit statement that our own goal was to hand to the participants the power of framing the conversation and shaping the discourse: as in the case with the Syrian initiative, we saw our role as facilitators who were there to help with the process, leaving the frameworks and the development of the content to the participants. Our repeated insistence that we had no agenda on our own other than helping the participants to develop their own shared agenda and content was met with suspicion. The more we repeated that we have no hidden agenda, the more often the question "so what is your true agenda?" was raised.

The organizers team at this stage of the initiative consisted of myself, a scholar-practitioner of conflict resolution originally from Armenia, residing in Washington, DC; a social anthropologist from Azerbaijan who worked in Berlin; an American facilitator and at the time the executive director of a conflict practice center in Washington, DC; and the representatives of the Imagine Center in Yerevan and Baku. A California-based American professor of conflict resolution acted as the external evaluator. The early target were the country representatives of the Imagine Center: as soon as one of them spoke up, she was interrupted by a participant who requested to keep the separation between the administrative support team of the project who should be responsible for logistics and the participants who are responsible for content. This has not been customary for our organization where everyone involved had a voice in both content and administration. However, in this particular initiative we had agreed as organizers that our role was to support those who were present explicitly as participants and that we could be helpful for them only to the degree that they would request. Consequently, we left the decision to the participants. The participants' opinions split on this topic with some supporting the full involvement of the Imagine Center's team in the conversation, and the others requesting role separation. As we were working through consensus and a consensus to include the administrators in the content conversation was not reached, we complied, and the country representatives left the table at the start of the first meeting, which effectively excluded them from the conversation for the entire duration of the project.

At the facilitators' request, the group then affirmed through consensus the role of the remaining organizers as facilitators. Some insisted that we should have voice in content discussions as well. This suggestion led to a further challenge to the organizers aimed at minimizing our voice. My Azerbaijani colleague and myself had initially positioned ourselves as Azerbaijani and Armenian facilitators, although living currently abroad. Yet our "Armenian-ness" and "Azerbaijani-ness" was questioned: some key participants suggested that having lived abroad for a number of years, we were not well aware of the situation on the ground. Further, being based in the western power centers of Washington, DC, and Berlin, we could carry biases and advance the interests of super powers, whether knowingly or not. Therefore, we were not well suited to represent our native countries. Representing Armenia and Azerbaijan was a claim that we did not have already, and as facilitators we had no intent of interfering in the content anyways. Therefore, we saw no contradiction between the request for us not to interfere with the content and how we saw our role. As we complied, the group showed more ownership toward the process and readiness to set their own agenda and develop their own content and the initial suspicion that some participants had toward the initiative was dropped. This seemed a positive development.

What surfaced later, however, during the interviews and reflections conducted for this research, was a major deficiency in our tactical decision back then. Our "ceding power" worked in achieving the immediate outcome as the group felt ownership of the process and worked collaboratively thereafter, producing a series of policy recommendations. And we, as organizers, did not cede anything tangible by accepting the participants' definition of our role, as our own definition of our role was similar to theirs. What we did not realize then, however, was the symbolic value of the move. For the facilitators, this was a simple acknowledgment of the hands-off role that we planned to play already. For those who led the charge of requesting facilitators to relinquish control, this was a successful coup, an act of intentional marginalizing of organizers in order to take control of the room.

The snowball of exclusions and marginalization continued: the participants from Armenia who had fought hard to have a group of Nagorno-Karabakh Armenians in the room were now asserting their dominance over the production of the "Armenian" end of the conflict discourse, politely overriding the views of the Nagorno-Karabakh Armenian participants at every occasion of disagreement. This was accepted rather well by the Azerbaijani participants, as the position of the participants from Armenia looked more conciliatory compared to those of the Nagorno-Karabakh Armenians. Yet here too the conciliation came at the expense of marginalization.

The Azerbaijani participants also worked on marginalizing the Nagorno-Karabakh Armenians, ignoring their presence and engaging directly with the participants from Armenia once a disagreement with the former group would arise. The Nagorno-Karabakh Armenian participants, in turn, used every occasion to veto the participation in our continuing series of meetings of new possible Azerbaijani invitees originating from Nagorno-Karabakh. There was a visible power struggle also within each of the groups, with the participants positioned closest to the governments striving for domination and marginalization of others.

All and all, this was a program of two extremes. It worked well in achieving its stated goals: externally the group looked relatively inclusive; it worked through consensus; it produced policy recommendations that were shared with policymakers and media; and the participants spoke publicly in one voice. All these virtues were rare for initiatives working in the context of the Nagorno-Karabakh peace process and were welcomed by both the participants and outside observers. At the same time the process of achieving these goals was problematic. Wholesale categories of possible participants were excluded. Many of those who made it to the room were marginalized in the process. Government critics, persons of mixed heritage, persons residing abroad, Azerbaijanis of Nagorno-Karabakh who were not part of the initial group, independent thinkers, to name just a few, were directly excluded from participation. In the room, the power struggle ensured the marginalization of the great many of those present, particularly the Nagorno-Karabakh Armenians and individuals who were not close to either Armenian or Azerbaijani governments. By the second meeting of 2013, the monopoly of voice firmly belonged to close-to-government participants from Azerbaijan and Armenia. The consensus was illusory—not more than a euphemism for compliance.

Implications of the Nagorno-Karabakh Analytic Initiative for recognizing power dynamics and resulting exclusion, and marginalization

Exclusion and marginalization have been manifested in both of the programs described here, the Syrian dialogue and the NK Analytic Initiative, while both aimed at conflict resolution and both attempted to be inclusive. If in the Syrian program, we started with exclusion and moved toward inclusion, in the NK Analytic Initiative, we aimed from the start to be inclusive, but new forms of exclusion would continuously emerge.

A few obvious instances of exclusion and marginalization have already been mentioned and are typical for the initiatives in the Nagorno-Karabakh context, where unofficial efforts follow the framework of Track 1, prompting individuals to engage in self-censorship and wary of participating in any format that might appear to contradict the policies set by their authorities. The nationalist groups and media who prey on peace activists also keep them in check, forcing those involved in conflict resolution to continuously prove their patriotic or even nationalist credentials. While some of the youth forums are able to stay under the radar and have more inclusive formats, the meetings that are similar to the NK Analytic Initiative featuring visible members of the society find themselves in the center of media attention, which keep the participants under added pressure, leading all but the few particularly courageous individuals to act with an extreme caution, putting forward demands that exclude and marginalize other populations.

When it comes to informal initiatives, by 2013, most Azerbaijani participants of high-stake Track 2 initiatives backed the official line that accepted either a "two-party format" with meetings between the representatives from Azerbaijan and Armenia only or "communal format," where the meetings are only between the Azerbaijanis and Armenians of Nagorno-Karabakh. The aim here is to frame the conflict either as a local and intercommunal one where the government of Azerbaijan can act as an arbiter or as an international one, and thus a case of aggression by Armenia that annexed the territory of Azerbaijan, and not a conflict where the Armenians residing in the former

NKAO of Azerbaijan felt discriminated against and demanded self-determination as argued by the Armenian participants. The Azerbaijani participants do not exclude the Armenians of Nagorno-Karabakh from the peace process altogether, but they limit the frameworks in which such participation is acceptable, confined to cultural initiatives and meetings with the Azerbaijanis of Nagorno-Karabakh, while excluding the participation of anyone representing the de-facto authorities. In practice, such formats deprive the Nagorno-Karabakh Armenians of a political voice, acknowledging only the voice of the governments of the Republics of Armenia and Azerbaijan in political matters.

By 2013, the Armenian participants of Track 2 initiatives appeared even less compromising and often demanded the outright exclusion of the Nagorno-Karabakh Azerbaijanis from all peace initiatives. Individual Azerbaijanis from Nagorno-Karabakh might be accepted, but with a condition that they represent Azerbaijan and not the Azerbaijanis of Nagorno-Karabakh. This stance, justified as a rejection of the previously mentioned Azerbaijani policy on advancing the "communal" format, is aimed at promoting the competing trilateral format that includes Azerbaijan, Armenia, and Nagorno-Karabakh as three distinct parties to the conflict and is seen as a way of legitimizing Nagorno-Karabakh as a political entity. With the legitimization and recognition of the Nagorno-Karabakh Republic seen by many Armenians as the ultimate goal of their efforts, Armenians who participate in the bi-lateral and communal formats preferred by Azerbaijan are criticized as unpatriotic and compromising the national agenda.

What this meant in practice was that at the start of many initiatives, the Azerbaijani participants would demand the exclusion of the Nagorno-Karabakh Armenians, while the Armenians would demand the exclusion of the Nagorno-Karabakh Azerbaijanis. Having accepted these conditions in earlier years and understanding that the NK Analytic Initiative contributed to the exclusion of key populations from the peace process, we were determined to make the process inclusive.

At the start of the NK Analytic Initiatives as we received the agreement of the key partners on the need to be inclusive, we tried to find solutions to the known exclusion patterns, namely the exclusion of Nagorno-Karabakh Armenians as political actors and the exclusion of the Nagorno-Karabakh Azerbaijanis altogether. Yet as we worked to address the known to us forms of exclusion and marginalization, many other patterns emerged, starting from the recruitment phase and continuing through the entire process. When considering new invitees into the Initiative, each new person's identity was discussed with the existing participants from Armenia, Azerbaijan, and Nagorno-Karabakh ad nauseam: many great candidates would be vetoed by one participant or the other, the downside of a consensus-based process. Prospective participants would be excluded for a variety of reasons: some were excluded because they were based abroad and therefore "not in the context enough," others had mixed heritage or heritage that was not of the "titular" ethnicity and were thus "not representative"; others yet were considered too controversial or too critical of the government or in some other way were not "Armenian enough" or "Azerbaijani enough." The participants of the NK Analytic Initiative would justify their adhesion to the close reproduction of the restrictive frames set by Track 1 negotiations by the need to have the recommendations produced acceptable to the officials, and therefore, with a higher chance to be implemented. The sacrifice for such a goal-oriented approach was the exclusion from the process of everyone other than a handful of individuals with impeccable patriotic credentials and whose Azerbaijani and Armenian identities and loyalties to the governments could not be questioned.

One tactic used by participants to exclude others was particularly frustrating for the organizers: almost every demand related to exclusion of someone else was accompanied by the threat of self-withdrawal. In other words, the threat of self-exclusion was used as a leverage to gain power in excluding others. This would force the organizers to constantly perform a balancing act: rejecting such an ultimatum would be interpreted as if we valued the potential candidate more than the one already active in the process. And the latter one in most cases was one of our key partners on the ground, with whom we had a long-lasting working relationship. At the same time, accepting the demands based on such an ultimatum and not on mutual agreement would not be constructive or ethical in regard to the would-be participant.

The NK Analytic Initiative discussed in this chapter demonstrated an example of an open power struggle for domination over the group discourse. The main products of that Initiative were policy papers produced through consensus, which prompted the participants to compete for gaining control over the group discourse. The persons controlling the discussion in that context were able, effectively, to formulate the content of the policy recommendations presented publicly as the united opinion of the entire group. The visibly inclusive format of consensus-based decision making gave incentives for power struggles, initially between or among the various delegations and later within the delegations, culminating in the authoritarian control of the Azerbaijani and Armenian government supporters over the group's discourse and resulting in the reduction of the dialogue to the simple reproduction of the Azerbaijani and Armenian official positions. The establishment of this discursive hegemony was achieved through the partial or complete marginalization of the majority of the participants and the suppression of the creativity or out-of-the-box thinking, bankrupting the format and leading to the eventual disintegration of the group.

Unlike the Syrian case where the conflict dynamics and the identities of conflict sides are still in flux, the conflict frames are well-established in the Nagorno-Karabakh context. The goal of striving for inclusivity, therefore, was accepted only theoretically. In practice, however, those on the two nationalist extremes who already assumed monopoly of voice by the time the NK Analytic Initiative had started, those positioning themselves as "pure and patriotic" Armenians and Azerbaijanis had little interest in expanding the boundaries of the conversation. Rejecting potential participants because of their identities was justified by the need to gain leverage in policymaking. Yet once exclusion as a price for political leverage was acknowledged by the participants as a legitimate tactic, an intense struggle for power within the room ensued, further limiting the number of those who had voice.

Part II postscript

You could think by this point of the book that sustaining exclusion and marginalization is not characteristic for conflict resolution work in general and that my colleagues and I are simply bad practitioners. And I sincerely wish you were right. But I am afraid that is not the case. As I will show in the next chapters, if anything, we are typical, and the specific dynamics in our work that I detailed here are reflective of patterns of exclusion and marginalization produced by one conflict resolution initiative after another.

I started this research with an assumption that exclusion and marginalization of the majority would be characteristic for a case like Syria where the conflict sides are not consolidated and the nonrepresentative extremes get disproportionate attention. I further assumed that most other conflicts are indeed binary, and in conflicts with consolidated frames bringing together two sides would be enough to have most everyone concerned well-represented. The refection on the NK Analytic Initiative and other cases discussed below, however, showed that exclusion and marginalization are manifesting themselves not less forcefully within the conflicts that are widely assumed to be binary.

For almost three decades now, virtually every commentator, myself included, have been framing the Nagorno-Karabakh conflict as "Armenian-Azerbaijani." The assumption is that everyone in the region of the conflict falls to one side of that divide or the other. Despite that, a critical look into conflict resolution practices shows that even today great many people affected by the conflict are left out of the process because of such framing. Regularly excluded are Armenians and Azerbaijanis of Nagorno-Karabakh, displaced, migrants, people of mixed heritage, minorities, as well as those who chose not to see ethnicity as their primary identity marker. Even in the successful looking peace initiatives, the binary frames tend to perpetuate exclusion and marginalization.

Part III

In Part II of this book, I took a close-up look at two cases where I was involved as a facilitator, reflecting on some patterns of exclusion and marginalization, which emerged in common conflict resolution practices, when approached uncritically. I offered this close-up look to show through the in-depth discussion of two very different cases how these patterns operate and help perpetuate conflicts at every possible stage of the initiative. Only a few specific patterns of exclusion and marginalization, however, were identified within these two initiatives. Many new patterns became apparent during this study and are presented in the pages that follow.

In Part III, I reverse the approach: I zoom out and present an entire system of patterns of exclusion and marginalization that serve to perpetuate conflict and that were identified in over 30 conflict resolution initiatives held primarily in Syrian and Nagorno-Karabakh contexts. Occasionally, when these colleagues referred to their work in other conflict contexts and I had their permission, I used these additional examples to examine the relevance of the discussed patterns of marginalization for conflict resolution work across various conflict divides.

Chapter 6
Influence of macro-frames on conflict resolution practice. Addressing exclusion perpetuated by binary conflict discourses of international relations

Marginalization and exclusion that perpetuate conflict, as I show in the next three chapters, can emerge at any stage of the conflict resolution process: during the framing of the problem, project conception, fundraising, project design, recruitment, implementation, or follow-up. Marginalization and exclusion can affect prospective or actual participants as well as practitioners. In this study, I do not aim to identify every possible pattern of exclusion and marginalization perpetuated by conflict resolution practice: compiling a full list would be impossible in a qualitative study, considering the multiplicity of conflict contexts and the large variety of interventions. I focus here on patterns that were present in most if not every initiative I studied and therefore proved to be widespread, as well as those that were repeated less often and were somewhat context-specific but had a major influence on perpetuating conflict discourses or marginalizing affected populations. The multiplicity of such patterns identified is enough to suggest that a deep re-conceptualization of conflict resolution interventions is necessary in order to develop inclusive practices that do not perpetuate conflicts. Further, what I discuss here is not every single pattern of marginalization or exclusion that I identified, but only those that the colleagues I worked with came to see as contributing to the perpetuation of the conflict discourses or as ethically problematic.

In this chapter, I focus on patterns of exclusion and marginalization embedded in macro-frames that have strong grip on the conflict resolution practice. Among these, the discourse of international relations has a particularly strong influence. The critique is followed by the discussion of possible alternative frames that have been tested through this PAR.

In the shadow of the international relations discourse

Conflict resolution, or at least the North American variation of it, is a field with a split identity that positions itself simultaneously as an alternative to international relations and a complement to it. As discussed in the introduction and review of theories, the present-day theory of conflict resolution understood broadly contains clear conceptual alternatives to international relations and other positivist approaches. The conflict resolution practice, however, remains closely associated with international relations as its soft substitute.

The constraining influence of international relations discourse on conflict resolution practice that prevents the latter from reaching its full potential is discussed in this chapter in the context of exclusion or marginalization of key constituencies as a result of a borrowed from the former binary framing of conflicts as a disagreement between defined sides.

The defacement of conflict resolution as an independent field starts with the common naming of many conflict resolution efforts as "Track 2" or "public diplomacy." As the second track of official diplomacy, it is then expected to follow the frames and conventions of the first track. I am not arguing against the term "Track 2 diplomacy" in conflict resolution work altogether. In cases when a certain initiative explicitly serves as the informal platform of direct support for the official negotiations, the term "Track 2" is justified, along with its derivatives such as "Track 1.5" or "consultations" (R. J. Fisher and Keashly 1991). One of the best-known examples of such efforts are the informal meetings in the Track 2 format that laid ground for the 1993 Oslo agreement (H. Kelman 2005). Track 2 work that supports official efforts, therefore, is important as one of the integral parts of a comprehensive peace process. What I am arguing against, however, is the reducing of the comprehensive peace process to its one part, the official negotiations, and the subsequent conflation of all the broader conflict resolution work with narrow Track 2 efforts aimed to support the official track.

I discussed the problem of terming all nonofficial efforts as "Track 2" in the introduction from a theoretical point of view. I argued there that the term "Track 2 diplomacy" is detrimental to conflict resolution if seen not as a small part of but a substitute to it. The track is numbered "2," making it secondary to Track 1, and signaling that the voice of influential but nonofficial actors in the societies is secondary compared to the voice of the political elites. Further, the work with the larger parts of the societies, including with those directly affected by conflicts in this hierarchy, is branded as Track 3 work or, by way of naming it, work of tertiary importance.

The second problem I outlined was that the term "Track 2 diplomacy" effectively has no independent meaning: as a derivative of Track 1 diplomacy, it gets legitimated only based on the degree of its contribution to the success of Track 1, constrained by its frames, vocabulary, aims, and methods. Yet diplomacy is not necessarily an endeavor aimed at resolving conflicts but one intended to serve the interests of the particular states, and these interests might or might not involve conflict resolution.

In this chapter, I focus on the practical implications of the use of the word "Track 2" in the cases I studied. The expectations donors attach to the initiatives known as "Track 2" are also delimiting. The Track 2 umbrella leads the organizations to frame the theory of change for their initiatives in terms of their support for the official process. This in turn assumes that the initiative works in some form of consultation with the officials, possibly with the inclusion of official or close-to-government participants, who almost invariably join in with a precondition that the initiative would conform with the policy of their government. As a result, the initiative loses its flexibility and ability to be inclusive or push boundaries.

Practical implications of naming initiatives "Track 2": impact on selection

In the Nagorno-Karabakh case, framing the initiatives as "Track 2" often results in the explicit concurrent requests to exclude the Nagorno-Karabakh Armenian leadership, almost all Nagorno-Karabakh Azerbaijanis, individuals who are not seen as loyal to the ruling regimes, and many others. The challenge has been known among the conflict resolution practitioners working in that conflict context as the "format problem" in reference to the two-party (Armenia and Azerbaijan), three-party (Armenia-Azerbaijan-Nagorno-Karabakh), or other "formats" preferred by either Armenian or Azerbaijani policymakers. This problem is not unique to the NK Analytic Initiative discussed in Chapter 5. Every colleague that led a Track 2 initiative in the Nagorno-Karabakh context had faced a similar "format problem." The framing of the initiative as Track 2 pushes practitioners to accept it as a complement to Track 1 coordinating the efforts with the officials and reproducing their frames, which in turn limits the circle of those who can be invited, excluding from unofficial work the groups that are already excluded from the official process.

Not all exclusion is done under direct official pressure: many practitioners have accepted and internalized the exclusionary frames favored by their government to a point that they themselves see them as necessary. For example, many Armenian colleagues working in the field of conflict resolution have stated categorically that the participation of the Nagorno-Karabakh Azerbaijanis in conflict resolution work for them, too, is unacceptable. The reasons for such an outright exclusion of a group who has suffered from the conflict varied:

- Some believed, on the personal level, that no one should be excluded from the peace process, but felt forced to comply with what they perceived to be the established policy by the Armenian and Nagorno-Karabakh authorities of excluding Azerbaijanis of Nagorno-Karabakh;
- Others set forth an expressly nationalist agenda, and saw conflict resolution as nothing more than a mechanism toward the normalization of the status quo and the eventual recognition of Nagorno-Karabakh as an Armenian state. This goal, they believed, could be threatened by the return of hundreds of thousands of Azerbaijanis who were resettled into the historically Armenian territory of Karabakh with an intention of outnumbering and dominating the Armenians. These practitioners, therefore, opposed any involvement of Azerbaijanis from Nagorno-Karabakh in conflict resolution work as it would give them voice and open up possibilities for their return;
- And most of who supported the exclusion were in between these positions and tended to deflect the responsibility from

themselves or the Armenian leadership. They blamed the Azerbaijani leadership for politicizing the involvement of the Nagorno-Karabakh Azerbaijanis using it to reframe the conflict into an intercommunal one rather than a self-determination struggle of the Armenian population against the oppressive regime in Baku. Working with Azerbaijanis from Nagorno-Karabakh, they argued, meant playing into the political agenda of the Azerbaijani leadership.

Some of the Azerbaijani colleagues, in turn, have been refusing to work with the Armenians from Nagorno-Karabakh, particularly with those representing the de facto authorities. This position had a range of explanations similar to the ones expressed by Armenians:

- Some practitioners did not personally agree with such exclusion, but followed the official line in order to preserve good relations with the Azerbaijani authorities and to safeguard their ability to work;
- Others who supported the exclusion, deflected the responsibility from themselves or the Azerbaijani leadership and this time blamed the Armenian leadership for politicizing the participation of the Nagorno-Karabakh Armenians by presenting it as a sign of implicit recognition of Nagorno-Karabakh Armenians as a side to the conflict, an agenda to which Azerbaijani practitioners would not want to contribute;
- I personally did not encounter any Azerbaijani practitioner who would take an overtly nationalist position of personally denying the Nagorno-Karabakh Armenians any right of participation. According to some of my Azerbaijani colleagues, however, such positions also exist but would not be shared with me openly considering my own Armenian identity. Specifically, my colleagues referred to positions held by some Azerbaijani practitioners who, similar to their Armenian counterparts, saw conflict resolution as a tool for advancing the restoration of full Azerbaijani control over Nagorno-Karabakh and saw the conflict exclusively as a case of aggression of Armenia against Azerbaijan. They preferred not to give voice to Nagorno-Karabakh Armenians, who as former Soviet Azerbaijani citizens would challenge this narrative.

Not all Armenian and Azerbaijani colleagues, of course, supported exclusionary positions. Many of them shared my frustration with the "format" problem and saw the need for the conflict resolution community to develop more inclusive frames. It was through the interviews and reflections with these colleagues that we identified framing of initiatives as Track 2, and the subsequent need to comply with the official policies, as a reason for the consistent exclusion of Nagorno-Karabakh populations from the peace process that should determine their future. In further confirmation of the limiting effect of "Track 2" terminology, we established that the initiatives framed differently, as the cultural or educational, had more freedom when inviting participants and as a result were far more inclusive. These initiatives, however, did not aim to address the conflict dynamics directly. The challenge remained, therefore, with developing frames where the initiative can both be inclusive and contribute to policy change or conflict discourse transformation.

Exclusions based on Track 2 framing are not unique to the Nagorno-Karabakh context. In the Syrian case, several practitioners critical of binary framing mentioned that they are actively encouraged by donors to build the capacity of the "opposition" preparing it for governing or for encouraging dialogue between the Assad government supporters and the opposition, making it hard to engage those outside of the established Assad-opposition dichotomy and involve populations who are refusing to identify with either. Many practitioners have internalized these international relation frames and see their work to be only in the empowerment of the opposition and the overthrow of the Assad regime or try to mediate between the supporters of Assad and the supporters of the opposition. Both of these frames, as I argued above and elsewhere, leave out the majority of the Syrian population who do not identify with either extreme (Gamaghelyan 2013).

The binary discourse of conflict sides borrowed from international relations, therefore, is a challenge that hampers creativity and potential inclusivity of conflict resolution efforts. The frames such as Assad-opposition, Turkish-Armenian, and Catholic-Protestant create dichotomies that exclude from participation those who are not one or the other. These binary frames privilege those at the extremes and exclude from the conflict resolution process the others—often the majority as is the case in Syria. Moreover, binary framing makes the conflict virtually insolvable. Identity-based conflict resolution theories have long pointed out that all individuals possess multiple identities and prioritizing one of them and reducing a group of complex individuals into a monolithic ethnic or religious group leads to nationalism and conflict (Roccas and Brewer 2002). Intersectional theory examines overlapping or intersecting identities in one individual and how marginalization, oppression, and domination occur on a multidimensional basis and do not affect more than one part of the person's identity (Crenshaw 1989). The identity-focused conflict resolution methods often focus on reversing this process, allowing the multiple identities of individuals to be revealed leading to understanding, empathy and sympathy, and eventually to reconciliation and partnerships across the conflict divide (see for example Rothman and Olson 2001; Halpern and Weinstein 2004; Cobb 2004).

Despite this awareness present in our field, however, most practitioners continue to frame conflicts in binary and ethnic terms, as if these identities are all that the people in conflict zones have, and as if these identities are indeed in conflict, a phenomenon that Brubaker calls an "ontology that leads us to talk and write about ethnic groups and nations as real entities" (Brubaker 1998, 292). Be it in the name of the project or the call for proposals or the program design and its selection criteria, many practitioners set up these binary frames. As we have seen in Chapter 4 and as supported by other colleagues, working in the Syrian context in 2011–2014, the conflict practitioners tended to categorize the participants as either pro-Assad or pro-opposition, excluding those who are neither. In the Nagorno-Karabakh case, the framing of the conflict as Armenian-Azerbaijani is even more entrenched and guides the selection. As the frames get repeated from project to project and year to year, those who do not fit the frames become permanently excluded.

Having framed the initiative as Armenian-Azerbaijani, the practitioners then feel pressured to determine who are these "Armenians" and "Azerbaijanis." And, more importantly, who is not. As we have a possibility of competing definitions and interpretation and the practitioners often look for the least common denominator, such framing creates a fertile ground for exclusion with the practitioners inviting only those who demonstrate a strong sense of belonging to one or the other. Yet identities are always complex. "Armenian" can have a geographic, ethnic, national, and other meanings. In the strive to ensure that the project is indeed Armenian-Azerbaijani, the distilling of the "real" Armenian excludes noncitizens, as well as many citizens affected by the conflict who do not fit the frame, such as an Armenian refugee from Soviet Azerbaijan who migrated to places other than Armenia or ethnic Kurds who were displaced during the war.

The words "true" or "real" Armenian or "true," "real," or "representative" Azerbaijani in the Nagorno-Karabakh case, "true" Muslim in the Syrian case were used by many of the colleagues to describe what guided their selection. They confessed to exclude those who do not conform to this image, as in their view, the "not true Armenians/Azerbaijanis/Muslims" would present narratives "not representative" of the society at large.

Very few facilitators I talked to in the Nagorno-Karabakh context would acknowledge this as a problem or even a potential problem. Others confirmed that they exclude those who live in the conflict societies but are "not a side" and defended this position. They considered those who do not belong to a clear side not to be party to the conflict and therefore irrelevant in the peace process. According to them, considering that the resources for conflict resolution are limited, it would be a waste to invite those who are "not a side."

Even in workshops for representatives of a particular profession the priority is often given to the ethnic identity and perceived representativeness of the participants. Professionals are often invited to fit the stereotypical definition of the "sides." While "impartials" who come from outside the conflict context, typically from the United States or Western Europe, can be welcomed as facilitators, trainers, or consultants, the organizers rarely find a role for insiders who are not "a side." This leaves out, either as a participant or as a facilitator, the unaligned, those of mixed heritage, those of identities that are not in conflict, empowering in the process the two "representative" extremes. To be sure, many programs that include nonconforming individuals or persons of mixed heritage exist as I discuss below. Such programs, however, usually focus on questions of diversity, human rights and others, and rarely on the question of the political resolution of the conflict.

Similar patterns are also present in other conflicts. The Armenian-Turkish dialogues confront an ongoing confusion as to who is qualified to participate. The following questions that haunt the practitioners during selection were mentioned repeatedly during my interviews: Are the dialogues for the citizens of Turkey and Armenia? Should then minorities be included? Can the nonethnic Turks from Turkey who have many problems with the county on their own represent Turkey? What about ethnic Armenians living in Turkey? How to involve them? As Turks or as Armenians? What about the diaspora? And how to decide who is representing diaspora and how to work with it? The default solution, particularly in Track 2 initiatives, have long been to exclude those whose identities represent a challenge for the initiative.

Practical implications of naming initiatives "Track 2": impact on dialogue

The binary frames dominate also the facilitation methodologies, even when the project selection is not dichotomous. I already discussed an example in Chapter 4 in the Syrian context, where the facilitators attempted initially to fit the participants into the Assad-opposition binary and had to back out only after encountering resistance. In most other cases, the binary frames were accepted as a given by both the facilitators and the participants without contestation. In a dialogue framed as Armenian-Azerbaijani, Assad-opposition, Turkish-Armenian, Arab-Israeli, Georgian-South Ossetian, and so on, most participants readily adopted the nominated identities with facilitators then mediating between these two groups. Those who do not readily belong to a side were either excluded at the stage of selection, self-excluded themselves prior to the dialogue by not applying or withdrawing, adopted a conflict side in the room, or were marginalized in the process, as we will see in the examples below. These exclusions filter out the participants and those who make it to the room adopt rigid identities, validating the theories that see identities as rigid "us vs. them" dichotomous constructs inherently in opposition to one another (Kriesberg 2003; Tajfel 2010).

The pressures to "fit" into a rigid frame of a conflict side did not end at the selection stage and continued throughout the initiatives. Both facilitators and participants communicate an implicit message that the participants should represent "their side's true" views, as if such unified views exist in any society. The core part of the PSW methodology, for example, is to ask the participants to break into sides and develop unified lists of needs, fears, concerns, and hopes of their societies (H. Kelman 1972, 2005; Babbitt and Steiner 2009). The colleagues discussed a number of cases in which participants from "one side" would articulate a point that was not seen as representative of the "mainstream view" or worse and was stereotyped as belonging to the narrative of "the other side." In such cases, the argument was mistrusted, dismissed, or otherwise marginalized even by the side that is "the other" in this case. Such examples came from a variety of conflicts.

During a dialogue in the Nagorno-Karabakh conflict context, some participants from Azerbaijan apologized to the participants from Armenia for the axe murder of Gurgen Margaryan by Ramil Safarov and the follow-up heroization of Safarov by the Azerbaijani authorities in the case described in Chapter 5. The Armenian participants did not seem to hear the apology and went on criticizing the Azerbaijani participants for the heroization of Safarov in Azerbaijan. When the facilitators pointed out that the Azerbaijani participants had agreed with this view already and also criticized the heroization, the Armenian participants expressed mistrust and disbelief. The later reflection suggested that Armenian participants saw themselves invited to meet "Azerbaijanis" and hear from them "Azerbaijani views," in return sharing stereotypically understood "Armenians views." In other words, they expected the exchange of nationalist narratives promoted through government controlled media and highly publicized speeches of the officials. One key stereotypical "Armenian viewpoint" was to be the criticism of the heroization of Safarov in Azerbaijan. The expected role of the Azerbaijani participants in this scenario would be to defend Safarov or at least to justify his heroization in the society. The participants from Armenia, as a consequence, did not know what to make of the Azerbaijani group sharing the presumed "Armenian viewpoint," so they dismissed the gesture and accused the Azerbaijani colleagues of dishonesty. Ironically, the incident was resolved when one of the Azerbaijani participants performed the expected role. He did not defend Safarov, but explained why he could be seen as a hero by many in Azerbaijan, suggesting that the narratives about the murder seem to differ in Armenia and Azerbaijan. According to the Armenian version, he suggested, Safarov axed the innocent Margaryan in his sleep for the only sin of being an Armenian. At the same time, the narratives circulated in the Azerbaijani media were more complex: Safarov was discussed as an IDP who lost his home during an Armenian invasion; Margaryan was described not as any Armenian but as an officer of the Armenian army responsible for his and his close ones' displacement and suffering; next, some Azerbaijani sources claimed that Margaryan disrespected Safarov and his loss, as well desecrated the Azerbaijani flag; finally, according to another version circulating in the Azerbaijani media, Margaryan was not asleep but was killed after an active struggle between the two. None of this, concluded the participant from Azerbaijan, justifies the murder, but in the atmosphere of an unresolved conflict and the inability of hundreds of thousands of displaced Azerbaijanis to return to their homes, the heroization of Safarov by some could be understood. A few Armenian participants then repeated their rejection of such a position arguing that a murder remains a murder and should be condemned, giving a chance to the Azerbaijani participants to once again express their agreement and apology, which in this case was accepted. The "dance" was now performed properly; the "sides" delineated; the "boxes" were reestablished.

In a similar situation in a Turkish-Armenian context, the Turkish participants' acknowledgment of the Armenian genocide during the very first day of a week-long workshop was met with mistrust. The situation was rectified after the retreat to presupposed positions of the denial by the Turkish group, the demand of recognition by the Armenians, followed by an extended dialogue, acknowledgment, and finally apology. Again, the structure of the binary discourse of the dialogue initially faltered, then got back on track by forcing the participants to perform "sides," allowing the dialogue to run its habitual course.

In another context, an Israeli participant was first criticized for "her country's" policies of suppression against the Palestinian population and the occupation of Palestinian lands with the assumption that the Israeli participant would support those policies and would deny the right of existence for a Palestinian state. When the Israeli participant instead harshly criticized the politics of the Israeli government and acknowledged the claims of Palestinians to own the land and to be a state as righteous, she was again criticized, this time for daring to call Palestine a state while the Palestinian communities are living under occupation. The views that the Israeli participant had were alternative to what the Israeli government holds, but these alternative views were nevertheless re-interpreted to fit into the conflict narrative that the Palestinian participant had. Only when the triggered Israeli participant retreated to an expected "Israeli" position defending her right to live in an Israeli settlement in the West Bank, she gained acknowledgment for "speaking the truth."

The reflections of this pattern that suggested many participants' need to have their stereotypes validated before the dialogue and change can occur supports Van Dijk's well-known thesis. He argued in his *Society and Discourse: How Social Contexts Influence Text and Talk* that the narratives of conflict sides form an ideological square by emphasizing everything positive about "us" and everything negative about "them" and de-emphasize everything negative about "us" and positive about "them" (Van Dijk 2009). These binary narratives of conflict sides, as this research confirms, follow a particular plotline that constructs stereotypes and prescribes actions and thoughts to both self and the other. In the initiatives that framed the conflict in binary terms and asked participants to assume a role of one or the other conflict party, those present interpreted this framing as a call to hold each other accountable to act from the position of the presumed shared national narrative. In the Nagorno-Karabakh conflict context, participants felt invited to perform the role of a group victimized throughout its history by various others, among them Turks and Azerbaijanis through massacres, as well as individual acts of terror, such as Margaryan's murder by Safarov. Armenians also portrayed their own group as peace-loving and constructive people. In the same narrative

Azerbaijanis were portrayed as aggressive, full of hate toward Armenians, heroizing acts of violence against Armenians. The confirmation bias (Plous 1993) then led the participants of such dialogues to interpret the information received from those framed as "the opposite side" in a way that fits the established narrative. A support or justification of Safarov's actions validated the Armenian narrative of Azerbaijanis as violent people. And to the contrary, the condemnation of Safarov by Azerbaijanis expressed in the early stages of the process when the attachment to own narratives of self and the other was still strong created a cognitive dissonance and was mistrusted rather than welcomed. With time, the relationships grew, and the participants started acting as individuals with varying opinions exposing a range of possible Azerbaijani and Armenian viewpoints. Eventually as all the groups, invariably, would prove to be diverse and not subscribing to any monolithic narrative, the image of the other would be transformed and the same condemnation of Safarov or the acknowledgment of the genocide accepted with trust and appreciation.

In the context of dominance of the binary discourses in understanding conflict, everyone is expected to take a side, at least initially. Those who refuse to take a side and try to break the binary are often marginalized or penalized. Acknowledgment of the wrongdoing of one's own side, therefore, is both crucially important for conflict transformation and very dangerous for the person taking this step. Both in the Nagorno-Karabakh and Syrian contexts, accepting the responsibility of one's own side in perpetration of mass violence against civilians is considered off-limits and instances of transgression are policed by many. Through my professional life, I myself have been called out repeatedly both in public and in private by other Armenians at every occasion when I would cross a line considered off-limits and criticized publicly the actions of the Armenian state. The examples cited above, therefore, were not common. Rarely would participants voice such acknowledgment or question the narrative of their side prior to going through dialogue or developing trust. Such self-criticism, at the same time, and the diversity within each presumed "side" is an integral part of a successful dialogue as it plays a central part in the deconstruction and transformation of exclusivist nationalist narratives and rigid identity-constructs through the acknowledgment of shared responsibility.

Discussions in small groups or in pairs, personal sharing, and the creation of an open atmosphere where the diversity of viewpoints is celebrated and learning from those one disagrees with is appreciated are all important steps toward such a multiplicity of discourses.

When encouraging the individuals to speak up and to act as individuals rather than performing a monolithic side, however, the facilitators should be aware of the risks potentially faced by the participants who cross lines early and risk the label of an outsider or worse a traitor or a "not-Armenian/Azerbaijani/Syrian" who can be excluded from further participation in conflict resolution efforts.

Leaving the shadow: addressing patterns of marginalization influenced by the international relations discourse

International relations theories, undoubtedly, continue to dominate the policy- and practice-level understanding of conflict and conflict resolution. There have been developments in the scholarship on nationalism and discourse analysis, however, that are increasingly part of academic programs in conflict resolution and offer conceptual alternatives. This literature contains not only criticism of the existing frames and approaches but also implicit or explicit conceptual innovations, which can be useful for conflict resolution in building more inclusive, ethical, and effective conflict resolution practices. Up to date, however, these alternative approaches have only marginally impacted conflict resolution practice.

Conceptual alternatives

Brubaker, as discussed in more detail in Chapter 1, argues that conflicts framed in binary ethno-national terms in principle cannot have a solution. In an ethnically framed structure, individuals have little choice but to continually reenact their preassigned roles that reproduce the ethnic framing of the conflict, consolidating the division, and turning the conflict intractable. The way out of ethnically framed conflict is never a negotiated outcome, but a gradual transformation of the context where the conflict slowly fades away (Brubaker 1998). Brubaker, not a conflict resolution theorist himself, did not offer practical mechanisms for achieving such transformation, though he made suggestions for transforming the language in which we write about conflicts as a step toward the transformation.

Specifically, he suggests to accept that it is not possible to have one correct way of analyzing the conflict or devise an objectively just and sustainable solution (Brubaker 1998, 274-80). He is also critical of concepts of "ancient hatreds" or searching for historical roots in the conflicts, suggesting that the conflicts of today are conditioned by the present-day structures and are "historicized" to justify contemporary goals (Brubaker 1998, 285-88). However, he does not see the conflicts as a direct result of rational elite manipulation either, since the politicians are a product of the same institutional and cultural frameworks that shape populations and thus driven by and not only the drivers of nationalist discourse (Brubaker 1998, 289-92). Finally, Brubaker criticizes the "groupist" language prevalent in most studies of ethnicity, the language that gives agency to ethnicity and is responsible for the binary ethnic framing of conflicts criticized in this book as well (Brubaker 1998, 292-98). Brubaker suggests to replace the static groupist language with one of a process or a performance that does not reify ethnicity and offers relational rather than categorical modes of identification (Brubaker 2004, 41-8).

In practice, I found that changing the language was more feasible than it might seem. Depending on the situation, specific descriptions such as "the Armenian government," "some of the colleagues from Georgia present in the room," "the state TV channel of Azerbaijan," "particular US Army officers," and "a few activists of the Black Lives Matter movement" could be used without implying that the situation concerns "Armenians," "Georgians," "Azerbaijanis," "Americans," or "African-Americans" in general. In no situation did I find it necessary to use these groupist alternatives. Whether one finds these particular terms applicable for analysis or prefers others more suitable for a particular context, groupist language is a trap that leads the constructivist analysis and respective interventions to self-destruct. Suggesting that groupist language always has alternatives, I do not imply that avoiding a groupist language is easy. We are socialized to use groupist categories and despite writing about this, I catch myself daily on using such language.

Making the change, however, can be transformative, as I witnessed consistently through this research. Naming the initiatives with words that focus on the future of Syria and Nagorno-Karabakh and not using identity terms encouraged the participation from many who did not see a role for themselves in an "Armenian-Azerbaijani" or "Assad-opposition" dialogue. During the dialogues itself, asking the participants to identify important identity groups affected by conflict and choosing which group to represent would inevitably result in a dialogue among a multiplicity of actors, some of whom were the typical conflict sides, but many others were not. At different times, I saw feminists, minorities (or a particular minority), LGBTI, progressive youth, human rights advocates, anarchists, even monarchists, to be represented.

The difficulty of consistently using constructivist language, however, becomes evident when one examines the language of many of those very writers whose work is devoted to the transformation of positivist language. From the discourse analytic perspective, Jabri's criticism of the positivist understanding of conflict and conflict resolution mentioned earlier is well-known. She argued against the generic reading of conflict and change as disconnected from time, place, and specific context. Conflicts of today, she continues, are both global and local. Reminiscent of Brubker, Jabri criticizes the tendency in positivist conflict resolution to assume "that social kinds ... have an existence that is independent of the discursive frames that render them meaningful" (Jabri 2006, 4).

Jabri is critical of the common assumption that conflict analysis can simply reflect the conflict without influencing it. She writes, "the third-party resolutionary is assumed to possess a language that is managerial to the core, aiming to solve the problem at hand, and hence not implicated. However, we know that the language of analysis is not simply a mirror-image of the world 'out there,' but actively constructs the world, in its choice of sides to a conflict, its understanding of the issues, the historical trajectory to a conflict, and its conception of desirable interventions and outcomes" (Jabri 2006, 5). Indeed, as illustrated in my discussion of Syria and other contexts, far from the role of passive observers, the think tanks, the media, the policy, abundance of constructivist conflict analysis. A comprehensive constructivist approach to conflict resolution, therefore, would be critical and reflective of its own vocabulary, and conscious and explicit that its analysis and interventions aim to co-construct a new reality rather than explain and solve a preexisting and defined problem. It would question the existing frames and explanations, as well as the basis and the consequences of its own frames. A comprehensive constructivist approach would do so continuously.

Evolving Designs: rethinking the language of mediation

Conducting research for this book, I worked on developing awareness about the influence that the discourses external to our work have on my own and my colleagues' framing of the conflicts and our interventions. Such awareness does not automatically assume rejecting all preexisting frames. Working with the existing discourse is not only necessary, but vital for the effectiveness of any effort. It is important, however, to be conscious of the influence that each particular frame has on the process, accepting those we see as ethical, while rejecting the ones we see as marginalizing and conflict promoting. I started gradually revising my language aiming to develop a vocabulary that is not groupist and discusses ethnicity as a category of practice and not analysis. As an example, I tried to refrain from using the terms "Armenians" and "Azerbaijanis" as nouns, or to denote with these words conflict sides. I used them as adjectives as a reference to a particular actor's self-identification, as in the "Armenian government." I tried to stop referring to conflicts as ethnic and instead referred to them as ethnically framed. I also started developing awareness about language and practices that contribute to exclusion of those affected by conflict. Specifically, as this research for this book progressed and I became aware of the consistent exclusion or marginalization of such people in my work, I increased my own efforts in bringing into the conflict resolution practice current and former residents of Nagorno-Karabakh, other refugees and IDPs in the South Caucasus, people of mixed or "not titular" heritage, and all others who in the past had been left out due to the design of initiative frames in binary terms. Moreover, many of the recent projects of the Imagine Center have been reframed as "regional" and the calls for applications specify that the initiatives are open for participants from all possible backgrounds.

Despite my efforts, however, I suspect that my language remains unconsciously groupist in some respects and many of the framings I use contribute to marginalization of conflict affected populations. I suspect this, as I see that even the much more experienced scholars as Jabri revert to positivist language in the very same text where they critique positivism. And on a daily basis, including in the process of editing this very text, I become aware of instances of groupist and positivist language I used the day prior. Transforming my own discourse and my internalized vocabulary is not an easy process and requires a sustained effort. I invite, therefore, any of my readers not to hold back from sharing with me their criticism, which I can take into consideration in my future work.[15]

After gaining an initial awareness of the limitations and marginalization that the uncritical acceptance of the established frames can lead to, I worked together with my colleagues involved in this research on developing an adaptive methodology of Evolving Designs for the initiatives we led. These flexible workshop designs would allow us to start off with a preliminary agenda, yet continuously work with various stakeholder on adjusting the frames of the initiative moving toward transformative and inclusive practices.

First affected was one of the major directions of the Imagine Center's work—series of dialogues, which are similar to the one we led for the Syrian colleagues and that was described in Chapter 4. Since 2007, the Imagine Center's dialogues have had three major components: analyzing our understanding of the past, rethinking the present, and visioning an alternative future. For years, our dialogue design relied on the binary frames that I am criticizing here. The discussions of history and the present assumed the presence of two identifiable "sides" who were to have the dialogue.

The dialogue projects were routinely named "Armenian-Azerbaijani," "Turkish-Armenian," or similarly, and the groupist language

---

15   With any questions or feedback please contact me at gamaghel@yahoo.com.

affected the selection process and carried on through the entire initiative. Aiming to bring about reconciliation between two antagonists, the discussion of history focused on dividing the participants between two sides who each would develop their respective historical timelines, the conflict narrative of each side. Then, in a big plenary, the two groups would work together to develop understanding and appreciation of each other's stories, humanity, and identity. The discussion of the present followed a PSW format, similarly dividing the participants into the same two sides, asking them to step away from the positions and analyze the conflicts from the point of view of the needs, fears, concerns, and hopes of their societies.

The approach we practiced, asking the participants to openly and constructively confront the historical narratives and the present-day dynamics of the conflict, had good results and was very popular resulting in a large network of dialogue alumni that the Imagine Center has developed. At the same time, while opening the doors to those who self-identified as a conflict party, it marginalized all others. This became increasingly evident in the PAR process. Once the binary framing of the dialogue was questioned, I started noticing that the selection process and even the language of program announcements tended to exclude; we saw time after time that dividing the participants into two neat "sides" to discuss history or the present was problematic. Which of the two groups should the ethnic Armenian citizens of Turkey go to? Or a refugee whose father was Azerbaijani and mother Armenian? What about an ethnic Russian residing in Georgia with family in Abkhazia?

Not all of our team immediately embraced the need to change the methodology. The dialogue approach we used for years, we all agreed, helped hundreds of individuals who consider themselves a side in a conflict to openly discuss the past and the present, finding ways for moving forward collaboratively. It had to be transformed, I argued, not to require any participant to necessarily assume a "side" allowing anyone interested to self-identify as they see fit. I agreed, however, that in some situations the binary framing could be appropriate. Examples could be initiatives where the officials from the two countries discuss a document they are authorized to sign or when establishing partnerships between institutions from two countries is the specific goal.

After securing the support of the rest of our team in trying a new approach by late 2014, we renamed most of our dialogue initiatives replacing the former binary tittles by more inclusive ones. Some of the latest dialogues I co-led have been named: "Joint Platform for Realistic Peace[16] in Nagorno-Karabakh" or "Summer School of Conflict Transformation." In other cases, we did not find it reasonable to remove the binary from the title. In one instance in 2015, we conducted a dialogue between two universities in Armenia and Turkey with the aim of establishing a longer-term bilateral partnership. In this case, giving the project a broad name would be artificial and not reflective of the purpose of the process. We named the initiative "Turkish-Armenian Dialogue and School for Conflict Transformation," preserving the binary while also making it clear that the intention was to work with participants on transforming the language of the conflict. In other words, the first half of the title had embedded in it the discourse of a conflict sustaining binary, which the discourse associated with the second part of the title aimed to challenge in the course of the project.

By 2016, we made gradual changes to the design of the initiatives also, aimed at addressing the marginalizing and conflict reproducing influence of the meta-frames of international relations and of sides. In conceptualizing new approaches, I was inspired by David Cavallo's concept of "Emergent Design," which in the field of education and technology describes a framework for conceiving and implementing systemic change. Cavallo proposed breaking "the 'educational mindsets' that have been identified as blocks to educational reform." Similar to the CDA approach that advocates for the elevation of the local knowledge, he also is critical of the assumption that "the population and teachers of rural areas lack the cognitive foundations for modern technological education" and developed his designs bottom-up,

---

16 The use of the word "realistic" has also been criticized by some colleagues as leaving a possible impression that the initiative follows the realist school of international relations.

based on the assumption that effective change has to be rooted in the needs and knowledge of the affected populations (Cavallo 2000).

The changes in the work of the Imagine Center inspired by the PAR process that started in 2013 have been gradual. Different from Cavallo's approach, our focus was less on "emergence" of a new design, and more on the continuous adaptation and evolution of the intervention to the particular context, thus the term "Evolving Designs." As of this writing, we kept those elements of the original design developed by the Imagine Center in 2007 that we did not find marginalizing or conflict promoting. At the same time, in the dialogues held in 2015–2017 we changed the language and design if those that we saw as problematic. If previously our work with history was aimed at presenting the narratives of two sides to each other followed by a joint analysis, the new approach would be to start from asking people to identify what are the groups whose historical narratives in their view influence the conflict. As collective historical narratives in the South Caucasus are heavily influenced by state policies and state-controlled media, so far the groups whose narratives we heard coincided with the "titular" ethno-national groups discussed above. Namely, our colleagues who were asked these questions identified the presence of "Abkhazian," "Armenian," "Azerbaijani," "Georgian," and "Ossetian" narratives. The division was not necessarily political. For example, those self-identifying as Armenians from Nagorno-Karabakh, while positioning themselves as politically separate from Armenians from the Republic of Armenia, never saw a need to present a distinct history.

Evolving Designs: rethinking dialogue and PSW

The Evolving Designs approach has been more pertinent in the part of the workshop focused on the present. Here we reframed the traditional to PSW question: what are the needs of your society? We start instead from acknowledging that no society is monolithic and cannot, therefore, have uniform needs, and second, the colleagues in the room can only represent their own views of the groups they identify with rather than the objective views of any societies. The reframed questions we pose have been: what are the key stakeholders to the conflict in your view? And what, in your opinion, are the needs of those stakeholders with whom you identify?

The new questions are radically different from the original one. When the original framing of "what are the needs of *your society*?" is used, the binary frame is established, the colleagues are restricted to act as representatives of one side or the other and asked to represent the generic needs of *their* side. And as society is never monolithic and therefore cannot have unified needs, those present are effectively sharing their personal stereotypes about the society in question, yet these stereotypes carry the weight of the objective representation of the needs. Not surprisingly, therefore, in years of my experience of facilitating PSWs, many colleagues struggled with the question how can they know for sure what are the needs of their society or how could they take on the burden of representing these. The reframed questions allow the colleagues to identify a multiplicity of groups, self-identify with any of these, and be explicit on subjectively and reflectively constructing rather than representing collective needs.

The comparison of the two examples listed below illustrate the difference between stereotype-building answers solicited by the traditional groupist question "what are the needs of your society?" and the later open-ended question inspired by the Evolving Designs methodology that allowed the participants to self-identify into groups.

In the first case, the lists of presumed needs, fears, concerns, and hopes of the Turkish society were developed during a Turkish-Armenian dialogue held in 2012, prior to the reformulation of the questions.

The Turkish Society's Fears, Needs, Concerns, Hopes[17]

Needs

- Need of democratization
- Need for the acknowledgment of the suffering of the Muslim populations during World War I and not only of Armenians.

---

17 Notes from the post-program internal report of the Imagine Center.

Fears

- Fear of legal ramifications for Turkey of the Genocide recognition, including fear of territorial and financial compensation
- Fear that reconciliation with Armenians could lead to loss of Azerbaijan morally, economically, and geo-politically.

Concerns

- Concern that recognizing the Armenian Genocide would damage the national image and prestige and dishonor Turks
- Concern that recognizing the Armenian Genocide can create a snowball/domino effect for other persecuted groups to also put forward demands
- Concern that cosmopolitanism could undermine the sense of Turkish unity.

Hopes

- Hope that all claims about the Armenian Genocide will go away
- Hope that Turkey will become a great power that no one could make any claim against.

The colleagues in this Turkish group self-identified as progressive, most of them openly recognized the Armenian genocide and worked for its recognition. That group was also very diverse and included individuals who further self-identified as an ethnically Kurdish Turk, an ethnically Armenian Turk, an ethnically Georgian Turk, a German-raised Turk and so on, all with very different senses of identity, memory, and needs. When asked to represent the "needs of the Turkish society," they did their best to reproduce the stereotypical image, focusing primarily on the presumed to be negative consequences of the recognition of the Armenian genocide, assessing it from the point of view of the tarnished national image, economic losses, and possible damage that the improved relations with Armenia could do to Turkey's alliance with Azerbaijan. The solutions implicit in the lists are for a stronger Turkey that can settle conflicts unilaterally and to its liking. As the one thing connecting this diverse group of individuals one to another was their Turkish citizenship, the only "common" perspective they were able to find was the state narrative. Any other approach would pull the group in many different directions. Very little attention, consequently, was given in this chart to the everyday needs of people or to the possibility that varying groups in Turkey having varying needs.

In contrast, the newly formulated questions, inspired by the emerging design method, allowed identifying diverse groups of stakeholders in each society and not only one monolithic side contributing to the thickening of the narrative. As we had seen in the Syrian example in Chapter 4, asking the colleagues to identify the relevant stakeholders helped map interrelations of dozens of actors, both internal and external, as understood by those present in the room. The second question is also openly subjective and asks to share their understanding of the needs of those stakeholders that each individual identifies with.

The below example is from a 2015 dialogue that followed Evolving Designs methodology included participants from Turkey, Armenia, as well as Georgia and Azerbaijan, and where the questions were already reformulated. It is important to note also that this dialogue took place three years after the previous one. In this timeframe, the relations between Armenia and Azerbaijan had been deteriorating with the violence between them increasing, and Turkey had more explicitly aligned itself with Azerbaijan, contributing to the worsening of the Armenia-Turkey relations. Armenia's accession into the Russia-led Eurasian Economic Union and other regional developments such as the wars in Syria and Ukraine and economic downturn further complicated the relationship, leading to concerns of economic instability.

The lists of needs, fears, and concerns of the group from Turkey were the following[18]:

---

18 Because of the shortage of time in this particular initiative, the "hopes" were not discussed.

Working Group: Turkey[19]

Needs

- Change in the state-society relations
- Reshaping the images of various groups in and outside the society
- Strengthening the social relationships (improving education, economy, communication, information).

Fears

- Sèvres Syndrome (fear of the breakup of Turkey and western racism towards Turks)
- Chaos as a result of internal and external conflicts.

Concerns

- Economic downturn and damaged economic relations with neighbors
- Loss of the prestige of the Turkish identity.

This list, unlike the previous one, does not contain even one mention of the consequences of recognizing the Armenian genocide. There is one indirect reference, in the subsection on fears, where the Sèvres Syndrome is mentioned and explained as a popular belief in Turkey that the "West" is conspiring against it together with neighboring Christian nations, and Armenia in particular, to weaken and dismember Turkey. The Sèvres Syndrome gets its name from the never-implemented 1920 Treaty of Sèvres that as to partition the Ottoman Empire between Armenia, Greece, Britain, France, and Italy. All the other items in the chart are focused on the interrelationship between various groups in Turkey and with the neighbors and the socio-economic needs of a number of stakeholders in Turkey.

The difference between the two lists is striking starting from the title, the first claiming to represent the needs of the Turkish society as a whole, and the second naming itself as a working group *from* Turkey. The content, in the first case, is rather stereotypical, state interest-

---

19 Notes from the post-program internal report of the Imagine Center.

driven, national and even nationalist, as the group was trying to present what they understood to be the needs of the generic and unified Turkish society. In the second case, as the needs were those felt by the colleagues who were in the room and representing a multiplicity of stakeholders with whom they personally identified, the items were predominantly socio-economic and much less confrontational in tone.

The benefits of the constructivist reformulation of the questions were many: the colleagues in 2015 did not feel forced to represent a generic Turkish or Armenian view as those in 2012 did, and it opened up a space for learning about many groups within each country, including religious, ethnic, ideological, or LGBTI, about their relationship to the state and to each other, and about the multiplicity of views that exist in regard to relations with neighboring societies.

In another dialogue in November 2015, the difference with all our previous work was even more striking. Given the opportunity to self-identify, six colleagues who would normally all represent the "Georgian side" split into groups named "Georgian progressive youth," "Armenian minority of Georgia," "Azerbaijani minority of Georgia," and "villages adjacent to South Ossetia." The colleagues from Armenia and Azerbaijan also split into small groups, some "groups" consisting of only one individual.

Freeing the questions about the past and the present from the grip of international relations and other positivist discourses transformed the future visioning conversation also. Previously, with the past and present conversation limited to the narratives of "conflict sides," in other words to national or nationalist narratives, the visions for the future derived from these would typically take one of the two types of scenarios: the first were the suggestions to devise an (inter) national political solution that would address the *national needs*; the second were the suggestions for improving the relations *between the two societies*. As contributing to the (inter) national-level political solution was typically seen to be out of reach of those in the room, the focus would be on the second type of scenarios. We would discuss how we can contribute to the improvement of relations between the two societies. This approach, even if problematic, was certainly valuable as many initiatives aimed at challenging stereotypes and improving relations followed the dialogues.

Such follow-up initiatives included screenings of movies of "the other side," cross-border video-conferences for youth, joint and parallel publishing, trainings in conflict resolution, and more. Yet we would continuously stumble on the question: how can our efforts aimed at improving relations between any given two societies counteract the massive state propaganda machines that work in the opposite direction and sustain the conflict? What we understood through this research and what I argue in this book is that initiatives frames in binary ethno-national terms simply are not in a position to transform the ethno-national discourse. The problem is not in the absence of resources or power. The problem is conceptual. "Armenians," "Turks," "Azerbaijanis," "Georgians," "Ossetians," and other groupist terms do not have agency as such. They gain meaning and are operationalized when appropriated by states or other ethno-national institutions and become, as Anderson would have it, products of "official nationalisms" (B. R. O. Anderson 2006, 83).

People self-identifying as Armenians, Turks and so on live outside the boundaries of the respective political nations as well, where the diasporic organizations can institutionalize narratives through schools and religious centers. Considering the dispersed nature of diasporas around the globe and scarcity of community schools that can attract a substantial number of diasporan children, it is hard to imagine, however, how an entire diaspora can develop and reproduce a unified narrative or exhibit signs of a monolithic group that has shared needs, in the same way that an ethno-national community whose groupness is mediated by the state (recognized or unrecognized) and state-controlled education does.

I argue, therefore, that the ethno-national discourse cannot be separated from the discourse of the respective state. Consequently, transforming the ethno-national discourse effectively means transforming the institutions of the state. And since the group (groupist) narrative and the official narrative are effectively identical, we are at the danger of falling into the trap of assuming that the work with the official narrative is the only meaningful one when it comes to conflict resolution. This is a trap I have fallen time and again and have seen many colleagues in there too.

Working to transform the official narrative is certainly a worthy effort. It is not always, however, the most effective road toward conflict transformation considering the investment that the nation-state institutions made and make into constructing and upholding these narratives. If we return to the beginning of the argument, we will see that its conclusion—the transformation of the conflict discourse equals the transformation of the official discourse—is based on the misleading initial premise that the role of conflict resolution is limited to the work with conflict "sides" understood as bounded ethno-national groups. In this book, however, I have problematized the concept of conflict "sides" both practically and analytically. Conflict "sides" undoubtedly exist and need to be included, yet these are only two of the multiple stakeholders affected by conflict and often the most extreme and violent stakeholders, as it was the case with Assad or armed opposition in Syria. Working with the official narratives and transforming the discourse of the two actors who act as conflict "sides," therefore, is only part of the conflict resolution work. Including the voices of all other stakeholders and through this transforming the conflict discourse is the other part.

Evolving Designs in practice: transforming the Analytic Initiative

The development of the Evolving Design methodology helped us transform many of our ongoing initiatives. Not limiting the selection processes to the clear representatives of the "sides" has been the first step in building an inclusive initiative. Once in the room, encouraging everyone to name the groups they most identify with consistently opens up the boundaries of the conversation to a kaleidoscope of new groups and relationships. With this approach, no two workshops have had the exact same composition of actors. The approach reminds a "kaleidoscope" as every particular figure formed is unique at the first sight and the landscape looks chaotic and unmanageably diverse. Yet as we look closely and systematically, the sets of key actors and relationships identified by participants repeat themselves and patterns emerge: never static or thin or binary or identical to the previous ones, but meaningful and manageable if not by the facilitator, then by the colleagues who formed that particular picture and have ownership of it.

The colleagues have always found a way to systematize the learning if empowered by the program design and facilitation, and the mosaic formed has been genuine and far more representative in the eyes of those present than the prestamped international relation's binaries. In the Syrian case, the black and white stamp we came with was to divide the peace-activists into Assad supporters and opposition, a stamp that the group rejected as artificial. The mosaic that they created by self-selecting into subgroups included, as we have seen: the same "Assad supporters," the subgroup that seemed devoid of people when we tried to impose this framing on the colleagues yet the one that gained recruits when it was named by the participants; "armed rebels," the subgroup that distinguished itself from the generic "opposition" by standing up for the right to wage an armed struggle; and the two most numerous subgroups called "civil society" and "minorities" who under the imposed "Assad-opposition" binary would have to choose a side or become voiceless. Inclusiveness that allowed for a more diverse picture to emerge in the group was not the only benefit of employing an emergent design. This new configuration allowed envisioning creative solutions for a future united Syria driven by the "civil society" and for the benefit of all and particularly of the "minorities," two groups that disappear in the "Assad-opposition" frame and along with which disappears the very hope for a solution.

Throughout this research, we increasingly relied on the emergent design approach allowing also the groups from areas with well-consolidated conflict discourses to question the established frames, reflect on the conflict, explore new sets of actors, and identify one's own place in all this. This approach worked well in dialogues that did not target policymakers or policymaking. The colleagues who participated in our recent work were students, academics, journalists, activists, and researchers, making it easier to step away from the international relations discourse and the discourse of sides. The initiatives that explicitly target policymakers, similar to the NK Analytic Initiative described in Chapter 5, present a different challenge. The question is: how can we reframe the conflict in the context of an initiative that targets policy-level change, and where upholding the international relations discourse is something many of those present do for a living?

To transform the conflict discourses in policy-focused initiatives specifically, one could start by challenging the conviction that conflict-focused policymaking and international relation theories are synonymous. International relations and economic theories today have a firm grip on policymaking, but this does not mean that they have it all figured out or that these theories are here to stay. International relations that has dominated policymaking is only one possible lens, and often a deficient one, for defining, preventing, or resolving contemporary conflicts. Alternative frameworks for analyzing conflict and designing interventions exist and a number of them were discussed in this book. And while the current power structures are invested in the reproduction of the status quo, there is not any inherent reason why CDA or elicitive practice or PAR, among others, cannot come to be used in policymaking.

The examples of consistent failures of the international relations frames are many, particularly in the context of the Nagorno-Karabakh conflict. And yet the initiatives branded as Track 2 in that very context have positioned themselves invariably as supportive and complementary to official negotiations, explicitly or implicitly accepting the realist lens adopted by the negotiators. Further, a great many of such initiatives took on the role of advocates of the so-called "Madrid Principles," the document proposed by negotiators as a possible settlement of the conflict. One such initiative was even named "Independent Civil Minsk Process" to make explicit the desired link with the "official Minsk Process" responsible for the Track 1 negotiations. For decades now, both the official negotiations and their civic counterparts are deadlocked, yet none would consider an alternative to the clearly dysfunctional "Madrid Principles" or the realist framing in which they are embedded.

The NK Analytic Initiative described in Chapter 5, while less explicitly, still adopted many of the frames of the official process and positioned itself as a link between Track 1 and Track 2. Starting from 2014, and inspired by the Evolving Designs methodology, we attempted to develop alternatives to the international relations frames for policy-oriented work through slowly reshaping the Analytic Initiative.

Once embarked on that journey, we realized that the very titles for the specific meetings of this initiative had been shaped by the international relations frames, such as, "Reassessing the Nagorno-Karabakh Conflict in the Aftermath of Russia-Georgia War," in reference to the August 2008 war, where even the naming of the war was problematic and political and excluded South Ossetia as an actor. In its new iteration, the initiative was renamed and here will be called "Regional Analytic Initiative" reflecting its more inclusive nature. The specific meetings had more inclusive names also, such as "Joint Platform for Realistic Peace in the South Caucasus." This new titles aimed to use language that is immediately understandable to donors and newcomers using familiar references to "realistic peace" and the possibility of finding common ground. At the same time, it steps away from binary frames and points to a transformative methodology focused on collaboratively developing a joint regional platform that does not predefine the actors.

Convincing colleagues involved of the need of letting go of the international relations frames, in which the NK Analytic Initiative was long embedded, was not very hard. What helped was the awareness of many colleagues that many of the known to international relations solutions have been tried in the Nagorno-Karabakh case and did not work: from confederation, federation, and power sharing to referendum for independence and to "creative" suggestions such as land swaps tried in a quarter-of-century-long negotiation process (Abasov and Khachatryan 2004).

Reframing the initiative into an inclusive one that follows Evolving Design brought immediate benefits. The selection process has been freed from the near impossible dilemma of finding the minimally acceptable "format" for the binary "sides." If in the past, we tried to balance competing demands to exclude Nagorno-Karabakh Armenians or Nagorno-Karabakh Azerbaijanis or opposition figures, the aim now was on building an inclusive recruitment process. With the focus on developing alternative frames and not on improving the Madrid Principles, it was not anymore paramount to keep the official representatives of the "two sides" in at any cost. While the presence of a few officials in the room at some stage of the initiative was agreed to be desirable as a step toward affecting policymaking understood in its conventional sense, this did not need to happen during the early stages of the initiative and certainly not at the expense of compromising the inclusiveness of the process. Instead, the initiative would build mechanisms of affecting the public discourse and by extension policy thinking, if not policymaking, through journalistic and analytic publishing, roundtables, TV appearances, briefings, and other methods that do not require prior coordination and the "blessing" from officials. Officials, as other stakeholders, would be able to participate when they see the value of the initiative and were ready to join without putting forward preconditions.

When it comes to the design of the policy-oriented initiatives, similar to the dialogues, we started opening up the floor for rethinking the meaning of the conflict by those present in the room, identifying the mosaic of stakeholders and categories of analysis that the group finds important to address. This new approach did not close the door on discussing the more traditional collective conflict narratives and the needs of the conflict sides. These could well be analyzed and discussed, as long as they were identified as relevant by colleagues present in the room.

During a policy-oriented workshop held in late 2014 in Tbilisi, the group of colleagues from Armenia and Azerbaijan included journalists, academics, NGO representatives, policy analysts, and youth activists. We resorted to Evolving Designs process and developed four categories of analysis in regard to which the colleagues found it important to build a common understanding: internal politics, geo-politics, peace processes, and conflict discourses. Initially in small sub-teams and later in the bigger group, each of these categories was analyzed, debated and a common understanding was developed. After that, the group refocused on strategic visioning and planning directions for future action that could be implemented by those present and their networks and that would address the needs that emerged as a result of the analysis.

Toward the end of the workshop, the group developed a series of recommendations for action. The analysis as well as the recommendations were shared during a roundtable for policymakers, donors and other international actors, and the civil society actors from Armenia, Azerbaijan, and Georgia.

In a stark contrast with all the previous years of the NK Analytic Initiative where many recommendations were developed painfully and rarely implemented, many of those present during the 2014 Regional Analytic Initiative took upon themselves the implementation and advancement of many of the developed recommendations. Most of them have become ongoing initiatives on their own, as of this writing. One reason for such a difference, undoubtedly, is the orientation of the 2014 recommendations toward the civil society rather than policymaking. This cannot be the only explanation, however, since many of the recommendations developed yet never implemented during the previous years similarly targeted the civil society. Moreover, they had been developed at times more conducive to civil society efforts as they were not actively obstructed by the governments and were even often supported and emerged a relative abundance of funding. The December 2014 recommendations, to the contrary, came at the time when the Azerbaijani government effectively outlawed all independent and international NGOs and froze their accounts, when many of the international donors left the South Caucasus or sharply reduced their presence, when the Nagorno-Karabakh conflict entered a new phase of violent escalation, and many existing civil society efforts folded.

The focus of the initiatives proposed was not qualitatively very different from the ones proposed in the past. The difference was in the method of developing these recommendations that created an open format where the participants could determine the identity group or conflict actors they could represent. The text of the recommendations developed during that meeting had the following language.[20]

> The expert group sees a need for increased support to programs promoting systemic changes in the spheres of education and media and institutionalized efforts that will conduct applied research on the development of alternative scenarios and a strategic vision for the South Caucasus. Such an approach will allow the existing conflict experts in the South Caucasus to unite forces and facilitate the emergence of extended networks of professionals across opinion-making fields that will advance reforms and collaboration in their respective areas.

---

20 From the document produced as the result of the workshop and that was shared with a wider audience during the roundtable in Tbilisi on December 5, 2014.

The group agreed on the necessity of going beyond short-term interventions and towards the formation of a regional conflict transformation center. Such a center can unite, empower, and maximize the potential of individuals and small groups engaged in peacebuilding work learning from the experience of Belgrade Open School in institutionalizing efforts for conflict transformation and development of democratic societies. The group committed to support the development of the South Caucasus Open School (SCOS) as a regional hub for the coordination and for increasing the resilience of the regional peace networks to tackle crisis. It is the vision of the expert group to transform the existing and emergent problems into opportunities and, through mobilizing the democratically-minded professionals in the region, work towards engendering sustainable peace, stability, and development in the South Caucasus. The expert group outlined the following directions of work for SCOS:

Professional and Ethical Journalism in the South Caucasus: It is necessary to contribute to the development of ethical and conflict sensitive media discourses in the South Caucasus and to encourage a culture of responsible, independent, and impartial reporting to counterbalance the prevailing mainstream coverage that serves the perpetuation of the conflicts in the region. To promote multi-perspective conflict sensitive journalistic practices in the region, it is necessary to expand the collaborative networks of journalists, engage them in on-going dialogue and capacity building, and facilitate a greater synchronization of methodological approaches to ethical and conflict sensitive reporting.

Dialogue and Capacity Building for Educators in the South Caucasus: It is necessary to work towards fostering dialogue and mutual understanding among historians and history teachers in the wider regional context of the South Caucasus. Joint capacity building for history educators, the adoption of conflict sensitive and inclusive approaches in the classroom, exchange of experience, increased sense of professional solidarity, and the expansion of that effect through their work with a wider network of teachers are vital components of this type of work.

Multi-Track Diplomacy in the South Caucasus: A new impetus to the coordination of Track 2 efforts with official peace processes is also deemed important. To do so, it is necessary to develop a platform for democratically-minded scholar-practitioners and conflict professionals in the South Caucasus to jointly develop and advocate for a new agenda focused on the transformation of conflicts and the development of inclusive and democratic societies in the region integrated into the world community. It is equally important to establish collaborative ties between the civil societies and all actors involved in official processes for engagement with each other that sets and advocates for shared vision, strategy, and action among professional networks, general public, and key actors in the region.

Dialogue and Schools of Conflict Transformation for Youth, Women, and Marginalized Populations: Efforts need to be dedicated to offering transformative social and cultural dialogue opportunities on vital issues such as gender, youth empowerment, conflict transformation, etc. It is necessary to facilitate a shift for these constituencies from adversarial, confrontational, exclusivist, and zero-sum views of situations toward collaborative and inclusive approaches to social and cultural issues that create equity in their communities. Through transforming different target groups' perception of themselves, of each other, their attitude towards the issues in their societies, and empowering them to explore their potential in instigating a shift for others as well, a great contribution to conflict transformation in the region will be made.

The number of the initiatives launched or restructured and implemented following the 2014 meeting with great enthusiasm included the restructured into Regional version of the NK Analytic Initiative itself, as well as a program initiated by journalists and focused on a design of an ethics code for covering the South Caucasus conflicts in media, a series of summer schools of conflict transformation that target their recruiting to minority populations and others traditionally excluded from the peace process. The NK/Regional Analytic Initiative, similarly, reformed from a two-party format into an open one, focused on recruiting those whose voices have been previously excluded or marginalized from having an input into the political end of the peace process, such as ethnic and religious minorities, LGBTI and women's rights activists, various voices from among the displaced populations and disputed territories, and others. Further, including these voices led the now Regional Analytic Initiative to see the advocacy for the rights of marginalized groups as an integral part of the peace process, and not a separate phenomenon. Cross-conflict divide research teams were formed that worked together and published analytic papers and policy recommendations on topics of Minority Rights as an Instrument of Conflict Resolution and Women's Rights and LGBTI Rights in the South Caucasus. The papers were published electronically and in hard copy, presented in numerous roundtables and other events in Yerevan, Tbilisi, Washington, DC, Istanbul, Stockholm, Berlin, New York, among others, for diverse audiences ranging from policy mappers to academics and youth.

The shift in methodology helped tremendously with inclusion and combatting marginalization. In all the previous years of the NK Analytic Initiative, the reliance on the preexisting international relations frames invariably privileged the actors close to the government who, establishing their dominance during the selection as well as in the room, excluded or marginalized all others. The Evolving Designs, built around the interest and expertise of those present, privileged inclusion and diversity during selection and collaboration in the room in terms of both the group composition and the range of topics that the initiative would tackle.

Chapter 6 postscript: gender and other binaries that affect conflict resolution practice

This chapter is devoted to the search of inclusive alternatives to the binary international relations frames as a central challenge for today's conflict resolution practice. It is important to recognize, therefore, that there are other dominant discourses present that routinely influence conflict resolution efforts. Some of these discourses today have a nearly universal appeal. Covering all possible macro-frames that influence conflict resolution work, unfortunately, falls well outside the scope of this book. Some of them have been covered by other authors. Galtung, in his discussion of cultural violence, addresses many frames that serve to normalize violence, namely religion with its doctrine of good and evil, ideology that presumes the existence of rights and wrongs, language or vocabulary that humanizes some and dehumanizes others, art that normalizes domination of some cultures over others, social science that promotes the neoliberal order, science in general as promoting dichotomies and intolerant to ambiguity, and more (Galtung 1990). All these frames if not approached critically can lead to reproduction of conflict and violence.

The gender binary, however, requires a special acknowledgment as it had a visible influence on all conflict resolution practices I studied resulting in marginalization. The gender binary does not have a separate chapter in this book, unfortunately, because it was not part of the original research design focused on the international relations binary. As a consequence, I started collecting data on it very late in the PAR process, and did not manage to go through enough reflection and action cycles to present meaningful findings. I intend to continue working exploring that topic in my future work and devote to it an article if not a book, ideally in co-authorship with colleagues who have been studying the topic longer than I have.

The gender binary privileges men over others and leads to the exclusion and marginalization of women, LGBTI, and other individuals nonconforming with the binary. The performance of the identity of the conflict "side," as I conformed through this research, assumes not only acceptance of a particular conflict discourse, it also requires the individuals to conform to the stereotypical look and behavior of the generic representative of that "side." Both the Caucasus and Syria share a heavily patriarchal culture where men are expected to be strong and "masculine" and women to be subservient and "feminine," each style understood to have its respective dress code, behavioral code, and roles in the society. Those who do not conform often get ostracized. I observed in numerous initiatives the marginalization of representatives of various subcultures, LGBTI, women who were subjected to violence, women who were known to date men from across the conflict divide,[21] men who were perceived as feminine, or women perceived to be masculine, or those dressing and behaving not according to perceived standards of the patriarchal societies of the South Caucasus and Syria.

Addressing marginalization resulting from the influence of heterosexual normativity that is implicit in the gender binary requires, but cannot be limited to, the increase of number of women who take part in peace processes. Including women and individuals not-conforming with the gender binary in peace processes is one step, out of many, yet insufficient step on its own. Further efforts are required for nonmale and nonmasculine voices to be heard. The often cited yet just as often ignored male privilege manifests itself forcefully in conflict resolution work. One illustrative scenario that I observed through this research continuously was the conversation that develops among men in the room, while formally the gender balance understood as a physical presence of a certain number of women is preserved. Women are invited, they sit at the table, and they get a turn to talk, but what they say gets dismissed as the men speakers, patiently or impatiently, wait for their turn only to go back responding to the latest man speaker effectively marginalizing the women's voices. Exceptions were women who held power external to the group (such as a position in the government), or when the group was actively aware and reflective of gender dynamics.

---

21   Men dating women of the other side rarely face the same problem.

My research, therefore, points me toward the need to go beyond what is self-obvious and not to equate inclusivity with the number of women[22] present in the room. Butler is perhaps the best-known author who argues forcefully against making the categories of "woman" and "women's equality" into the subject of feminism as within the dominant hetero-normative discourse, "woman" is a construct that denotes a dominated category. She illustrates that accepting the essentialist notion of "woman" is counterproductive as in that case "to have a gender means to have entered already into a heterosexual relationship of subordination" (Butler 2006, xiii).

Butler also questions the essentialist approach to the category of "woman" as an identifiable monolithic group disconnected from the political context it exists in, color-blind to categories of race, class, and culture, an approach echoed by many who critique the mainstream feminism that prioritizes the problems vital for the white upper- and middle-class "western" women, while ignoring the distinct needs of those who are identified with other genders, races, classes, nationalities, and so on (Frankenberg 1993; Newman 1999; Roth 2004; Ortega 2006). This critique is also consistent with the Intersectional Theory concerned with studying overlapping forms of oppression within society. It illustrates that racism, sexism, homophobia, xenophobia, and others are in play not concurrently but simultaneously, and those who are underprivileged in more than one category are particularly vulnerable (Knudsen 2006).

It is not enough, therefore, to address the marginalization embedded in the gender discourse simply by bringing "more women" into conflict resolution work, as those who do not fit the binary will still be excluded and those physically present still can be marginalized in the room and not treated as equals.

---

22   In this text, the words "man" and "woman" are used as social constructs denoting a discursive gender binary. I tried to avoid using the words male and female, which can be understood as biological categories. When using the words "man" or "woman" was not phonetically appealing and I used the words "male" or "female," I understood these to be representing the same social constructs and not biological categories.

Chapter conclusions

Macro-frames affect virtually every human activity, and conflict and conflict resolution are not an exception. These frames condition much of the marginalization and exclusion in conflict resolution practice. In this chapter, I examined the international relations discourse of conflict sides as one such macro-frame. Through the PAR process, my colleagues and I explored and I presented in this chapter the patterns of exclusion and marginalization of populations affected by conflict as a result of the uncritical acceptance of the international relation frames by conflict resolution practice.

In building more inclusive and transformative practices, I suggest starting from reframing the initiatives, when possible, to avoid binary titles replacing them with transformative language. During recruitment, I suggest paying particular attention to the patterns of exclusion that we follow unconsciously. This can be done by asking ourselves question such as: are we privileging the violent extremes and the "true" representatives of conflict parties over others? Are we excluding any group affected by the conflict based on our perception of their race, gender or absence thereof, political or professional affiliation, mixed heritage, history of participation in dissident work, and so on? How can we ensure a more inclusive selection process?

At the Imagine Center, when we realized that the frames of our initiatives were restrictive and did not allow for an inclusive selection, we were able to reframe the initiatives and develop more inclusive processes, resorting to affirmative action when necessary encouraging women and various minority groups to participate. As we learned through our work, accepting exclusion and marginalization as a necessary evil is not only unethical, it is also ineffective. The initiatives that started with exclusion were very likely to perpetuate further exclusion, privilege the existing dominant discourses that sustain the conflict, marginalize all others, and remain closed to innovation and transformation. More often than not, the very possibility of a new discourse was conditioned by the inclusion of previously excluded or marginalized voices, as was the case with civil society and the minorities in the Syrian initiative.

The inclusive selection, of course, is only part of building an inclusive process. The macro-frames continue influencing every step of conflict resolution practice. Instead of asking the colleague in the room to fit into the preestablished frames such as "Assad-opposition" or "Armenians-Azerbaijanis" and "man-woman," we could offer those present to map the conflict, creating a kaleidoscope of numerous stakeholders, and consolidating them when possible into a more manageable number of groups. The colleagues present could then be asked to choose which groups they identify with and share their subjective understanding of the narratives and the needs of these groups. Such an approach can move the initiative away from simplistic binary frames that sustain conflicts and develop instead a thick description of the context from which various possible ways forward can sprout, and motivate colleagues to undertake follow-up as the picture created is their own.

Chapter 7
Marginalization specific to conflict resolution initiatives. Addressing the formation of dominant factions

In Chapter 6, I examined exclusion and marginalization present in an overwhelming majority of initiatives as a result of the uncritical acceptance of discourses external to conflict resolution practice. In this chapter, I focus on patterns of marginalization that emerge within particular conflict resolution initiatives themselves through a process of formation of dominant factions. These patterns are context-specific and therefore less permanent and more amenable to transformative actions compared to the ones influenced by the external macro-frames.

The dominant factions, the subgroups in a bigger group that hold discursive power, can form thanks to dynamics such as the structures and parameters established by the donor or as a result of the presence of actors holding power positions external to the initiative, for example, government advisor or head of a university department. The discursive frame of the project methodology could also privilege some, while others can build voice by relying on the internationally accepted norms, such as human rights regimes or international law. The discursive frames that can come to dominate are many. Oftentimes a number of discourses can be in a struggle, and it is possible that more than one discourse can become accepted and dominant within an initiative. Which factions come to dominate, therefore, is highly context-specific and can be influenced by dynamics and discourses both internal and external to the initiative.

In this chapter, I discuss a few patters of domination and resulting marginalization that I came to encounter most often. First, I focus on patterns when *one* faction comes to dominate thanks to structural or discursive advantages such as the "cultural intelligibility" of some participants for the organizers or the reliance of organizers and participants on a dominant discourse external to the initiative, such as nationalism or the human rights discourse. In the next section, I focus on cases when *a number* of discourses are in a struggle and more than one become accepted and co-dominant, marginalizing those who represent the nondominant discourses. Toward the end of the chapter, I focus on CDA as a methodology that can help practitioners in recognizing and addressing domination and resulting marginalization.

Formation of a single dominant faction within initiatives

The dominance of some discourses over others takes place in almost any initiative and can be conditioned by either the criteria for participant selection set forth by the politics of the funding agency or the implementing organization or by the aims, design, and the driving discursive bias of the workshop.

Cultural intelligibility to the organizers

With the organizers having a major influence over the selection, they are often looking for participants who are "culturally intelligible" for them, excluding others, many of whom might be in a greater need of conflict resolution initiatives.

The examples of selection based on "cultural intelligibility" I observed were many. In an initiative for Armenian, Azerbaijani, and American teenagers led by a young practitioner from the United States, the participants recall that the entire group was selected representing "hipster," English-speaking, socially liberal, "western"-behaving youth. Similarly, in a few Syrian initiatives where the selection was conducted by a team of young Europeans, the participants all espoused "western" values. The positive discrimination toward "western"-behaving folks is not limited to the organizers from the "West" only, it is also practiced by the local facilitators educated in the "West." This often leads to the recruitment of individuals who either also studied in the "West" or have already participated in previous conflict resolution work and have learned the social skills necessary to interact with the "western" donors and organizers. As a result, we have a commodification of conflict resolution work, when the participation in cross-border and international events becomes a ticket to many others, helps build a professional network, and opens up doors for employment.

In all these situations, therefore, we privilege those culturally intelligible for us and marginalize the others. As organizers, we are never just "another person" in the context of the initiatives we lead. We hold positional power, decide who is in and who is not, how the space and the conversation is structured, what the content is, and even who speaks and when. By privileging some during recruitment, we exclude others outright; by privileging the discourses of some in the dialogue, we deprive others of voice; and by privileging some during the social time, we reinforce the message to the rest that this particular behavior is more welcome than others and that the carriers of particular discourses stand closer to organizers than the holders of others.

Such selection in some cases can be tactical, aimed at creating a network of conflict resolvers who share values. Often, however, the selection is not intentional and has no aim of network creation. This can be the case with various skill-building trainings in peace journalism that are common in the South Caucasus, with dialogues for those who suffered from the conflicts such as refugees, families of deceased soldiers, border populations, and many others. In such cases, many of those who truly need the dialogue might be journalists or affected by conflict people who do not share values or cultural similarity with the organizers and the colleagues from across the conflict divide, yet are left out of the process. In other words, forming and sustaining committed networks of peacebuilders is a necessary part of the peace process, but it does not negate the simultaneous need to engage those affected by conflict and not fluent in international settings.

Instead, as it became evident through the PAR process, a small group of regular participants shuttles between various programs irrespective of the aims of these programs, reproducing a specific discourse that is pleasant to the ears of facilitators yet often hollow. New participants also join in, and are often "mentored" by the seasoned colleagues, pressured to conform and play within the acceptable discourse. The presence of a large number of regular participants forms a culture in which "representatives of conflict sides" meet regularly, behave politely and professionally, focus on the common ground in public discussions and avoid at all costs any sharp angles or areas of potential disagreement, and do not engage with the conflict directly. The downside of this culture is that no hard topics, often central to the future of the societies in conflict, get named, addressed, or resolved. Moreover, the individuals who are not familiar with the culture, come across as unpolished or confrontational, labeled as difficult, nationalist, or nonconstructive for raising challenging questions. They then get marginalized and later excluded. Exclusion or marginalization is also often the fate of those who are not fluent in English, Russian, or otherwise the common language of the initiatives, those from rural areas, and those without advanced degrees, in other words those who do not appear "cultured" enough to participate.

Reliance on a dominant discourse external to the initiative

In the previous chapter, I discussed the influence of the binary discourse of international relations on continually privileging the violent or nationalist extremes and marginalizing the nonconforming individuals and those who do not fit the image of "conflict sides." The reverse pattern I observed far less frequently, yet at the same regularly. In certain cases, the representatives of subcultures turn the tables, particularly when they are culturally intelligible to the organizers. Some conflict resolution initiatives create spaces welcoming of subcultures, and when the organizers are supportive, the ratio of representatives of subcultures or their supporters compared to others can be significant, and the dominant discourse can be constructed accordingly. I have witnessed more than one initiative in the Nagorno-Karabakh context where many participants had nonconforming alternative looks, views, behavior and, because of the numbers, could not be marginalized and were a vocal voice, gradually forming some alternative dominant discourse. In such cases, those who are seen as mainstream or "not progressive enough" can be marginalized or ostracized.

The framing of the program and its theory of change play a big role in this. PSWs and dialogues, as already discussed, aim to bring about resolution between the preestablished conflict sides and, as a result, frame those invited as belonging to "sides," privilege the mainstream discourses, and marginalize those who do not "fit" unless they accept a "side." At the same time, many other initiatives I observed were focused on bringing together the representatives of subcultures and discriminated groups explicitly forbidding to talk about the conflict, suggesting instead a focus on commonalities. In such cases, the aim is the empowerment and network building, and it is often used in cross-border educational programs, initiatives focused on human rights, cultural exchanges, and so on. In these cases, the frames favor the discourse of subcultures and those who are seen as not progressive enough are marginalized. Mirroring the cases described in the previous chapter, now the participants labeled as nationalist or patriarchal can be marginalized not only for the positions they take on conflict related issues but also for their identity: this most often affects rural residents, military personnel, and conservative heterosexual men who find themselves in the unusual position of an actively ostracized minority within specific initiatives.

A number of colleagues who self-describe as critical or progressive or queer accepted during the interviews that they have contributed to marginalization of colleagues seen to be "not progressive enough." The PAR process revealed that I too, as a facilitator driven by the desire to empower representatives of subcultures who I see as discriminated in their daily life, would often grant them privilege in the program, thus contributing to the marginalization of others. During a number of initiatives where I was a facilitator I befriended gay, lesbian, or bi-sexual colleagues. In an attempt to empower them and ensure that their voice is not suppressed, I often sat beside them during the formal sessions and watched for and addressed signs of disrespect or discrimination. I still do not see anything problematic in this approach, as long as the assumption behind it holds, and these participants are indeed facing the risk of discrimination as it is often the case. In some specific contexts, however, the typically alternative voices could be the majority. And those holding more mainstream positions could face a coalition of the majority of the participants and the facilitators, retreating and losing voice. In such cases, my support for the stereotypically discriminated voice crossed into what I described above as giving privilege to those culturally intelligible for the organizers. As a facilitator, I need to be conscious of the context and differentiate between the situation when I support the silenced voice and the one when I support the silencing of voices. I have to acknowledge also that the line between these is hardly clear, and one can easily flow into the other, leaving the facilitator with hard choices in high-pressure situations. And while it is rare to come across a situation with one "correct" course of action, ongoing work on critically reflecting on the group dynamics and one's own role in them could lead to more self-aware decision making.

The reflection conducted in the framework of this book leads me to problematize the facilitator's role in marginalization of anyone's voice. Many of those who are labeled as "nationalists" are often individuals who are new to conflict resolution work and are simply not aware of the cultural norms of such initiatives, they also often come from rural areas or underprivileged groups within the majority demographics. And even those who are not newcomers to conflict resolution work and yet stick to "mainstream discourse" are typically open-to-collaboration individuals, which is not common in any of the societies I am discussing here. At the very least, they have taken the step to leave their comfort zone and meet "the other side," which very few individuals in Azerbaijan, Armenia, or Syria are willing to do. This also applies to the government officials who support conflict resolution work. From the point of view of conflict practitioners, the representatives of the governments who agree to take part are often seen as necessary yet destructive and status-quo-maintaining actors. Yet considering that the governments in the studied cases have explicitly hawkish policies and are actively engaged in hostile rhetoric, arms race, and armed conflict, those individuals who support conflict resolution efforts are the doves among their ranks and can serve as a bridge between conflict resolution work and policymakers. Participating in a dialogue with the "other side" or joining a workshop on LGBTI rights are not common activities or popular choices for the majorities in the Syrian or Nagorno-Karabakh contexts or for government representatives. Those who "look" and act as mainstream, but are in dialogues, therefore, can serve as bridges helping to bring alternative discourses into the mainstream. Rejecting these folks as "nationalists" or marginalizing them in the context of the programs, we end up marginalizing the conflict resolution work itself, turning down the chance to gain voice within the larger society.

Competition for domination and shifting marginalization

Up to this point, I discussed in this chapter cases where the discourses that dominated in any particular initiative had a sustainable character. The dominants could be the nationalists or the supporters of the LGBTI causes; the domination could be a result of the theory of change of the initiative or of the presence of high-ranking government officials. Often established from the very start, a particular discourse and a particular group would sustain its domination. Another pattern, however, also emerged through this study: in some initiatives, a number of competing discourses were at play, and which ones dominated could change over time.

Often the groups arriving from one country socialize separate from one another during the initiative by convening in single-party spaces and developing strategies for acting as one unit. Even when the space within the program itself is structured intentionally to minimize the formation of factions, the organizers face an uphill battle. Participants from the same locality often know each other well; further as extended travel can be required to reach the program location, the participants from the same country have hours or days of intense interaction, sleeping together in train stations and airports, sharing food and road-related discomfort. One colleague from Armenia recalled her first encounter with Azerbaijanis as a 16-year-old. The program was to take place in a remote location in the United States where their group of teenagers had to travel for two days from Armenia. The shared stress of traveling for the first time without their families, the anxiety from having to meet Azerbaijanis who many considered enemies and to spend a month with them while living in American families, brought the group members very close. The Azerbaijani group had a similar experience during the travel bonding well prior to meeting the Armenians. As the organizers of the initiative did not proactively address this dynamic and did not invest an effort into team-building with the assumption that the weeks spent together will create cross-border relationships, the two groups remained apart and socialized separately for the entire duration of the program, each acting as a unit that was in confrontation with the other. The divide and conflicts only deepened as the time passed. During the final public event of the initiative, the tensions grew so high that the participants from Armenia and Azerbaijan refused to be in the conference room simultaneously. One group made its presentation with the second one demonstratively absent. Only after it finished and left, the second group came in to deliver its presentation. The American teenagers who hosted the Armenian and Azerbaijani peers in pairs in their homes through the duration of the first phase of the program were in tears, telling during the presentation that the initiative had a great promise but ended for them as a disheartening and disempowering experience.

The interactions of individuals in such separate spaces often result in the establishment of a consolidated group narrative which might or might not be representative of the official discourse of their "side." It becomes, however, consolidated enough to prevent the dissenters from gaining voice. As these two monolithic discourses enter into competition, they establish a shared domination and marginalize any nonconventional discourse. Further, the presence of a unified narrative raises a question of representation leading to power struggles within each group and the emergence of spokespeople who act as gatekeepers of the discourses. Politicians, historians, or individuals with leadership qualities, as well as the acknowledged victims of the conflict such as refugees, are often well-positioned to occupy the role of such spokespeople. Once such a unified narrative and its spokespeople are established, intensive efforts by the organizers are necessary to create space where diversity and dissent are welcome, where individual voices can again emerge contesting the dominant discourses.

We have already seen a different example of some discourses gaining domination through competition in the Syrian dialogue described in Chapter 4. There, the initial PSW approach privileged the supporters of Assad and the political opposition. However, once the Assad-opposition binary was questioned, the door was opened for the supporters of the discourse of diversity, civic solidarity, and a united Syria to gain voice. The participants whose identities emerged as associated with this discourse were urban, secularist, feminist, and NGO-affiliated. This in turn brought into the conversation many strong women's voices, as well as those activists who prior to that point did not find a place for themselves in the conversation that had been led by the two violent extremes. The breaking of the binary frame started favoring the discourse of diversity, and this new subgroup of secularists gradually emerged as dominant. And while inclusivity was their mantra, they were effectively marginalizing and dismissing as "regressive" everyone who had a strong religious identity be they from the Sunni majority or any of the minority groups. Some religious groups were easier to marginalize than the others, with the Sunnis and the Alewites already having gained a strong voice thanks to their association with the militaristic discourse.

Gradually, the group developed two and not one dominant discourses (and three dominant groups): one dominant discourse was centered around the masculine militarism of (1) the Sunni militants and (2) the largely Alewite Syrian Army; the other discourse was centered around (3) the civil society advancing ideas of secularism, Syrian unity, civic solidarity, and diversity. The dominance of these three groups left out a number of participants not belonging to any of them.

Following the formation of these two dominant discourses, we conducted an additional exercise where the participants themselves identified the categories of actors in the Syrian conflict, helping to further close the representation gap. The three of the categories identified lined up neatly with the groups that already had voice: the Assad supporters, the armed opposition supporters, and the civil society group. Not everyone was satisfied with the comprehensive nature of this breakdown, however, and a Kurdish participant named "minorities" as a new possible group. It quickly gained recruits. First to join were the other Kurds, the Christians, and one Palestinian all of whom left the larger civil society group, feeling that their voice as a minority was drowning among the wider concerns of the civil society. Then a few folks "defected" from the "pro-Assad" group, adding Alewite voices to the minority group.

This fourth group emerged from those who up to that moment were either marginalized or had reluctantly joined one existing group or another. Their voice was complementary but distinct from the civil society, the latter comprised from affluent, well-educated folks from the big cities, who for the most part renounced their religious or ethnic affiliation or at least did not see it as a politically salient part of their identity. Those who self-identified as minorities had a different agenda: they deeply cared about their ethnic or religious affiliation and saw their groups as discriminated and in need of representation and acquiring rights. The minority subgroup capitalized on the international human rights discourse, appealing continuously to respective UN conventions.[23] They acted in close coordination with the civil society group, forming a strong faction.

In this particular dialogue, the participants worked hard to establish an inclusive process. Big credit here goes also to the Syrian organizers who recruited a diverse group and made an effort not to discriminate or exclude any particular identity. Such selection was key in making it possible for us to try to build an inclusive program.

Various subgroups gained voice throughout the process, and all the subgroups combined included every single participant of the dialogue, making the initiative relatively inclusive. I would not claim, still, that at any point, everyone had an equal voice. Each subgroup had its own hierarchies of voices: in the minorities group, Kurds and Alewites dominated, with the Christian and the Palestinian needs hardly heard; the civil society group was so diverse that only some perspectives were heard, while others remained voiceless; in the group of the rebels, where the participants were all religious, the men dominated and women were silenced or migrated to the other groups; in the pro-Assad group, individuals close to the government had the loudest voice, while others followed.

As we can see in this and other examples, the discourses that dominate are not static and can develop or evolve overtime, their numbers can increase or decrease, and who is marginalized in the group can change depending on the identity that the participants or organizers politicize or prioritize the role they perform. Examples of such shifting marginalization that I observed were the cases where the dialogues started in a form of a binary confrontation of two nationalist discourses, and everyone who shared the discourse was part of the two dominating groups. As the dialogue developed and had a transformative effect, and particularly when the number of participants

---

23 http://www.ohchr.org/en/professionalinterest/pages/ccpr.aspx. Accessed on April 4, 2017.

sharing a peace-oriented discourse grew, the initially dominant participants holding nationalist narratives who did not keep pace with the change and would try to fight the group's transformation could become seen as "regressive" and their position in the group could shift from mainstreams into marginalized. The shift away from nationalism, of course, is an evidence of conflict transformation and should be encouraged. It is possible, however, to leave behind the nationalist discourse without leaving behind the individuals who had been socialized to accept it.

Recognizing and addressing domination and resulting marginalization

In this section I address the discourses that influence the relationships between organizers and participants, the marginalization resulting from formation of dominant discourses within an initiative and particularly discourses that dominate thanks to their cultural intelligibility for the organizers. The reflection and action in this section combine reconceptualization of conflict resolution from the perspective of CDA with respective experimentation and changes made in practice itself.

Every relationship, to some degree or another, is influenced by larger discourses in which the actors are embedded. Some discourses and macro-frames, however, have a stronger influence over the conflict resolution field than others. The binary discourse of conflict sides in the international relations frame influence almost all conflict resolution initiatives in similar ways, as we saw in Chapter 6. Other discourses also influence conflict resolution initiatives, but unevenly. The conflict resolution practitioners who act as organizers of these initiatives often have the power to tip the balance and privilege one or more discourses over others. They can also act to balance the power dynamics.

The hierarchy between the trainers and the participants is critical in perpetuating systematic marginalization as it gives the practitioners a leverage in privileging some groups over others. The move away, therefore, from conceiving of those involved in conflict resolution practice as organizers and participants and approaching everyone as colleagues can help minimize this effect. This does not mean, of course, that the roles people play cannot be different one from another. The difference, however, does not have to mean domination, and with some effort, we have seen it to be possible to develop an inclusive vocabulary and less hierarchical relations.

Instead of terms that indicate identity and hierarchical relationships such as "conflict resolution professionals" and "participants," we could talk about process roles people play depending on the situation leading to the evolution of hierarchical discourse into collegial. For example, when the experience of those present is of importance, we could refer to "those who are involved in conflict resolution work recently," "those who participate in it occasionally," "those experienced in conflict resolution work," and "those who do that work professionally." Those with extensive professional expertise in a particular subject can be valued for their particularly crucial input and contribution. When the roles played in the room are important, we could refer to "administrators," "facilitators," and "participants" of a particular exercise. The role-centered terms are not direct replacements for the identity-centered terms. Some "participants" can have much longer experience in conflict resolution than the "conflict resolution practitioners" who have initiated the meeting or a particular exercise can be facilitated by a newcomer to the scene while the organizers of the initiative are participating.

There can be cases, of course, such as skill-building workshops, where a certain level of hierarchy is justified and the presence of trainers can be valuable. Even in such cases, however, various models of relationship between the trainer and the rest exist. Through the PAR process, I encountered numerous complains about authoritarian trainers who would ignore the needs and opinions of those in the room and lecture them from a position of a know-how. Such trainers could be both insiders and outsiders to the conflict. The alternative approaches, the best-known of which was the elicitive training model (Lederach 2008), and other experimental and interactive models that solicited active input from participants from the very early stages of the process received much more appreciation and built the motivation of those present to stay involved with conflict resolution work. The positive news was that a number of initiatives in the recent years, if yet small in numbers, in the Nagorno-Karabakh and Syrian contexts, as well as in other parts of the South Caucasus and Turkey, have been moving in this direction, with the organizers empowering those who were once participants to take control of the initiatives.

Moving away from hierarchical language might be difficult still, when a person or a group combines a number of power-related positions, for example has the longest experience, a PhD or a diplomatic title, is assigned the role of the facilitator, and is the administrator of the initiative. In such situations, a conscious effort is needed to identify the strengths of others in the room and assign the roles in a way that would empower and give voice to others present. Those who are not involved in conflict resolution work, are new to it, or are involved only occasionally are at a disadvantage compared to their more experienced colleagues or those employed in the field. Individuals falling into the latter category are often formally in charge of organizing conflict resolution initiatives, deciding who participates and who does not, and what is the design and the format of the conversation, thus are well positioned to dominate others whom they selected and who are often expected to look at the experienced folks for guidance in the room.

To understand who we marginalize during the initiatives and how to address it, I build on the learning on *how* we marginalize. As discussed above, in all initiatives, certain discourses become dominant. Depending on the framing of the initiative, its methodology and design, selection criteria, the views of the organizers, and other dynamics, the discourses that come to dominate can be as diverse as nationalism or peace, majority rule or minority rights, discourse of honoring and privileging the military or discourse of vilifying the military, and so on. Once the dominant discourses are formed, they marginalize those who are not part of them.

Organizers and facilitators who often hold particularly strong positional (facilitator, trainer) and personal (gender, age, experience, etc.) power are able to establish the frames of the conversation and influence the formation of dominant discourses. They have, therefore, the primary responsibility in reflecting on their own role when it comes to marginalization through formation of a dominant discourse. Even if they do not dictate the frames directly, as we saw above they can contribute to the formation of dominant discourses by privileging those present who are most culturally intelligible for them and share their discourse. In my work, I found it effective to employ CDA as a method of raising the self-awareness of the facilitators as well as the awareness of the entire group and working on the development of inclusive discourses.

CDA, as discussed in Chapter 2, calls us to make our values explicit and assess our work against these values, identify where we fail, where we can improve, particularly when it comes to power relations and inequalities. More specifically, the *critical* language awareness within the CDA approach directs us toward a reflective analysis of practices of domination implicit in the transmission of information and insists that the "critical language awareness should be built from the existing language capabilities and experiences of the learner. The experience of the learner can [...] be made explicit and systematic as a body of knowledge" (Fairclough 2010, 531–38).

Working to address marginalization created by the formation of dominant discourses within conflict resolution initiatives, whether they are developed through internal power dynamics or as a result of the influence of external macro-frames, I started increasingly incorporating critical discourse awareness advocated by CDA into my work. As the organizers often have the first word in the design of any initiative and in deciding who can participate, it was important to start the work of critical discourse awareness from ourselves. As I learned, the projects at the stage of conception and fundraising rarely resort to critical discourse awareness or other reflective methods. The initiatives can be conceived either as a response to a call for proposals by a donor or independent of such a call and with a plan to fundraise. In the initiatives that are conceived as a response to a call for proposals, the organizers' primary concern is with fitting the requirements of the donor, typically without much thoughts given to possible marginalization or other harmful impact that the initiative can lead to. In the other often-repeated scenario, the organizers first conceive an idea and then "shop" for funding. When the potential funding is in sight, the organizers then are forced to reframe the idea to fit the donor requirements. In cases when the donor is an individual or a small private foundation that supports the original idea, the organizers have a better chance of focusing their time on being reflective and not worrying about fitting another actor's agenda.

In all these scenarios, still, I found it possible to build critical discourse awareness starting from the stage of the project conception and design, followed by recruitment and implementation. At the stage of initiative conception and recruitment, at the Imagine Center we now ask questions such as: are we excluding affected categories of people? How are we addressing the influence of outside macro-frames such as gender, nationalism, and others? How can we frame the work in a nonbinary way? These pre-program reflections changed our work tremendously. As already mentioned above, we moved away from binary frames such as "Armenian-Azerbaijani" conceptualizing our work as inclusive. This helps to expand the boundaries of the program during the recruitment to include those who would not fit into any binary frame. It also helps with critical awareness when the conversation in an open-ended Evolving Designs format opens to reflection and change. In cases when we do accept an initial binary term because of grant conditions, we do so with an intention to approach the initiative critically and transform the very meaning of the groupist terms such as "Armenians" or "Turks." If in the past, we would try to imagine the boundaries of these terms and fit the participants into these boundaries, we now approach these categories as conditional and open to shaping and reshaping.

As we have seen in the above discussion, of course, exclusion and marginalization take place not only during the conception of the idea or recruitment but also during the program itself as well. Cultural intelligibility of some but not others for the organizers is a likely at all stages of work from selection to the implementation. Applying critical language awareness and building inclusive relationships in the program, therefore, cannot be built in some instances but be disregarded in the others. Building inclusivity should be approached as a holistic process. During selection, we need to make a conscious effort to recruit diverse groups, and necessarily invite those not regularly invited to conflict resolution work, folks outside capitals and especially from conflict zones, those who suffered from the conflict directly, and those of non-titular heritage. In this process, we keep the conversation open among organizers to check ourselves against privileging those culturally intelligible to us. This is not always easy. Those from underprivileged backgrounds do not always have access to internet to see the call for applications, do not have resumes ready or the skills to write an application, do not speak the language of the workshop (often English).

A number of organizations, including ours, have attempted to address the language and skills barrier by expanding the scope of the initiatives in the Nagorno-Karabakh and other conflict contexts in the South Caucasus. Starting from 2011, the Imagine Center has been complementing the dialogues with local trainings, movie screenings, discussion clubs in local languages. We have also been providing translation when possible. A Tbilisi-based partner organization, GoGroup Media also has a number of programs explicitly aimed at giving voice to the marginalized and affected by the conflicts. They hold televised talk shows in which the speakers are not experts but regular people; they travel to remote regions in the South Caucasus, hand interested people cameras, teach basic recording and interviewing skills, let them film what they see relevant to their life, and later work with them in editing the footage into a documentary. After that, they not only show these on mainstream TV and on the internet but also tour other regions organizing screenings in collaboration with local organizations or at homes. They then offer the audience members the opportunity to take on cameras and make their own films and talk shows as well.

Such initiatives greatly expanded the circle of those engaged in peacebuilding work, involving many from the conflict and border zones, from minority groups and mixed families, from LGBTI and feminist organizations. The diversification of those who participate and the inclusion of many not previously involved, on their own, had only a limited impact on the conflict discourses in binary-framed initiatives where the voices of those who represented the official narrative dominated. The inclusive recruitment coupled with the emergent design-inspired approach where the conflict sides were not predetermined, however, changed the discourse considerably. As the participants were able to reflect on the conflict individually, name the actors who they would like to represent and complicate the picture, the binary discourses disappeared, and very complex pictures of actors, populations, and needs emerged. The ethnic and religious minorities, feminists, and LGBTI activists, as well as various other groups that emerged in one initiative or another, such as retired combatants, journalists, artists, refugees, perhaps not surprisingly brought in discourses in regard to the influence of conflict on the groups they represent and their needs in the resolution process vastly different from the standard monoliths reflective of the official discourse offered by the binary groups.

The emerging diversity of conflict discourses catalyzed by this new approach, in turn, raised the interest and enthusiasm of many other feminists, human rights activists, and researchers who were previously apathetic to the conflict resolution work and saw it irrelevant to their struggles. An analytic project was initiated in late 2015 that brought together over 40 analysts, journalists, and researchers from all parts of the South Caucasus, as well as Turkey and Russia who devised nine lenses through which the conflicts on the South Caucasus could be looked at. Their joint work resulted in the publication titled "The South Caucasus and its Nationhood: From Politics and Economics to Group Rights" (Gamaghelyan et al. 2016) featuring nine articles on a variety of topics ranging from the politics of sanctions and economic isolation and transnational networks to minority rights, women rights, and LGBTI rights as instruments of conflict resolution. Each article was coauthored by a number of researchers each representing different actors and identity groups. This was a unique case in the South Caucasus where representatives of conflict sides would coauthor and jointly sign under analytic articles on the conflict topic. What made it possible was the commonality of the struggles against oppression perpetrated by the ongoing conflicts faced by activists, feminists, LGBTI rights advocates, ethnic minorities, and others across the conflict divides. It was also unique in bringing together the questions of violent conflict on the one hand and the rights of various groups that are not traditionally seen as part of the conflict on the other under one umbrella. For once, the conflicts were not analyzed as an interaction of Armenians and Azerbaijanis or Georgians and Abkhazians or Ossetians, but as an interaction of a multiplicity of actors with diverse needs and agendas.

We have been working toward developing holistic and inclusive programs at the Imagine Center where not only the formal but also the informal time is considered as its integral part. Such an approach is taxing on the organizers as they need to be conscious of their behavior and relationships not only from 9am to 5pm but around the clock. The formal part can end at 5pm, but the relationships continue. Conversations at dinner and in the afterhours, chats or social gatherings, all matter in developing an inclusive space. In cases when we did not invest into the evening time, the colleagues present tended to quickly retreat into small groups of people who had known each other previously or those who are culturally similar reinforcing existing divisions. Currently, we organize all-inclusive evening activities for the first night or two at the start of every initiative, inviting other colleagues to take the lead in days to come. When spending individual time, we try to ensure that we are accessible to everyone. We start by having short individual conversations with every person present, inviting further conversations, consultations, and feedback and follow up with periodic check-ins. Ongoing team checkups during the evenings and organizer reflection sessions are also important to ensure that we do not start privileging some others as the time goes by, and that each colleague present has a voice and if not, make adjustments.

The organizers' and facilitators' self-awareness is an important step, yet colleagues who do not have an organizational role also can marginalize others. As we have seen in case with the Syrian dialogue, factions form in the group, and some discourses start to dominate. Whether the dominant is a masculine military discourse, a nationalist discourse, or a co-existence discourse, all of them have the tendency to alienate—in these examples women, nonconformers, or the nationalists respectively. The critical discourse awareness practiced by the organizers, therefore, should be shared with the participants as well. Explicit discussions of power and marginalization and introducing elements of reflective practice have shown to be empowering and ensuring that the group also takes responsibility for everyone's voice. This happened in the Syrian initiative organically as we searched for a solution to the dilemma of facilitating a nonbinary group. Yet we should not wait for the problem of marginalization and exclusion to become as painfully obvious as it was in the Syrian initiative, before we start practicing inclusion. Challenging the facilitator-participant dichotomy and asking everyone to take responsibility for the dialogue and inclusion of each person present is at first unsettling for many as it breaks the common expectation of the participant as a listener and recipient of knowledge, but empowering as we go through with it and build the program together.

Inviting everyone present to join in as creators of knowledge rather than as recipients of it opens up the horizons of what is possible. And respectively allowing a few discourses to dominate forces people to limit their outlook only to these few, joining one or the other, and leaving out new possibilities. To return to the Syria example, when the Assad-opposition and later Assad-opposition-civil society discourses dominated, everyone split themselves among these three, even if reluctantly. As we had seen, however, with the possibility open for the formation of new subgroups and new discourses, soon a "minorities" sub-group was formed uniting the Kurds, Alewites, Christians, and a Palestinian. Once the sub-group was formed the minority rights discourse, prior to this moment nonexistent, became central in the search for a solution by the participants. Many of the Alewite participants leaving the "Assad supporters" subgroup for the minorities was an important statement on its own. The power in the room was not limited anymore to the two dichotomous discourses of Assad and opposition. The Evolving Designs created space for such a shift to occur, space for new discourses to flourish.

Chapter conclusions

In building inclusive initiatives based on Evolving Designs methodology that can open the horizon of what is possible in conflict resolution, it is critical for practitioners to remain conscious of the power held by factions, and particularly by the privileged position they themselves hold in facilitating the formation of dominant factions. Gravitating toward those who are culturally similar to us is convenient. Yet that also contributes to the formation of factions, and the production and reproduction of discourses that dominate in that particular setting implicitly, often without a space or procedure to be challenged. In the context of conflict resolution initiatives, the presence of a faction and a dominant discourse supported by the facilitator often means the marginalization of those who are not part of it. The organizers, facilitators, and participants who hold policymaking or otherwise important for the conflict context offices are often the actors who can tip the balance in one way or the other, privileging some discourses over others, and therefore have a particular responsibility in behaving ethically and reflectively. CDA, reflective and elicitive practices, Evolving Designs and other self-critical approaches adopted by practitioners are useful in developing innovative solutions for addressing the conflict dynamics in the wider society.

Chapter 8
Addressing marginalization patterns within the conflict resolution community

Marginalization affects not only the participants of conflict resolution initiatives but also practitioners and entire organizations as well. In this chapter, I examine the relations within the conflict resolution community itself. Struggle for domination and resulting marginalization are perpetuated here by competition over resources, gate-keeping behavior, and power struggles within teams. Similar to the section on the emergence of dominant discourses, the power dynamics within the conflict resolution community are often context-specific and, as a result, the transformation of relations is within the reach of the practitioners involved.

This chapter starts with examining competition over resources between organizations and gate-keeping practices that tarnish the image of conflict resolution practice and alienate many potential allies and supporters, followed by the discussion of steps taken by some organizations to advance practices of cooperation within the field. The second part of the chapter looks into less visible to the outside eye marginalization that takes place within teams in one organization as a result of struggles for power and business-like hierarchical relations that disempower those in the lower-ranked positions and into possible ways of building inclusive and horizontal teams that value everyone's input.

Competition among organizations

The professionalization of violence calls for a professionalization of conflict resolution, as a field that can systematically oppose perpetuation of violence of all kinds. Because of this normative aim, the field of conflict resolution and organizations and individuals practicing it professionally take on the implicit obligation to act ethically and practice the values that they promote. Acting ethically, in turn, creates a need for continuous introspection and self-evaluation that can help prevent the descent of conflict resolution into one of Illich's *"Disabling Professions."* Illich criticizes the professionalization of certain aspects of human life, such as education or health, as crippling institutions that have taken away the people's ability to provide for their own needs and turned societies into passive clients of the will of the professionals. The professionals hold a monopoly over deciding what is a norm and what is a deviation or a disease prescribing human needs, while simultaneously having a monopoly over the remedy as holders of professional knowledge (Illich 1987). Conflict resolution as a young profession aiming to help societies to transform into violence-free and socially just structures has to work hard to ensure that it addresses the challenges posed by Illich and others.

The debate in favor and against professionalization of the conflict resolution field dates back at least to 1982 (Wedge and Sandole 1982) and continues to generate arguments in favor (Hansen 2007) and against (Sword 2009). The arguments in favor of professionalization discuss the need for more systematic and institutionalized response to conflicts. They also look for protections of participants who could suffer at the hands of unqualified conflict resolvers. Those against argue that professionalization will halt innovation and diversity of the inherently interdisciplinary field, and do little to protect participants as conflict resolution practices are often confidential and take place in remote locations. The debate about the merits of professionalization, or rather standardization, of conflict resolution exists also among evaluators who are continuously struggling to find appropriate methods for evaluating its nonquantifiable practices (see Ross 2001; Pearson d'Estrée et al. 2001; Church and Rogers 2005).

The warning signs provided by those who agree with Illich are not abstract. Throughout the process of this PAR, I came to observe or learn about many practitioners and organizations that saw conflict resolution as a little more than another form of business. Such framing in turn led to the legitimization of "business practices" such as elimination of competition, exclusion of many groups and individuals, and prevention of newly emerging voices from entering the field or growing in it. The consequence of such practices, as discussed below, was the stagnation, growing cynicism in regard to the capacity of the field, absence of innovation or formation of a critical mass needed to bring about social change. Similar to professionalized medicine criticized by Illich for preference for diagnosing, sustaining, and continuously treating chronic diseases rather than for healing, the professionalized brand of conflict resolution is at the risk of becoming too concerned with justifying its own existence, with working to diagnose and sustain conflicts chronically in active opposition to the stated goal of conflict resolution.

More specifically, a number of colleagues working in the Syrian, Nagorno-Karabakh, and other contexts explicitly referred to conflict resolution as to a job in a field where the resources are limited and therefore saw the sabotage of "competitors" as a legitimate course of action. Others mentioned the necessity for the existing actors to stop the new ones from entering the field to prevent the competition from expanding or, when not possible, to keep their work under control by making them subcontractors or junior partners. Two practitioners, both outsiders to the conflicts they worked in, went further and confessed during informal conversations that they would not want to see the conflicts they are working on resolved as this would "push them out of the job market." One of them, a scholar-practitioner working primarily in the Balkans, recalled that he used to be an expert in nuclear nonproliferation once, and the fall of the Berlin Wall put him out of business once. He concluded that he would not want the Balkan conflicts to end as then he would be out of business again. My probing explained the ease with which such visible problematic positions were voiced: colleagues holding these narratives assumed that this was the shared norm in the conflict resolution field. They saw the alternative views of conflict resolution as a vocation aimed primarily at resolving conflicts as a well-sounding pretense, suited for fundraising rather than private internal conversation and argued that everyone was in this for money and that those who claimed otherwise are dishonest.

"Gatekeeping," controlling access to the field, emerged in my research as one of the primary methods of exclusion both when practitioners framed conflict resolution as business and when they saw themselves as better than others. Interestingly, in most cases the colleagues I talked to were well aware of instances of gatekeeping from which they suffered. Rarely, however, did I find anyone to acknowledge an instance of gatekeeping they had perpetrated. All of us were victims of gatekeeping, apparently. None of us was the gatekeeper.

Gatekeeping, to be sure, does not have to be negative. As discussed by Christian in regard to access of researchers to inherently dangerous and hard to reach conflict zones, gatekeepers can provide vital access. The same gatekeepers, however, can also have a disproportionate influence on the researcher and the research restricting the information that can be accessed (Christian 2017). In conflict resolution practice gatekeeping, if not performed reflectively and with caution, can lead to the monopolization of access and resources by a small number of local and international actors.

As I learned through the process of the research for this book, the local gatekeeping is often performed in the form of monopolizing the access of international actors and donors to the area and preventing the entry of new local actors into the field. Such gatekeeping is most visible in the smaller and unrecognized or partially recognized states of Nagorno-Karabakh, South Ossetia, and Abkhazia. Considering the limited human resources, as well as the tight control of the authorities over all the spheres of public life, very few individuals in Nagorno-Karabakh, Abkhazia, and South Ossetia have been able to rise to the position of civil society leaders who have the clearance from their authorities to operate. As the access to these territories for international actors is limited, they are forced to compete for the partnership with those few actors who have ability to operate locally. This in turn gives further power to these few individuals or organizations who control the local field preventing any "competition" or a younger generation from emerging. The local gatekeepers typically command groups of loyal followers and control who from their society participates in a given initiative. They also ensure that the participants follow "the party line" established by the authorities. Active young people who exhibit nonconforming behavior or thoughts when invited or those who try to initiate endeavors on their own are sacked from the arena, sometimes through intimidation locally and other times often through threats to international actors to withhold from them future support should they continue collaborating with the alternative voices. These practices preclude the entrance of new actors into the scene creating a vicious cycle that deepens the dependence of the international actors on the local gatekeepers, making in turn the entry of new actors even less likely. What local gatekeeping does, in addition to its ethical repercussions, is the prevention of the development of local peace constituencies and the limitation of the potential impact of conflict resolution work.

Gatekeeping is also common among international actors and bigger NGOs operating in the recognized states. The absence of local ownership has been acknowledged by the donor community and theoretical literature as one of the main reasons for low effectiveness of conflict resolution efforts. According to Lund's recent study, "Few themes have been sounded as loudly in the policy discourse of international peacebuilding and development as the need for 'local ownership.' However, the international approach to peacebuilding and development is criticized for still being driven largely by mandates, preconceptions, and programs defined outside the countries being served, and often taken from the standard menu and designed along certain sectoral lines" (Lund and McDonald 2015, 5–6). In Armenia and Azerbaijan, and to a lesser extent in Syria and Georgia, the conflict resolution field and the money flow to the civil sector is often controlled by consortiums of international NGOs. Despite the often-uneasy relationship among themselves, these NGOs cooperate in preventing others from entering or growing in the field. Similar to the gatekeepers in the smaller societies, they create an illusion of diversity by allowing the functioning of a limited number of smaller actors who depend on the bigger counterparts financially as sub-contractors. The cycle is enabled by the funding schemes, when the bigger donors rely on well-established international actors trusting them with the administration of large sums of money, making it impossible for emerging actors to institutionalize or grow. Having control over the financial flows into the field, the bigger NGOs use it to deepen the financial dependence of the smaller actors. The alternative actors and new voices, therefore, have little avenues to develop institutionally. As they have no direct access to program-level funding, they have to rely for project-level financial support on bigger NGOs, who in return demand loyalty and "knowing your place." This form of gatekeeping by big actors, coupled with gatekeeping locally, severely limits the possibility of bringing fresh ideas, new organizations, and alternative voices into the field, stalling development, contributing to stagnation, lack of enthusiasm or big visions, and cynicism or loss of motivation by potential peace constituencies.

One particular pattern that illustrates how gatekeeping operates in case of the multiyear multimillion funding for the conflict resolution processes in the South Caucasus became visible during my research. In the 1990s, soon after the collapse of the Soviet Union and the onset of the conflicts, a few big international NGOs received millions for local capacity-building. Over the decades of operation, the capacity was indeed built and local NGOs started emerging. They initially worked as subcontractors of the international NGOs that helped to establish them and train their staff. Eventually, some of the local NGOs built their own networks and methodology, institutional memory, experience, and rooted locally (and at least in one case having offices and networks on all sides of conflict divides), some of them started demonstrating the ability to conceive, design, and operate initiatives that equal or surpass in scope and efficiency the work of their "parent" NGOs. Having reached that stage, the emerging NGOs started facing obstacles for operation that ranged from the cut-off in the funding from the "parent" NGO to the difficulty of establishing direct contacts with the international donors as the latter relied on the international NGOs assessment of the field. The local NGOs have been continually deemed not having the capacity to administer funds and in need of continuous capacity-building and supervision. Moreover, those local NGOs that continued working as sub-contractors to the international ones also fell in line, some accepting the terms of the international parent NGO. Others did not want to see any of their peers getting ahead and becoming independent players with a voice in the peace process that surpassed theirs. As a result, many of the emerging NGOs that strived for independence and sustainability lost access to funding. Eventually, their core team members had to accept positions in the private sector or with the international NGOs, gradually depleting the human resources. Eventually, most of the emerging NGOs either disintegrated or returned to the position of a client NGO to the international ones. Consequently, the development of the conflict resolution-focused civil sector in the South Caucasus stagnated in its most promising years in mid- to late-1990s and early 2000s as the institutionalization of local NGOs was made unsustainable thanks to the sabotage, be it intentional or not, by the donor agencies and the big international NGOs, the very actors charged with building the local capacity. The rise of authoritarianism in the late 2000s and early 2010s and the crackdown on the NGO sector especially pronounced in Azerbaijan and South Ossetia practically outlawed and destroyed the rest of the civil society sector pushing the remaining activists into immigration or into the shadows. The majority of conflict resolution NGOs today in the South Caucasus that still function are one- or two-person operations dependent financially on the international NGOs, despite 25 years of "capacity-building" and "institution building."

The behavior of those who are excluded or sabotaged is not always transformative either. This research showed that many practitioners were concerned primarily with their own inclusion into otherwise exclusive frameworks rather than concerned with the problem of exclusion itself. During one interview on the topic of gatekeeping and exclusion, an experienced scholar-practitioner was complaining about her exclusion from some high-level coordinating forum where she used to be a regular in the past, but not any longer. As I tried to move the conversation toward possibilities for reforming the forum to make it inclusive, the scholar-practitioner protested that her interest was to be part of this exclusive club and not in making it inclusive. This and many other conversations, including the private confessions of the former leaders of the international NGOs, have shown that gatekeeping and exclusion of new peacebuilders from the field was not always innocent, accidental, or even structurally determined: there was a clear interest articulated by a number of colleagues to keep the field closed and exclusive.

Conflict resolution as a business with gatekeeping as its tool is not the only discourse that justifies exclusion and marginalization. Many of us, as I learned, hold a narrative that we are better professionals than others and therefore deserve a privileged position. We are more experienced or more innovative, better educated or more directly affected by the war, more neutral or more local, and so on, always better than others who would do damage to our efforts by their involvement. Such narratives were very widespread: almost every colleague who participated in this research held some form of a narrative of one's own superiority compared to others.

I too have not been an exception. In the initial draft, this section contained the following paragraph:

> "I want to stress that I am not arguing against business models or financial motivations in general. Instead, when the primary motivation is financial, there are many fields where making a career with an aim of generating high income is appropriate. Better yet, these fields tend to pay more. There are fields, however (i.e. medicine or conflict resolution), where the other's livelihood depends on us, and in these cases, having a financial gain as primary motivation is unethical and harmful." I continued, "I am not arguing against the need for conflict resolution professionals to make a decent living either. Many of us are skilled and well educated folks who believe that we deserve a comfortable life. It is still possible, I have seen, to make a decent living without sacrificing one's integrity and having one's commitment to peace and nonviolence guide their work, with the compensation coming second."

Deservedly, one of the dissertation committee members, Dr. Jessica Srikantia, pointed out that my approach was not qualitatively different from the business approach that I criticize. When reflecting on Jessica's challenge, I did not have to look too deep to realize that indeed, my belief that I am a professional and therefore deserve a certain level of financial well-being was not different from the frames held by colleagues who called conflict resolution a business; or that like those who I criticized, I also held a narrative of myself as a better professional than many others. And if these answers were right on the surface, why did I not see them before? Likely, I simply did not want to look until Jessica's questions made it impossible not to. And then, what else is there that I do not see? How disturbing can these new revelations be?

I had started my research with the intent to explore whether the positivist macro-frames of international relations were influencing the conflict resolution practice in a way that contributed to marginalization of key groups of population and reproduced conflict discourses. Through the process of this PAR, I learned that marginalization and other practices that sabotaged the effectiveness of conflict resolution practice could result not only from the influences external to the field. They were often conditioned by power-play within the conflict resolution community itself, and specifically from practices that treated conflict resolution as nothing more than a well-sounding lucrative business where profit-making takes priority. Certainly, these were dynamics shaped by the larger context of capitalist economics within which the contemporary conflict resolution operates. When the profession has a normative claim, I remain convinced, the economic rationale cannot take priority without corrupting the profession. And conflict resolution is a profession that has a normative claim.

Walking the talk: the case for the organizations preaching cooperation to lead by example

The two specific patterns leading to marginalization and resulting from the relations between and among organizations that I studied were the framing of conflict resolution work as a business, and gatekeeping. A number of other patterns supported these practices. These included the commercialization and professionalization of the field that disqualifies those affected by the conflict, but not possessing respective training or experience, from contributing to conflict resolution, as well as the monopolization of the conflict resolution practice by big donors and NGOs concerned more with upholding hegemonies rather than contributing to social justice.

Similar dilemmas exist in the field of human rights where the critiques maintain that dominant frames serve the reproduction of the hegemonic discourse and not the advancement of social change. Many neocolonial practices, that can be considered actions of oppression and domination, are reconfigured as actions of emancipation and liberation if carried in the name of human rights. As a consequence, the debate has been developing whether human rights can at all be used in a counter-hegemonic way (see, for example, Crépeau and Sheppard 2013). Similarly, if in practice, actions carried in the name of conflict resolution routinely help to uphold dominance and marginalize those on whose behalf the field acts, it is time to ask whether conflict resolution discourse, in principle, is positioned well to contribute to social justice or not.

Such a critique of conflict resolution is not new and comes from within as well as from outside the field. From outside the field, it has been criticized heavily from the human rights perspective that sees conflict resolution as value-neutral and concerned with upholding the status quo rather that contributing to justice (for the summary of the debate between the human rights paradigm and conflict resolution, see Mertus and Helsing 2006. And for a more detailed discussion of synergies and tensions between human rights and conflict resolution practitioners and the survey of the core principles, goals, and values as well as the methods used by practitioners in each field, see (Lutz, Babbitt, and Nannum 2003)). Conflict resolution, and particularly its once popular form ADR, was also famously criticized as "an instrument of social control, not social change" by anthropologist Nader in her book *Harmony Ideology* (Nader 1993). This line of thought blames the conflict resolution field for working effectively to pacify the oppressed upholding the interests of the powerful.

My views on this topic have been evolving in the past few years and through this research especially. I most certainly share the concern raised by Nader regarding conflict resolution understood in the ADR sense, as a value-neutral tool-box or professional endeavor aimed at helping parties find a mutually acceptable solution. I can attest through my experience, be it in real-life dialogues and negotiations or in simulations, that a neutral and technical approach to conflict resolution that brings two sides together serves the interests of the party of relative power and disempowers and pacifies the representatives of the weaker party without allowing them to achieve their goals as well. In this book, I developed a further critique of such approaches as excluding or marginalizing any discourse outside of the dominant binary. The traditional "weaker side," therefore, coming second, is not in the worst position. An example I have discussed in the previous chapters is in the Nagorno-Karabakh case: the governments of Azerbaijan and Armenia are accepted as the main protagonists by the international community marginalizing another known actor, the leadership and the population of the unrecognized Nagorno-Karabakh Republic that gets an unequal voice. Yet there are populations affected by the conflict, such as the hundreds of thousands of displaced, who are nearly silenced. Worse yet, there are populations who are deprived of voice entirely, such as Kurds who have also been displaced en mass and other groups not called "Armenian" or "Azerbaijani" and are rarely if at all mentioned or consulted in connection to this conflict. Similar dynamics are in place in Syria where only known factions engaged in violent confrontation receive consideration, with the majority of the population who is not identifying with any of the violent actors deprived of voice.

Of course, the conflict resolution field is not limited to the ADR or other positivist approaches. Nader's and others' critique has been heard by some, and alternative approaches have been emerging with a number of constructivist and concerned with power and capitalism theories becoming prominent in conflict analysis. The practice concerned with political processes, however, by and large, continues to marginalize and contribute to sustaining the status quo. The question remains whether professional conflict resolution practice can, conceptually, contribute to social justice or as Illich would have it, the professionalization itself is the problem (Illich 1987).

While appreciative of Illich's critique, I do not fully agree with it. Over-professionalization understood as technical expertise that dismisses the contribution of all others is marginalizing and is the one extreme, and the absence of any systematization of conflict work is the other. The South Caucasus in the early 1990s and Syria in the early 2010s had many people with no strong sense of ethnic or religious affiliation and with inclusive visions committed to a united South Caucasus and a united Syria respectively. Motivated by the need to address the conflict that recently turned their lives upside down, yet without emotional or analytic experience of handling ethnic and religious mobilization and mass violence, in my interviews with them, I often heard them speak of the difficulty in developing a coherent strategy that would offer alternatives to the well-structured nationalist and sectarian discourse. In post-Soviet conflict contexts, the newly formed states adopted nationalism as an ideology, institutionalizing it through constitutions and commemorations, and the education and media ensured that the new generations are growing up with an internalized sense of enmity and readiness to fight the other. As the conflict discourses are institutionalized and professionalized, they require matching interventions.

I do see a need, therefore, for a systematic, institutionalized, and even professionalized approach to conflict resolution. However, professional conflict resolution does not need to be the only form of peacebuilding and can exist side-by-side, and in alliance with, various nonprofessionalized expressions of it in art form or in everyday life. And conflict resolution certainly cannot afford becoming its own antithesis, serving to perpetuate conflict or marginalize the populations affected by war, and retain the claim to serve peace and justice. Professionalized, reflective, and self-critical conflict resolution can have its place in addressing the institutionalization of violence. Yet the engagement of broader populations affected by war or conflict as well as educators, media, and other groups who influence the conflict discourses not as subjects of work but as stakeholders are just as critical for an eventual transformation.

The professional (and particularly paid) engagement of anyone in this field should be very self-aware, conscious of its goal and the effect of its approaches. Isolated from the grassroots and without a commitment to foster inclusiveness, conflict resolution becomes an extension of international relations perpetuating marginalization and sustaining the conflict producing frames. In order for conflict resolution to address successfully the critique aimed at it and become a field that promotes social justice, it should make central to its project the voice of the marginalized and building inclusive processes. The role of conflict professionals, therefore, far from upholding a monopoly of own voice and status in the peace processes should be working to give voice to all those affected who do not have it already.

The respective changes we made in Imagine Center's work included selection processes that did not privilege well-known professionals and known representatives of the "sides"; expanding the circle of those we work with to include colleagues from various regions, particularly those most affected by conflicts and irrespective of their ethnic identity; asking the colleagues to identify the relevant actors and self-identify with the groups they choose instead of assigning them to predetermined categories; opening up the *Caucasus Edition*, Imagine Center's journal that previously published only professional analysts and scholars, to nonprofessional voices.

I do not argue, of course, for any particular initiative to be all-inclusive as it is not practically possible. I argue, instead, against active practices of exclusion of the voices that could have an important contribution to the respective conversation, with particular attention paid to bringing in those who would typically be excluded or marginalized. If working toward social justice through fostering inclusion and empowerment are to be core criteria to what is conflict resolution, then competition and gatekeeping simply have no role in it. One cannot have a mission of giving voice and working for inclusiveness, while also actively preventing others from entering the field or having voice. And its mirror, irrespective of the proclaimed goals, the organization and individuals who practice competition and gatekeeping, cannot be considered as part of the conflict resolution process, but rather part of a conflict-sustaining process; they should be exposed as such and invited to reconsider their methods.

The challenge to the competence and bias of the local NGOs, a charge often leveraged by international NGOs trying to keep monopoly over the resources available to any particular peace process is surmountable: the local NGOs can build a reputation and engage in own public relations campaigns or look for alternative funding sources. None of these are easy of course, as the local NGOs rarely can match the access or the voice that the big international NGOs based out of Brussels and DC have, but it is possible.

At the same time, the hiring of the leader of local institutions as a method of sabotage, whether intentional or not, is particularly potent and hard to address. Mark Duffield who critiques liberal interventionism qualifies the structures of NGO support as part of global governance system in which governments and civil society, knowingly or unknowingly, police the gap between the mass consumer society of the Global North and those living beyond (Duffield 2007). As a consequence, it is institutionally nearly impossible for a local NGO to compete with internationals when it comes to hiring or retaining human resources.

We have experienced this within the work of the Imagine Center. Until 2014, the Center functioned as a US-headquartered NGO. Consequently, our salaries were set according to the US standards for the team members based in the United States or internationally. For the staff based in the Caucasus, the donors insisted that we set salaries lower, adjusted to the living expenses of each place, and comparable with salaries of the local staff of international NGOs. Even the salaries for the local staff of an international NGO, however, have been considerably higher than the salaries for comparable folks in local NGOs. In fact, at the time, we were puzzled as to why the local NGOs would not increase the pay-scale of their employees and thus have a better chance of retaining them. We learned why, soon after we moved the headquarters of our organization from Washington, DC, to Tbilisi and positioned ourselves as a Caucasus-based NGO. Suddenly, we started experiencing difficulties in reaching out to international institutions and donors and securing appointments. When we had a meeting, our capacity would almost immediately be questioned and a suggestion made to invite a European or American specialist to the team, something we never faced as a US NGO, even when we were newly established and indeed lacked experience. The hardest struggles were the salaries: we were directly asked by a number of donor agencies to substantially lower the salaries and cap them at about half of what the international NGOs operating next door pay their local staff. We were facing an impossible dilemma: on the one hand, we would lose the donor support unless we lowered the salaries well below the level of the international NGOs; on the other hand, we were risking to lose the organization were we to lower the salaries to a point where our hard-built team would be constantly tempted to move working for the better-paying neighbors. The risk was not abstract. Job offers were periodically made to our team members, myself included, and they are hard to resist.

As of this writing, we weathered the storm. We refused to accept the cap. And we lost many prospective donors. Yet we retained a small team comprised of individuals committed to each other and to the work we do, and who are critical of the business approach to conflict resolution. No one, yet, left the team for financial reasons. Many of us turned to other work, mainly in academia, for financial sustainability, while staying involved.

One organization, of course, can only transform itself and not an entire field. Many organizations have done just that. I have been inspired by a number of colleagues who went much further than us in taking out financial gain from their work. A colleague of a Japanese background who conducts an active practice not only does not accept any payment for his work but subsidizes the projects he leads from his salary as an educator or from his consultancy work. An Ukrainian friend who is a peace activist and an independent filmmaker subsidizes her activities in the field through her work at a restaurant. Many others have given up more lucrative options in Track 1 and consultancy to work in grassroots activism.

Any structural change in the mainstream professional conflict resolution practice that would prevent or eradicate gatekeeping and competition, however, is hard to expect in the near-future. These practices are normalized today with most organizations engaging in them as a common practice. This normalization is in tune with the hegemonic neoliberal discursive frames of the capitalist society that celebrate competition and promote it as a driver of progress. Moreover, considering the centrality and depth of market economy in regulating every sphere of life, a radical change in one field alone might well bring that field down depriving it of resources and a place in mainstream academia or practice.

Working toward such structural change is important, however, from the normative position. Competition directly contradicts the values of equity, inclusion, and collaboration that conflict resolution claims to promote. It is important, therefore, to start problematizing the competitive and gatekeeping behavior, framing it as unacceptable and contrary to the spirit of the field, exposing such practices. The question of the impact of a competitive behavior of a conflict resolver on the general state of the field is not raised often enough in academic discourses either. A number of authors, particularly those working in the intersection of international development and peacebuilding, have addressed the challenge of decolonization of civil society work in general and peacebuilding in particular. Victoria Fontan is unequivocally critical of peacebuilding led by "western" organizations calling us to consider the destruction and injustices that such efforts bring about, making an argument for nonconventional initiatives for peace (Fontan 2012). Others argue against romanticizing "the local," pointing out that no "local" exists in today's interconnected world untouched by global economic or cultural influence (Richmond 2011). Others yet, without posing an existential challenge to the rights of either international or local actors to exist, look for strategies to develop best practices. Allen warns us against the dangers of exclusive networks and advocates for the value of inclusivity in peacebuilding (Allen Nan 2008), while Anderson develops an extensive systems of checks aimed to ensure that the organizations professing peace or humanitarian values "do no harm" (M. B. Anderson 1999).

Following the above discussion, I call on donor agencies to support emerging voices and particularly the local voices. The big international NGOs and long-established local NGOs perhaps have more effective grant management practices and are easier to work with than the lessor known actors. The former are also culturally intelligible for donors and better positioned to implement longer-term programs in terms of following the established guidelines and procedures, which is critical for sustainable peacebuilding. The support for existing actors, however, should not get to a place where a few NGOs monopolize the field. Such monopolization is not only unethical but also counterproductive as it prevents the formation of a critical mass necessary to change the tide, and it also suffocates the development of the civil society locally.

In sharp contrast to the millions operated by the international NGOs, most local institutions have little resources available to develop institutionally and become sustainable. The very few grants available are small and rarely enough to build an organization. The bigger infrastructural funding provided by the EU, the USAID, and the World Bank is distributed in coordination with the state structures. This leads to the development of organizations registered as NGOs but in practice are supervised by officials and channel the resources away from the development of the independent civil society rather than in its direction. Such organizations are so widespread that even have a name, the oxymoron Governmental Non-Governmental Organizations or GONGOs (Naím 2007).

It is also important to revise the approach where the international NGOs act as perpetual capacity builders and the locals as perpetual capacity receivers. Ongoing growth and capacity-building are certainly necessary for any civil society organization or academic institution, local or international; as the world changes, new research becomes available and new practices are developed. This does not mean, at the same time, that all international NGOs have the necessary capacity or that no local actor is competent. Seth Cohen discusses the power asymmetries, funding challenges, and other crucial dynamics that impact on North–South partnerships as a form of a dependency. Driven by competition over scarce resources and the need to survive, many local actors feel forced to "adjust their mission, objectives, and perhaps even values ... when the local Southern-partners' interests are discarded for the larger political agenda of the foreign or national government that is backing the typically more financially stable Northern-partner" (Cohen 2014, 69). Cohen concludes that the empowerment of local partners requires to giving them, or at least sharing with them, the financial and programmatic control that is typically monopolized by the international NGOs (Cohen 2014). Richmond, similarly, makes the case for a "post-liberal" form of peace, where the international and the local collaborate in developing hybrid institutions that reflect parts of each and where the local has a significant level of agency (Richmond 2011).

With sustainable support directed toward the institutionalization of local civil society actors that follows their capacity-building, international support for peacebuilding can be transformed from the process that privileges some actors over others into a collaborative process of ongoing mutual learning and impactful peacebuilding.

Power struggles within teams

Power struggles take place not only between organizations but also within them, similarly leading to the exclusion, marginalization, and disillusionment of many. And these struggles are rarely waged between equally positioned individuals. My observations, interviews, and focus groups showed that most organizations practicing conflict resolution, as well as specific teams assigned to particular projects are hierarchical, often involving a director and subordinates or a lead facilitator and junior ones. In some cases, the same person can combine a few positions of power (for example, director and lead facilitator), while another one can have a few subordinate positions (for example, administrative assistant and junior facilitator). Those in the subordinate or junior positions are the majority, who come to the field full of enthusiasm and big dreams. If continuously dismissed, overpowered, and marginalized, they eventually lose interest in the field or belief in own ability to influence change.

All the cases shared by my colleagues, many fascinating, were sensitive, and as I write about ongoing initiatives and existing organizations I might unintentionally make both the colleagues I worked with and their co-workers or supervisors recognizable, thus damaging projects and relationships. Therefore, I will bring only two examples in this section, both from my own practice—one from a position of relative powerlessness and the other from the position of relative power. According to my research for this book, both of these cases are fairly representative of experiences faced by practitioners and highlight dilemmas of trying to build an inclusive and empowering team and process.

The first incident took place over a decade ago, when I was an MA student in conflict resolution and a starting facilitator having had only one prior experience of initiating and facilitating a student dialogue. As I conceived a more ambitious PSW program that would involve Turkish and Armenian diaspora community leaders, I understood that I would need the support of experienced colleagues and started networking. My proposal caught the attention of an experienced facilitator affiliated with one of the top universities in the United States. After the initial discussion, she agreed to collaborate. The fundraising was conducted under the name of a well-known center in that top university and with my new colleague listed as the Director. Soon after, we recruited a Turkish facilitator to balance me, as well as another senior colleague from a second major university with whom the Director had years of experience of working together. Once the team was formed and we sat to discuss our roles, the Director informed us that she was, well, the Director and therefore the ultimate decision maker; that, as a Turk and an Armenian, the two of us in the team were necessarily biased and as a result should accept the positions of observer-advisers; that this role, not part of the original PSW design, was added later in the adaptation of the method for facilitators in training. As the Director explained, the observer-advisers are junior members of the facilitation team, often from the conflict sides, who are silent during the dialogue and advise the impartial senior facilitators prior to the dialogue, during the breaks within the dialogue, and during debrief afterwards. The benefit to the observer-adviser was described as educational as they can learn from their senior colleagues in action. After some resistance connected with a more active role I foresaw for myself, as well as with the discomfort of sitting in a three-day event as a silent observer, I decided to trust the experience of my senior colleagues and accepted the challenge. The payment also played a role. As a student, I had few other sources of income and had a hard time renouncing the job and with it the honorarium.

This turned out to be one of the most disempowering experiences in my career as a conflict resolution practitioner. After having invested months of effort into the idea, its design, and the recruitment among the Turkish and Armenian diaspora where my Turkish colleague and I had to spend a considerable social capital, we found ourselves sitting through a few days of intense dialogue literally voiceless. As our contract explicitly stated that we cannot say a word during the process other than when introducing ourselves, we had to watch our friends and colleagues from Turkish and Armenian communities engaging in an emotional journey, at first appealing to us to get into the conversation as they trusted our input. Later they grew increasingly uncomfortable with two silent notetakers who would not utter a word to their open calls to speak up and would only whisper to the senior facilitators during the coffee breaks, keeping their distance from everyone else. The voicelessness turned into an explicit emotional torture toward the end of the dialogue as my relations with the friends and other representatives of the diasporas present started deteriorating to the extent that to date, a number of them refuse to greet me when we cross paths.

There was a learning in this exercise that influenced my future work: I understood the importance of every person in the room having a voice; I learned that I have a strong preference for the horizontality of relations among the team members of a conflict resolution initiative; that the "local" voice in the teams is of great importance and that these are the people who have the most to contribute and the most to lose; that the observer-advisor position is very disempowering and therefore not effective as an educational approach; and that the financial compensation acting as an important motivator for involvement can have a silencing role.

Later in my career, I found myself in situations when I was in the position of relative power compared to my teammates. One instance that particularly stood out and was followed by lengthy reflections was a dialogue for a group of close to 50 participants from Azerbaijan and Armenia organized in 2014 by the Imagine Center. The previous programs we held were smaller, and were usually facilitated by a group of three or four facilitators, consisting of one experienced facilitator from the United States who in some programs would be supported by another "outside" facilitator, as well as one experienced facilitator from Azerbaijan and myself as the facilitator from Armenia. Maintaining horizontality of relations in a smaller team was relatively easy, particularly as time went by and personal and professional trust developed, although it still required ongoing efforts.

In the mentioned dialogue in 2014, however, the team was much bigger. We had developed a winter camp for 50 individuals divided into three dialogue subgroups. The camp, in addition to dialogue, also intended to serve as a training of trainers where the three of us with extensive experience would serve as mentors for six younger team members in their first experience of facilitating a dialogue. Our team involved every single person employed by the Imagine Center at the time, a total of ten people, and was divided among the three dialogue groups each consisting of three people—one Mentor and two Facilitators. The tenth person acted as the internal Evaluator.

Despite our enthusiasm to have the entire organization present in the event, and all the efforts that we had put into the preparation, the facilitation turned out to be stressful and led to more conflicts within our team than any of the previous programs. In two subteams, disagreements and misunderstanding developed between the Mentor and either one or both of the Facilitators in regard to role definitions and responsibilities, as well as in regard to decision making in and outside the dialogue room. During the dialogue, we focused on ensuring that the participants could get the most out of the program, keeping the conflicts latent and did not engage in a deeper reflection until after the program. The post-program reflection helped us identify a number of structural causes that, in combination with relational dynamics, had contributed to the emergence of the conflicts, mostly having to do with role definition, power, and competing hierarchies.

Lukes challenged the one-dimensional view on power as a behavioral attribute that applies to individuals to the extent that they are able to modify the behavior of others. He advanced a multidimensional view, where power in addition to behavioral control can also manifest itself through the ability to shape the agenda or the discourse and the ability to have the powerless act voluntarily against own interest (Lukes 2004). The book called *The Art of Facilitation* operationalizes the concept of multidimensional power in the context of facilitation and identify five types of power: positional power (based on the person's position imposed externally that cannot be revoked by the group), assigned power (position assigned by the group itself and that can be revoked by the group), knowledge power (based on the relevant professional competence of the person), personal power (can be related to the age, gender, charisma, experience, or leadership qualities), and factional power (when a number of people in a group act in coordination) (Hunter, Bailey, and Taylor 1995). While these categories are of course fluid, transformable, and situational, they helped us partially in analyzing the conflicts that took place during the dialogue. Within each of the three subteams each Mentor and Facilitator had an assigned role, at the same time exercising various combinations of power. This could have been beneficial had we been reflective prior to the dialogue about the complementarity of the roles each of us was assigned to play with the experience each of us brought, the positions we held or did not hold in the organization, the prior relationships and other power dynamics. Instead, we simplistically looked only into one power dynamic, prior experience of facilitating dialogues for the Imagine Center or absence of it when assigning the roles of the mentors and facilitators.

The powers people exercised in practice, however, did not always align well with the stated roles. In one of the subteams, the Mentor was a relatively young woman, well-experienced in facilitation, yet a latecomer to the Imagine Center compared to the other two Mentors who were among the founders of the organization. While she also held an institutional position as a board member and co-director, she was not actively involved with the organization for over a year. At the same time, the two Facilitators in her subgroup happened to be the country directors of the Imagine Center in Armenia and Azerbaijan, close friends, and people who conducted prior trainings in the countries, recruited the participants for the dialogue, and had a lasting relationship with them and a strong sense of ownership. The Facilitators, therefore, could exercise positional power as country directors, personal and knowledge power as the recruiters, trainers, and friends of many of the participants, as well as factional power as they acted as a team. In this subgroup, conflicts developed in regard to the interpretation of the role of the Mentor who had the dilemma of having to position herself as the mentor, yet struggling to find voice in the already well-established group of the two Facilitators and the participants who, having prior relationships, in her view disregarded her input. At the same time, from the point of view of the two Facilitators, their Mentor appeared resigned and not willing to invest in her role. During a post-program reflection, the Mentor came to the realization that she should have been explicit about this discomfort at the time and should have requested an open conversation aimed at restoring the relationships, rethinking the roles, and developing a new design that would be beneficial for the entire group. One of the Facilitators, similarly, shared that she had interpreted the initial hesitation by their Mentor as unwillingness to contribute and, being comfortable in her good chemistry with the other Facilitator, did not attempt to reach out to look for a solution. In her words, the conflict "was a consequence of the misunderstanding of the role division and the load of work our roles implied. What I clearly see in our group's dynamics though is factional power [...] because the described situation created a clear division and formed a coalition, which, I agree, we preserved till the end, because in the coalition you feel safer than alone. Thus, there was no attempt from either my or [the other Facilitator's] side to address the issue. There should have been though, clearly. At least because there were two of us and she [the Mentor] was alone. At the time, unfortunately, the absence of our critical awareness of power structures influencing that subteam, combined with the tendency to 'stick to our guns' in a conflict situation, contributed to the marginalization of the Mentor and her inability to contribute fully in that role".

In another subteam, the Mentor was an older man, one of the founders of the Imagine Center, and on multiple occasions in the past, the well-liked trainer of the Facilitators. As a result, he was assumed to exercise considerable personal power within his subgroup. At the time of the program, though, he was working at the Imagine Center only occasionally as a consultant, while one of the two Facilitators, a young woman, was the deputy director of the Imagine Center involved in managing the organization's daily operations, including the implementation of the that very dialogue, and was in charge of hiring the consultants, among them her own Mentor. The other Facilitator in this subteam, also a young woman, was an experienced trainer, a person displaced by the war, a former powerful participant of Imagine Center's initiatives whose personal tragedy, contrasted with her bubbly personality and courage, had inspired the great many of us in the team to stay committed to conflict resolution. She long cooperated with the Center, but never had any organizational role. Unlike the first group, being in different organizational positions and not having a strong prior relationship, the two Facilitators did not act as one team and did not exercise any factional power, yet similar to the first subgroup, here also a misunderstanding developed in regard to the roles in the dialogue. In this group, the Mentor, being conscious of the possibility that his age, experience, gender, and past experience as a trainer of the Facilitator might lead the participants to turn to him marginalizing the Facilitators, assumed a rather distant role from the beginning, aiming to empower the two colleagues who in his view would co-facilitate as a pair. The tactic, however, backfired with the subteam acting as three individuals rather than a team. The Facilitator who had organizational position took responsibility and control over the process and leadership in the room, confused by what she saw at the time as absence of mentorship by the Mentor. As the dialogue progressed, and the Facilitators requested the Mentor to assume a more active role, the mentioned Facilitator and the Mentor started cooperating and alternating in leading the sessions. The second Facilitator, typically a very charismatic trainer, could not find her role in this developing dynamic. She also did not understand the intention of the Mentor to empower them by stepping back. Not having any organizational role, she did not feel that she knew enough about the needs of the program to take leadership into her own hands. When she saw the Mentor and her co-Facilitator alternating in leading sessions, she sat back, and contributed periodically, but felt marginalized. Here too, during the post-program reflections, the Facilitators and Mentor involved took responsibility for their personal actions and discussed how they could have acted differently making the process more effective. Similar to the first case, the absence of a process for developing timely awareness and addressing the power dynamics contributed to a confused relationship among (a) the Mentor struggling to strike a balance where he can be helpful without dominating, (b) one Facilitator who was also the deputy director and felt responsible for the program and as a result ended up dominating, and (c) another Facilitator without an organizational role who in the process, lost voice and became increasingly marginalized.

The third subteam involved me as the Mentor. Similar to my colleague mentoring the previous group, I was also an older man and one of the founders. Different from him, however, I was now a board member and the acting executive director of the organization. As a result, I was seen as exercising a series of powers: positional power as the director, assigned power as a Mentor, knowledge power as an experienced facilitator, and personal power as an older man who in the past trained almost everyone in the group of facilitators. One of the Facilitators in this subteam, an experienced woman, was the development director of the Imagine Center, a key position in the organization, yet subordinate to mine. While the second Facilitator did not have any organizational role, the two Facilitators happened to be close friends and acted as a team, exercising factional power that prevented the marginalization of the Facilitator without a positional role. In this subteam, the Facilitators requested for all three of us to work as a team and co-facilitate together with the learning happening in action. We further divided the roles where the Facilitators would take the lead in the majority of the sessions and I, as the Mentor, could back them up periodically, but not intrusively. At the same time, I would take the lead in some of the most challenging sessions with the two Facilitators backing me up. I would also facilitate the evening's reflection of the subteam where we planned the next day's sessions. Conflicts in this subteam were rare and quickly addressed and we worked effectively.

The relative calm in the last subteam could not be explained strictly by conflict-averse behavior of individuals, a possibility that we considered. Structures mattered. We have been known to have conflicts in the Imagine Center's team, including one between myself and the development director who was one of the Facilitators in the current subteam. This time we managed to avoid the conflict as we were well aware of the existing power dynamics and managed them proactively.

However, we were much less aware of the power dynamics that crossed over the boundaries of the subteams, affecting particularly strongly the big team meetings that we conducted once a day and that involved all 10 of us. If in our particular subteam, we had no miscommunications in regard to my role, in the bigger team we had. There factions were formed differently, further strengthening those with positional roles in the organization vis-a-vis those with assigned project-based roles, many of whom became marginalized in the process. As we understood only after the program, I carried too much power compared to everyone else as I combined the roles of the co-founder, at the time the executive director of the organization, an older man who trained most of the younger facilitators involved. With my power unchecked, I had the ability to overrule any other individual, including the other two Mentors. As a result, when in big team meetings, we would discuss the work and conflicts in individual subteams, and each of us was sharing opinions about self and others, the voices we had were not equal and mine carried disproportionate weight further disturbing the already fragile balance of powers in the subteams. This dynamic became clear during the post-dialogue reflections, when we understood that the assumed role division of three equally positioned Mentors and six equally positioned Facilitators did not take into consideration all other power dynamics present in the team and subteams.

The two cases discussed above were reflective of dynamics in other teams as well. Hierarchical relations and power dynamics were always present and had a strong potential to marginalize and disempower. This was particularly true in NGOs that espoused a business-model and were highly hierarchical. There the mid- and lower-ranked colleagues consistently complained about the lack of voice, input, interest, or motivation and communicated intention to leave the position once there was an opportunity. The well-functioning teams where the team members felt valued and motivated showed a high degree of awareness of power dynamics and made conscious efforts toward balancing powers and relationships and valuing the input of all core team members.

Of course, the problems with hierarchies are not unique to the conflict resolution field. But here too, I am convinced that our field, one that strives to bring social justice to societies it works with, should lead by example. The questions I try to answer next, therefore, are: is it possible to build a nonhierarchical team or organization? Can it be effective or viable in a world where hierarchy is the norm? Or can hierarchy and other power relations remain but be managed in a way that everyone is valued and the team culture is cooperative? Will such efforts change the quality of the programs delivered?

Addressing marginalization within teams

Similar to the competition between the organizations in the field, the competition within teams affects the perception of conflict resolution for everyone involved. Hierarchy and other power differentials also affect the relations and the atmosphere within the organizations leading to cynicism and resentment. As I showed in the example of the Imagine Center's team management of a large dialogue that involved 10 team members, the roles of mentors and facilitators in training assigned for the management of a particular initiative came into conflict with the administrative hierarchy of the organization. Remaining unacknowledged and unaddressed through the duration of the dialogue, these dynamics sabotaged the work of the previously harmonious team.

In his longitudinal study of what helps or prevents the Israeli and Palestinian alumni of dialogue programs led by the NGO Seeds of Peace to stay engaged in peacebuilding, Lazarus cites the organizational conflicts within the Seeds of Peace as one of the reasons for the young people's disappointment in conflict resolution work in general. One of his interviewees commented: "One devastating result was that the 'Seeds of Peace' management and staff, all of whom work for an organization that exists to teach respectful dialogue and treatment of others, ironically did not enact these codes-of-conduct with one another" (Lazarus 2011, 404). The sentiment was repeated by one former participant of Seeds of Peace after another, explaining their feeling of alienation and apathy.

The norms of behavior of conflict organizations and individuals involved in conflict resolution are critical to the sustainability of the field. These norms should be reflective of the values we promote. Whether it is our intention or not, we serve as role models to those who we invite to join us in conflict resolution work. This is particularly true when it comes to the initiatives engaging youth. As Lazarus shows on the example of the Seeds of Peace, and as I saw through the process of this research, when the initiators do not practice what they preach, those initially motivated to commit to conflict resolution often develop cynicism and disappointment.

It is critical, therefore, for the organizations and individuals committed to conflict resolution work to be aware of their own behavior and norms, work continually and intentionally on fostering collaborative and inclusive relationships and environments, expanding rather than constraining the reach of the field and building toward a critical mass.

This PAR revealed a few key dynamics that motivated the peacebuilders to stay involved with an organization. Those who felt valued, empowered, and motivated identified the following dynamics as key to making a workplace a cooperative and inclusive place:

- the management of hierarchy and power;
- a clear role distribution and a team culture built around the needs and strengths of the members;
- a near-absence of micro-management and the presence of transparency;
- and space for sharing frustration and managing conflict, as well as providing acknowledgement and recognition.

The *management of hierarchical relations and other power dynamics* was seen as perhaps the most critical component of building a cooperative team. The teams where members felt happy, accomplished, secure, and fully realizing their potential had the same common characteristics.

Some of them were nonhierarchical. This applied primarily to smaller organizations with a team of 2–5 members. Others that were bigger than that, yet had no more than 15–20 team members, had nonhierarchical relationships within the core team. In the bigger organizations, there were usually team members who were not satisfied with the relationships; the most satisfied colleagues who worked in low- and medium-ranked position in big organizations were those who work without direct supervision and in relative independence. All of the diverse cases above had one characteristic in common: absence of direct supervision over daily activities. Although fewer, there were also those who had supervisors and felt happy and fulfilled: these were either individuals who recently started at entry-level positions and felt that the work allows them to learn and grow or those whose supervisors acted as mentors or friends and not as bosses.

At the Imagine Center, for a number of years, we believed the solution to be in building a team that was altogether nonhierarchical. After the initial power struggle, we adopted a nonhierarchical framework that worked for us between 2008 and 2010 when the team consisted of only three co-founders who had an equal decision-making power and were acting through a consensus, and between 2010 and 2012 when one of the co-founders left and a new team member stepped in. As the organization grew, however, some of the initial team members left, and a number of new colleagues joined in, sustaining nonhierarchical relations and consensus-based decision making became challenging. This led to the rethinking of our organizational culture once in 2013–2014, when the team grew in numbers thanks to former participants joining the Imagine Center and initiating their own projects; and the second time in 2015–2016, when a new group, this time of established professionals, joined the team allowing Imagine to engage in new directions of work, but also bringing in diverse organizational cultures. That we were working long-distance and at our peak, had team members based in eight different countries, made the task even more challenging.

With communication taking place mainly online, and consensus building on every topic becoming very time consuming, we changed our approach and aimed to institute not a hierarchy but a role-division with people responsible for a particular direction of work having the deciding voice in regard to that direction. At the same time, the power had to be kept in check to avoid domination and not to disenfranchise any core team member. To do this, we eventually abolished the position of co-directors that gave disproportionate power to those holding the roles. One of the co-directors stepped out all together to pursue a different career path, maintaining her position on the board but not in the management, and I (as the second co-director) assumed the position of the director of programs, responsible for the development of new projects and fundraising for them, as well as for the methodological design of the existing initiatives. Other core team members assumed the roles of country directors for Turkey, Azerbaijan, Armenia, and Georgia, as well as the positions of the development director and the methodological director. We also have had project managers, often from within the same group. Therefore, each person has primary responsibility and decision-making power for her or his direction of work or area, while working in close coordination with the rest. As different directions of work or projects gain priority, the team would shift enough people-power to support the particular person in fulfilling the task. When power struggles still arise, the agreement has been to discuss them openly first between the people involved, and if needed within the larger team. Maintaining open communication and conflict resolution mechanisms long-distance, however, has been challenging, and we have had to use every opportunity to meet in person in advance of workshops or stay for a day or two longer and work on maintaining the team.

Asked whether the structural hierarchy affects the friendships, one colleague noted that most relationships, including friendships, are hierarchical as well: age, gender, social standing, personal insecurity, and other dynamics create a power differential, and not only at work. The solution, therefore, in not in the complete absence of hierarchy, but in the acknowledgement of the power dynamics and use of it for the benefit of everyone involved. The role of a mentor and a friend was cited as an example of a role that the older and more experienced colleague at a higher position in the organization could assume, instead of that of a boss.

While having no supervisor or having a supervisor as a mentor/friend, and having space to learn was deemed important, this alone was not enough to make a cooperative and inclusive team. The cases where the team members loved their work, felt empowered and motivated had in common also a *clear role distribution in the team, built around the personal and professional strengths of each team member*, complemented by a *near-absence of micro-management* and enough independent decision-making space when it comes to the fulfillment of tasks for each team member; informal relations and often friendships with those in hierarchically higher positions; and space to have one's voice heard and safety to challenge anyone's decisions. The colleagues who worked in cooperative environments said that they do not think of the persons in hierarchically higher positions as their bosses. To quote one colleague at an entry-level position who said about the head of the organization: "[…] He just wants to get things done; he never commands or sounds commanding. He never shows that he is the boss; he is equal to the others. However busy he might be, he always has a moment to engage with or help others. That does not mean we let him do all the work. Seeing how he works, I also do all I can, and only then ask for help." Others worked best in environments where they were on the first name basis with everyone, and where superiors were mentors or friends, the work was fun, and the responsibility and enthusiasm for the mission and efforts was shared.

Another key dynamic that differentiated cooperative and inclusive teams from others was the *transparency*, both in access to people and information and in decision making. A colleague from Armenia recalled her shock when she started her fellowship in a big media organization in the Netherlands. The first thing she noticed were the open doors and that any team member could approach any other at any time, including the head of the organization. Related, she was surprised by the involvement of the fellows in the "big-picture" conversations on a regular basis. This contrasted sharply with her experience in the South Caucasus, where to reach even a medium-level manager or ask a question about the strategic direction of the organization, one would have to go through a number of "doors," both figuratively and literally.

Primarily the benefits of transparency were discussed in the context of decision making. Colleagues, at varying levels of organizational hierarchy, who felt that they had adequate information and adequate voice, were comfortable with the decisions made in the organization. When the process of decision making was clear and transparent, the team members were often comfortable even when they disagreed with the decision. At one rather extreme example, a recently laid-off colleague expressed appreciation for the organization's practices and for the transparent way that particular decision was made, with a six-month-long advance notice, conditioned by loss of a stream of revenue that affected her particular position, and with a prospect of getting rehired.

The transparency and space for open communication were linked to another important pattern—*space to safely share and address frustrations and resolve conflicts and miscommunication*. Some teams had specific procedures devoted to this, others dealt with this on an ad hoc basis. In both cases though, the team members felt responsibility to address any frustration they had directly and constructively, and were confident in the rest of the team in supporting them in this.

As important as it is to create space for open expression and resolution of conflict for building inclusive and cooperative teams, it is just as important to share acknowledgments and recognition, ensuring that each team member feels valued for her efforts and contributions. At the Imagine Center we have long developed a "clearing session" where potential conflicts are surfaced and resolved is followed by an acknowledgment session.

Chapter conclusions

This study suggests that when organizations in conflict resolution field engage gatekeeping, competition, and monopolization, they sabotage the trust of populations toward the field and reduce the impact of their own work. And yet such practices are presently the norm. Not surprisingly, in my interactions with the major donors funding conflict resolution efforts in the South Caucasus, they often cited the visible lack of expansion of the civil society and building of a critical mass despite years of investment, and the confinement of conflict resolution work to the small circle of international NGOs as one of the main reasons of losing interest and belief in nonofficial efforts. The competition for resources and the effective squeezing out of "competition," ironically, did not benefit even these active competitors in the long-run as it had led to the shrinking of the resources available.

My study showed also that the sustainability of the conflict resolution efforts is closely linked to the culture of the organization in handling the relationships within it as well as its relations with other organizations, a conclusion supported also by the research of Lazarus. When we invite people from across the conflict divide with a history of violence to give a chance to cooperation, inclusivity, and mutual respect, without practicing these in our own organization or in the relations between organizations, it is not only hypocritical but also visible, disappointing, and disillusioning to those we invite. The businesslike relations between organizations based on a competition for resources and mutual sabotage hamper the development of the field and its impact. And to the contrary, teams that practice what they preach attract strong following.

Chapter 9
Lessons learned

In today's violent world, the relatively young field of conflict resolution is struggling to make a tangible difference or find enough recognition and traction in affairs concerning conflicts. It is tempting to blame this apparent shortcoming on various "others" to the field, such as the grip of the military-industrial complex or the realist school of international relations on policymaking. However, a critical look inside exposes many contradictions internal to the field. These contradictions result in mass exclusion and marginalization, as well as the reproduction of the conflict frames and should be addressed for conflict resolution to stand on solid foundation and offer alternatives that are inclusive, conceptually sound, and comprehensive. These contradictions are the most pronounced precisely in the constructivist wing of conflict resolution where many authors and practitioners actively critical of positivist approaches routinely use exclusionary essentialist frames in their own writing and designs.

One key learning from the research conducted for this book has been that many of the challenges in building inclusive and effective conflict resolution initiatives, while certainly not easy to overcome, are also not unsurmountable. The practitioners I worked with were able not only to identify patterns of marginalization, exclusion, and conflict reproduction but also to conceptualize and test alternative and inclusive methods that rely on evolving intervention designs. Some of the alternatives, particularly the convening of PSWs without preconceived sides, were well tested in a few cycles of reflection and action through the life of this research. Learning from adjacent fields of CDA and critical studies of nationalism has been particularly helpful in building alternative practices that were consistently constructivist in language and frames. For other patterns, particularly those identified later in the research as was the gender binary, we were able to design conceptual alternatives, but they remained only partially tested. Many of these patterns warrant a further research and testing in practice as outlined in the "Questions for further research" section below. I see a strong need in the conflicts I work on to experiment with alternatives, criticize and reflect on them, conceptualize new ones, and develop effective and holistic approaches able to transform relations, for the conflict resolution field to leave its paradoxically marginal position in the wider conversation on the phenomenon of conflict.

I start this final chapter with a section called "Reflection," meant as a summary of conceptual learning and findings of this book. The "Reflection" section is followed by the "Action" section, the discussion of some specific changes made in conflict resolution initiatives led by the practitioners at the Imagine Center and other colleagues working in the Syrian and Nagorno-Karabakh conflict contexts who aimed at building more inclusive approaches based on learning from the reflection and action cycles of the current research. I recognize that every conflict context and every particular initiative has its own sets of circumstances and challenges, and, therefore, what worked for us is presented here not as a blueprint or a toolkit for others to replicate, but as a conversation starter that can stimulate other practitioners in engaging in their own reflection and changes.

I conclude the chapter and with it the book with a set of new questions identified during this research that require further research and experimentation in practice.

Reflection: the learning and the key findings

I started this research with the assumption that marginalization and exclusion of affected populations were rare and unfortunate occurrences in conflict resolution practice, primarily conditioned by the overreliance of the field on the binary frames of international relations. The process of this research, however, led me to the gradual realization that the problem was deeper and not limited to the influence of international relations on conflict resolution practice. Other macro-frames, such as the hetero-normative binary, as well as processes pertinent to conflict resolution practices themselves also manifested patterns of marginalization and exclusion that led to perpetuation of conflict discourses.

This book begins with a critical review of conflict resolution theories that conceptualize the phenomenon of conflict and prescribes respective solutions. The most dominant trends in literature pertaining to conflict, the realist and liberal schools of international relations that follow the positivist paradigm, despite their overt differences, share many base assumptions. Among others, they propose a rigid understanding of conflict as a confrontation between well-defined sides, privileging the actors at the two extremes of the conflict continuum and forcing the rest to either join one of the extremes or remain voiceless. The mainstream conflict resolution literature, despite proclaiming itself as an alternative to international relations, simultaneously positions itself as a complement to the official track, effectively borrowing the terms of reference from international relations and reproducing its discourse. I then shift to constructivist and postmodernist literature, which offers conceptual alternatives to such a rigid understanding of conflict, helps transform the language through which we understand conflict, and yet up to date, remains primarily theoretical and underutilized in conflict resolution practice.

The postmodernist lens through which I approached this research led me toward nontraditional research methodologies that would help me to look critically at the discourses I myself, as a scholar-practitioner, and my colleagues were embedded in. I adopted PAR as a method that flips the traditional relationship between the researcher and the research allowing not only me to investigate the assumptions and practices of others but also to others to investigate my assumptions and my practices. The reflection and action cycles of the PAR provided a framework for my colleagues and me for designing theoretical alternatives to the practices we identified as problematic and testing them in real-life initiatives before returning to the reflection space.

The research for this book also provided a space for a methodological innovation, collective auto-ethnography, where the self-reflective critical inquiry was conducted by a team of colleagues and not an individual researcher. Chapters 6–8, and particularly Chapter 5 on the NK Analytic Initiative that provide a close-up look at real-life conflict resolution effort with all its aspirations and challenges, are all a result of this collective auto-ethnographic inquiry. They uncover disturbing patterns of exclusion and marginalization of key populations affected by conflicts and of perpetuation of conflict narratives in these successful from the standpoint of achieving their stated goals initiatives.

Chapter 4 devoted to a Syrian dialogue is the centerpiece around which this book is built, and details the challenges of applying conventional methods of conflict resolution practice in an evolving conflict environment.

I devoted Chapters 6–8 to uncovering further patterns that contribute to exclusion, marginalization, and reproduction of conflict discourses, and to building alternative frames and intervention designs. Chapter 6 looks into the patterns perpetuated by the influence of macro-frames of international relations. Chapter 7 explores marginalization of participants through the formation of dominant discourses within conflict resolution practice. Chapter 8 looks into the competition and domination between and within organizations practicing conflict resolution. Such patterns, present at every stage of conflict resolution interventions, ranged from the framing of the conflict followed by respective intervention designs that privilege the violent extremes to selection biases and to further exclusion and marginalization within the initiative of those who are not part of one or another dominant discourse. In each chapter, the analysis of patterns that contribute to marginalization and perpetuation of conflicts was followed by the discussion of possible conceptual and practical alternatives based on Evolving Designs methodology that can promote inclusive and transformative conflict resolution.

The routine binary framing of conflicts as an affair that includes defined "sides" borrowed from the international relations paradigms emerges as the key problem in conflict resolution theory and practice that leads to the reproduction of the conflict and its intractability. These binary frames are normalized today to the extent that it is hard to conceive or describe conflicts in any other terms. Yet there is nothing natural or permanent about such framing or understanding of conflicts, even on the policy level. There is no inherent reason why policymaking itself should be limited to the realist paradigm. As pointed out by Avruch, the dominance of realism even within the international relations field is a relatively recent phenomenon, and a consequence of the disillusionment in Wilsonian idealism and the liberal approaches in the aftermath of World War II (Avruch 2012, 141). Further, policymaking, the approach toward and the act of managing intra- and interstate relations, should not be confused with the field of international relations, liberal or realist. International relations is one of the many possible theories for approaching policymaking. Acknowledging this and advancing alternative frameworks is clearly challenging. The groups in power who benefit from the status quo are rarely keen on adapting emancipatory approaches that might question their power.

Despite this resistance in any specific time-period, on a larger scale, paradigms, epistemologies, and meaning-making mechanisms have been in constant transition and are subject to ongoing contestations. Instead of acting as an uncritical follower, the conflict resolution field is well positioned for leading the charge in contesting the meaning and the mechanisms of conflict and conflict resolution. And the challenge I suggest is not to policymaking itself, but specifically to the primacy of the war-reproducing realist approach to policymaking, as well as the inefficient liberal approach to policymaking. Constructivist, reflective, and critical frames might seem complicated for today's political systems that function on the basis of two-page briefs and public-opinion polls. Yet these oversimplified procedures are not only irresponsible, but judging from the dismal standards of international or interstate affairs of practically any state, also spectacularly ineffective.[24]

The shifting of paradigms does not need to start at the policy level. The conflict resolution field itself has a road to traverse in incorporating the existing alternatives to the realist paradigm into its lexicon and practice. Further, my appeal is not to the positivist wing of conflict resolution, whose theory and practice are internally coherent. My appeal is to the constructivists in the field as we have a claim to representing a challenge to the established models of thinking; yet our

---

24 Hundreds of millions of people live in poverty, including in liberal democracies; climate change is reaching a point of no-return; migration is endemic and mismanaged; societies grow multi-cultural resulting not in rich diversity but far-right backlash and violent conflicts that involve both intra-state bloodshed and active geo-political rivalry. The list goes on, with no policy options in sight.

practices conform with these same models as we accept the binary frames and terms such as "Track 2 diplomacy."

During my research, I found that in principle many of my colleagues share my criticism of conflict resolution as we have it and conceptually agree with the need for developing constructivist alternatives. At the same time many are inclined to stay with the tested if imperfect methods as their skepticism toward the effectiveness of alternatives is strong. One reason for skepticism that I often hear is that developing new approaches can take decades. Yet we do not need to invent entirely new approaches. Alternatives are long available, some of them not implying binary opposition, such as peacebuilding or conflict transformation. In practice, currently, these might not be very different from "Track 2 diplomacy" and might represent terms used interchangeably to describe the similar nongovernmental efforts aimed at complementing official negotiations. Yet they have the potential to forge an independent path. Peacebuilding means efforts toward the establishment of harmonious, equitable relations within, between, and beyond societies. Conflict transformation suggests the transformation of not only the relationship between the actors but the transformation of the actors themselves. None of these imply a binary division or diplomacy as a process.

Other skeptics argue that the actors we have today and the relations between them might have been socially constructed, but they are here now, they are real, and our task is to deal with what we have. This approach is based on the implicit assumption that we are at the end of the long road of historical transformations that culminated in the present-day identities and their interrelations, and these identities are here to stay in the form they have now. Yet the formation, reformation, and transformation of actors, relationships, and identities are ongoing processes and continue as I write these words. Ethnicity was conceptualized or institutionalized as a state-forming instrument as late as in the early nineteenth century; states have been transformed from city-states to empires to republics to political-economic unions in different times; most of the nations that are members of the UN today are recent constructs, as is the UN itself; Syria, discussed here, is disintegrating before our eyes; the European Union and the entire liberal order seem very vulnerable; and today's militant ethno-nations of the South Caucasus, ironically, emerged right out of the cocoon of the presumed post-nation-state communist utopia. And there is hardly any reason to believe that these transformations are about to stop, neither that they have to be necessarily violent. We have witnessed the positive transformation of long-standing conflictual relations in Europe in the late twentieth century followed by political and economic integration; we have seen the parallel descent into violence and fragmentation of the Balkans and the South Caucasus resulting also in the transformation of actors, identities, and relationships.

Further, not only do actors and identities transform, but so do the paradigms through which we understand the world and conflict. Instead of reproducing the readily available frames and reacting to processes initiated for us by conflict promoting discourses, our field should be at the forefront of articulating alternative visions and leading to positive transformation. Examples of visions that laid a path for transformation are many: from the ideas behind the French and American revolutions to Gandhi's philosophy of nonviolence, Martin Luther King's "dream," and the vision for the European Union. These groups and individuals did not play by the rules; they created the rules. It is time for conflict resolution to leave the shadow of international relations and cast its own light.

Action: Evolving Designs
in Imagine Center's recent initiatives

The PAR process contributed to learning from conflict resolution practices that my colleagues and I have been engaged in and in turn influenced these very practices. The examples chosen here to illustrate changes to the conflict resolution practice of the Imagine Center in direction of Evolving Designs are that of a recent Dialogue for civil society actors and a recent phase of the NK Analytic Initiative that has been transformed into the Regional Analytic Initiative aimed at contributing to policy-level thinking. I chose these two here as illustrative examples, as they are the direct descendants of the two initiatives described in depth in Chapters 4 and 5 and consequently best positioned to showcase the transformation of our approaches.

One major change concerned the framing of the conflicts and the initiatives. As a result of this research and other reflective conversations, we, at the Imagine Center, have been moving away from framing the conflicts in binary ethnic terms. Related, when naming the initiatives, one alternative has been to name them after the problem that we are aiming to address or the processes through which we are trying to address these problems rather than the ethnicity of the participants. The latest dialogue initiatives we conducted, which would previously be named as "Armenian-Azerbaijani Dialogues" or similar, now carry activity or method names such as "School of Conflict Transformation," or "Joint Platform for Realistic Peace in Nagorno-Karabakh." The change in framing had an immediate effect on the recruitment: if an "Armenian-Azerbaijani Dialogue" sounds exclusive and encourages applications only from people identifying as one or the other ethnicity, the issue-based "Joint Platform for Realistic Peace in Nagorno-Karabakh" communicates openness to those who can contribute to the topic, irrespective of their ethnic or national background.

We have been intentional in building an inclusive recruitment process during our latest South Caucasus-wide Dialogue for journalists held in November 2015. We made it explicit in the call for applications that the program is open for residents of the South Caucasus of all backgrounds. Further, we reached out to regions and not only capitals, encouraging the participation of those whose voice is rarely heard in dialogue initiatives. This required making efforts during the selection process toward the recruitment of applicants from outside the capitals whose resumes were considerably less impressive, lacked prestigious diplomas, and were often written in broken English or Russian. The journalists from outside the capitals were far from geopolitics and have been writing primarily about life in the regions, bringing to the table the everyday experience of people who are most hard-hit by the conflicts and often ignored. Our efforts paid off, and we had participants of diverse backgrounds and from all parts of the South Caucasus, including from the Javakheti and Kvemo Kartli regions of Georgia and from the Georgian villages adjacent to South Ossetia, later also from the Georgian villages in South Ossetia.

During the Dialogue itself, as I already discussed in Chapters 4 and 6 on the examples of groups from Syria and Turkey respectively, the methodology was amended and Emerging Designs employed. Traditionally, PSWs bring together two sides of the conflict, and ask each side to reflect on and share the needs, fears, concerns, and hopes of their society, later jointly looking into solutions that could satisfy the needs of both sides. As I argued in this book, such a binary approach affects the selection excluding affected groups from the conflict regions that do not identify with any of the two "sides." Further, such an approach effectively asks those present in the workshop to construct and present to the "Other" a unified narrative of "one's own side," thus pushing the participants to perform the roles of a "side." In the Syrian dialogue described in Chapter 4, we did not divide the participants into predetermined groups and did not ask them to represent the generic needs of their entire society. Instead, we worked with the group to codesign a methodology that would work for their context. We asked them first to identify the range of groups affected by the conflict, and after mapping these, to self-identify with the group whose views each colleague present in the room would like to represent during the particular event. We conducted a similar self-identifying exercise in the November 2015 Dialogue in the context of the South Caucasus conflicts. The change might seem to be that of a nuance, moreover, each element of it is not new as such as mapping or self-identifying are methods used by many practitioners and well-discussed in conflict resolution literature. Yet the combination of these methods aimed at encouraging inclusivity that started with an inclusive selection, followed by giving those present the voice in mapping the conflict and then positioning themselves in it, transforms the conversation as evident from two meetings facilitated with these changes in methodology and described above. The mapping exercise in the Syrian dialogue in 2013 ended up with over 40 stakeholders. Further, asking the colleagues to self-identify with the groups they would like to represent and to form factions with others of similar views creates some unexpected configurations that can vary from meeting to meeting, even in the context of the same conflict. The 40 stakeholders identified initially were consolidated eventually into Assad Supporters, Rebels, Civil Society, and Minorities. In the South Caucasus conflicts context, the self-identifying exercise held in November 2015 led the group to break into ten stakeholders, some represented by a single individual as only 16 colleagues were taking part in the initiative. These stakeholders were diverse, ranging from the Georgian Progressive Youth to the Society of South Ossetia and the Azerbaijani Displaced Population. The picture painted through the discussion of the needs of a multiplicity of groups with whom the colleagues present self-identify is substantially more nuanced than the one painted in the two-sided initiative. In a more nuanced configuration, many of those who in the binary setting would find themselves in the opposite sides end up in the same group, as was the case in the Syrian dialogue when the Civil Society and Minorities groups involved colleagues from both sides of the Assad-opposition binary.

Our facilitation process has also become more conscious of the likely formation of factions and dominant discourses resulting in marginalization. In the Syrian case, those on the two militant extremes, the Assad supporters and the rebels, enjoyed an immediate discursive advantage provided by the initial binary format of the PSW and the discourse of conflict sides. As we abandoned the rigid two-sided format for a more evolving and inclusive one, the Civil Society faction emerged uniting the voices of those who were advancing the vision of civic solidarity and Syrian unity and drawing power from the discourse of a civic patriotism. Thanks to facilitation conscious of the marginalizing dynamics, a number of those who initially aligned themselves with either Assad Supporters, Rebels, or Civil Society yet felt marginalized in these groups, eventually united to form the Minorities faction capitalizing on the international human rights discourse and enjoying the backing of the Civil Society group and sympathy from both the Rebels and the Assad Supporters.

Gender-based marginalization is also prevalent and needs to be addressed in most initiatives, although the dynamics vary greatly from one context to another. In groups with strong feminist voices present or the facilitators encouraging open and taboo-free communication, the gender dynamics in the initiative can be brought into the open and addressed transparently. In my experience, when the topic is discussed openly and explicitly, the holders of overtly sexist attitudes usually find themselves in an overwhelming minority. Further, once called out and not suppressed, the gender dynamics tend to remain as an ongoing topic of conversation. In cases with no strong feminist voices present, the facilitators might assume that voice.

To summarize the lessons from the application of learning in civil society dialogue contexts: when in the name of ensuring the effectiveness of the conflict resolution effort we rely on binary and rigid frames, exclude many of those affected by the conflict, privilege the nationalist extremes, dismiss sexist and other marginalizing behavior as irrelevant, we further minimize the appeal of conflict resolution for those affected by violence and turn it into another instrument of the reproduction of the existing conflict discourses and power relations. And to the contrary, employing Evolving Designs open to input from the participants, reframing the conflicts, including those typically excluded, and challenging the power relations open new horizons for what is possible and what previously could not be seen.

Applying Evolving Designs to transform projects that have a political focus, such as the NK Analytic Initiative of Chapter 5, showed to be considerably more challenging compared to civil society dialogues. A fully inclusive recruitment is harder to imagine in such cases as the focus on policy requires the presence of professionals from respective disciplines and politicians. What we found possible, however, was the considerable expansion and diversification of the identity and belonging, the professional background, and the political positions of those involved. Further, when full inclusion proved difficult, we ensured the absence of intentional or politically motivated exclusion safeguarding that no one, who would be invited otherwise, is excluded based on their ethnicity, political views, gender, or other identity markers. Increasing the diversity and avoiding politically motivated exclusions required a significant expansion of the number of colleagues engaged in the NK turned Regional Analytic Initiative and we went from 12 to 18 people we invited to the past iterations of the initiative to over 25. The expansion of the professional and personal background of the colleagues involved contributed to an out-of-the-box thinking and immediately revealed the nonsensical nature of the stale state-imposed exclusionary frames that we had been struggling with from the beginning of the NK Analytic Initiative in 2008 and until recently. If during these initial years, the initiative included only policy analysts and government advisers, currently it includes analysts, journalists, economists, as well as scholar-practitioners from the fields of history, sociology, anthropology, and gender studies, all from an extended regional geography.

Similar to the recent Dialogue initiatives, the transition away from the binary framing of the conflict and the related expansion of the profile of the colleagues involved resulted in a much more nuanced language in describing the Nagorno-Karabakh conflict, as well as the other conflicts in the South Caucasus. Factions were formed along professional lines or based on shared topical interests rather than ethnic or national identity. With a diverse group involved in the conversation as stakeholders, maintaining the structure of the discussions along the "us vs. them" lines proved to be much harder as many of those present did not self-identify with any "side." Instead, the conflicts were analyzed from the position of the various fields in which the colleagues present in the room had expertise. To ensure that marginalization embedded in the gender discourses is addressed, we included feminist researchers in the group. Their presence ensured that gender relations were openly addressed during the meetings and named as one of the key cultural dynamics that contribute to the perpetuation of the culture of militant masculinity in the South Caucasus.

After a number of dynamics that influence the conflicts in the South Caucasus were identified, they were broken into specific research topics requiring further exploration. Working groups were formed to collaborate on each of the following three blocks:

- a politico-economic block with three interlinked topics: analysis of global and regional actors in the South Caucasus, analysis of the politics of isolation and self-isolation, and economic benefits of regional cooperation;
- a block focused on human rights, including: analysis of ethnic groups and conflicts in the South Caucasus and Turkey with a focus on majority-minority dynamics, followed by a discussion of minority rights as an instrument of conflict resolution,

transformation of gender relations as an instrument of conflict resolution, and case studies of minority language schools in Georgia, as well as South Ossetia;
- and a final and integrative solution-focused block that discusses the possibilities of federative solutions to conflict resolution, as well as nonstate integration processes.

If in the past, the NK Analytic Initiative focused primarily on the international relations dimension of the conflict, the current approach helped us identify a range of dynamics, all of which are critical for the more nuanced understanding of the conflict. Topical transnational teams of co-authors were formed around each topic, and close to ten analytic papers were published on the *Caucasus Edition*, the periodical of the Imagine Center. Interestingly, the initiative presently has promise not because it unites like-minded individuals, but to the contrary, because it provides an inclusive frame in which diverse colleagues with differing perspectives can collaborate constructively. It is precisely that diversity that allows us to put the pieces of the kaleidoscope together drawing a complex and multicolored picture of the conflict and what is needed for resolution.

An important achievement of this new framing and more inclusive design of the Regional Analytic Initiative was the visible absence of previously persistent ethnic divisions and adversarial positioning, even despite a major escalation in the zone of the Nagorno-Karabakh conflict in April 2016. Conversely, it was the clear division into sides resulting in the exclusion and marginalization of nonconforming voices within each side that had kept the NK Analytic Initiative in stagnation for years. With the new design, the colleagues engaged have been collaborating extensively and the ground is set for developing the initiative into a permanent transnational virtual think tank. That had long been the goal of the NK Analytic Initiative, yet for years, it remained elusive, due to the ongoing confrontations between the participants from the conflict "sides."

Questions for further research

While proud of certain progress in developing inclusive programming in the context of the Imagine Center's and other colleagues' work achieved through adoption of the Evolving Designs, I acknowledge that we are only at the beginning stages of critically reassessing our own language and discourse and our own contribution to the perpetuation of marginalization and conflicts. Many questions pertaining to conflict resolution practice remain open, and even more remain well-hidden from our sight in the collective blind spots of the conflict resolution field.

An example of a question called into the open is the formation of dominant discourses and related factions within initiatives that results in marginalization. This can be successfully mitigated through the development of awareness by the conflict resolution practitioners and the intentional introduction of additional factions or through bringing the challenge into the open. At the same time, the ability of practitioners to recognize the presence and marginalizing influence of external discourses and to address them is severely constrained as we are all part of the society and embedded in these discourses ourselves. As critical theory comes closest to exposing structures that contribute to marginalization and oppression, a closer and trans-disciplinary engagement with postcolonial studies, critical race theory, critical feminist theory, CDA, and others could contribute to building the necessary awareness of discourses of marginalization in the field of conflict resolution that are hidden from view.

A further challenge is posed by the attempts to develop inclusive practices within conflict resolution organizations. Some of the smaller teams have been successful in this, through practices that involved the elimination of hierarchy and the establishment of clear roles and responsibilities, open communication, and the absence of micro-management. However, can these approaches work in larger organizations? If not, what could an inclusive and effective team within a larger organization or a university look like?

Finally, the marginalizing patterns I found hardest to address have been the business-like practices in the field of conflict resolution, such as competition, monopolization of resources, gate-keeping, and others deeply entrenched in the modern-day bureaucracy that fit well with the dominant neoliberal discourse. My research showed that the damage done by such practices is great and hinders the development of local civil society in conflict zones, contributes to cynicism and disillusionment among the donors and the participants, and harms the name of conflict resolution. A great many colleagues from conflict zones stressed the need to end the dominance of the field by big international NGOs, expanding the local presence in conflict resolution practice, and institutionalizing the civil society in the conflict zones with the external actors acting as a support group, forming peace movements, and doing similar support activities. How to achieve this, however, remains a question.

Postscript

I started the exploratory stage of this book with the intention of addressing one particular problem: the marginalizing effect of the binary framing of conflicts in PSWs and dialogues. The reflection and action process, however, uncovered one marginalizing pattern after another, and a number of them were addressed in this book. Further, having started with the proposition that positivist methods and frames served to reproduce rather than transform existing power relations and conflict dynamics through the use of essentialist language, I uncovered that much of constructivist theory and practice of conflict resolution shows great inconsistency and relies on the same essentialist language it aspires to criticize. The challenge to building inclusive approaches to conflict resolution, therefore, is much greater than I initially assumed. The findings of this book give us reasons for cautious optimism. Once particular patterns contributing to marginalization and conflict perpetuation were identified, and the practitioners engaged in reflection and action developing alternatives or adapting existing alternatives to the situation, we saw great improvements in our work. Encouragingly, in many cases, the conceptual critique and alternatives were well-known, as is the case with Brubaker's discussion of groupist language in constructivist writing and the articulation of possible substitutes that we successfully applied in our initiatives and writing.

The key takeaway from this study is the feasibility of developing consistently constructivist and inclusive conflict resolution practices. Such transformation, however, requires our attention at every step of the process starting from the naming of the conflict when we conceive the intervention to the last step of the project implementation. In naming and analyzing conflicts, the distancing ourselves from the customary binary frames that essentialize ethno-religious groups proved to be easier than one would think. When naming the actors, in almost every instance a reference to a particular person or institution such as "the government of Armenia" or "a director of a Baku-based NGO" would anticipate the reference to a generic "Armenian" or "Azerbaijani" side. In naming the initiatives, it proved possible to focus on the goals of the proposed project and in rare cases, the countries or the regions involved, rather than the ethnicities. The nonethnic naming of the initiatives opens the door for participants from mixed backgrounds and others who defy the binary ethnic or religion identity and who are typically excluded from the peace process. The final step in ensuring inclusive recruitment, the "affirmative action" approach that overlooks the shortcomings of resumes, is often necessary in order to encourage individuals from the conflict zones, from regions populated by minorities, from LGBTI communities, and others often excluded to apply.

In the process of dialogues or PSWs, it proved transformative not to preassign the participants to any preconceived conflict "side," allowing them instead to name the identity group or actors who they see critical in understanding the conflict and self-assign to one of these actors. This creates a kaleidoscope of identities and actors that often unites individuals who in case of a binary framing would find themselves at the opposite end of the divide. Further, during the implementation of the initiative, we found it critical to engage in continuous debriefing or other forms of reflective practice that question our assumptions, keep in check the power relations among the participants, between the facilitators and the participants and within the team of facilitators. The domination of some participants over others can take numerous forms: some might rely on outside to the group position of power; others can form factions and establish a dominant discourse that marginalizes others; and yet others can rely on their cultural intelligibility to the organizers.

A final yet critical principle is the management of relationships within the conflict resolution community or at the very least, within the project team. Strong hierarchy, competition, and silencing or marginalization of team members all send unmistakable signals to those new to the conflict resolution field that the principles and values of inclusivity and collaboration we preach in conflict zones exist in words only.

The conflict resolution field holds a great promise: to transform the world into a place free of violence, a place the path to which is yet to be forged. It is only fitting then to lead by example. As the Spanish poet Antonio Machado would have it, "wanderer, there is no road, the road is made by walking."

Bibliography

Abasov, A. S., and Arutyun Khachatrian. 2004. *Karabakhskii Konflikt: Varianty Reshenia: Idei I Real'nost'*. Izd. 2., I dop. Moskva: Mezhdunarodnye otnosheniia.

Allen Nan, Susan. 2008. "Social Capital in Exclusive and Inclusive Networks." In *Social Capital and Peace-Building*, edited by Michaelene Cox, 20084324:172–85. Routledge. http://www.crcnetbase.com/doi/abs/10.4324/9780203887837.ch11.

Allen-Collinson, J., and Hockey, J. 2008. "Autoethnography as 'valid' Methodology? A Study of Disrupted Identity Narratives." *The International Journal of Interdisciplinary Social Sciences* 2: 209–17.

Anderson, Benedict R. O'G. 2006. *Imagined Communities: Reflections on the Origin and Spread of Nationalism*. Rev. ed. London; New York: Verso.

Anderson, Mary B. 1999. *Do No Harm: How Aid Can Support Peace – or War*. Boulder, CO: Lynne Rienner Publishers.

Annan, Kofi. 2012. "Security Council 6736th Meeting: In Presidential Statement, Security Council Gives Full Support to Efforts of Joint. Special Envoy of United Nations, Arab League to End Violence in Syria." http://www.un.org/News/Press/docs/2012/sc10583.doc.htm.

Avruch, Kevin. 2012. *Context and Pretext in Conflict Resolution: Culture, Identity, Power, and Practice*. Boulder, CO: Paradigm Publishers.

Avruch, Kevin, and Peter Black. 1996. "ADR, Palau, and the Contribution of Anthropology." In *Anthropological Contributions to Conflict Resolution*, edited by Alvin W. Wolfe and Honggang Yang, 47–64. Southern Anthropological Society Proceedings, no. 29. Athens: University of Georgia Press.

Babbitt, Eileen, and Ellen L. Lutz, eds. 2009. *Human Rights & Conflict Resolution in Context: Colombia, Sierra Leone, & Northern Ireland*. Syracuse, NY: Syracuse University Press.

Babbitt, Eileen, and Pamela Steiner. 2009. "Combining Empathy with Problem Solving: The Tamra Model of Facilitation in Israel." In *Building Peace: Practical Lessons from the Field*, edited by Craig Zelizer and Robert Rubenstein. Sterling, VA: Kumarian Press.

Bamberger, Michael, Jim Rugh, and Linda Mabry. 2012. *Real World Evaluation: Working under Budget, Time, Data, and Political Constraints*. Thousand Oaks, CA: SAGE.

Brubaker, Rogers. 1998. "Myths and Misconceptions in the Study of Nationalism." In *The State of the Nation: Ernest Gellner and the Theory of Nationalism*, edited by John Hall, 272–305. Cambridge: Cambridge University Press. http://works.bepress.com/wrb/13.

———. 2004. *Ethnicity without Groups*. Cambridge, MA, and London: Harvard University Press.

Burton, John W. 1969. *Conflict and Communication: The Use of Controlled Communication in International Relations*. London: Macmillan and New York: Free Press.

———. 1990. "Human Needs Theory." In *Conflict: Resolution and Prevention*. New York: St Martin's.

Butler, Judith. 2006. *Gender Trouble: Feminism and the Subversion of Identity*. Routledge Classics. New York: Routledge.

Cavallo, David. 2000. "Emergent Design and Learning Environments: Building on Indigenous Knowledge." *IBM Systems Journal* 39 (3&4): 768–81.

Christian, Patrick James. 2017. "Gatekeepers in Conflict Research Settings: Ethics, Access & Safety." Accessed January 2. http://www.academia.edu/1494659/Gatekeepers_in_Conflict_Research_Settings_Ethics_Access_and_Safety.

Church, Cheyanne, and Mark Rogers. 2005. "Designing for Results: Integrating Monitoring and Evaluation in Conflict Transformation Programs." http://www.sfcg.org/programmes/ilt/ilt_manualpage.html.

CNN, Nick Thompson. 2017. "Syria's War, Explained in Graphics." *CNN*. Accessed March 19. http://www.cnn.com/2015/10/01/middleeast/syria-russia-war-in-graphics/index.html.

Cobb, Sara. 1994. "A Narrative Perspective on Mediation." In *New Directions in Mediation: Communication Research and Perspectives*, edited by Joseph P. Folger and Tricia S. Jones, 48–66. Thousand Oaks, CA: Sage Publications.

———. 2003 Interview by Julian Portilla. Beyond Intractability. http://www.beyondintractability.org/audiodisplay/cobb-s.

———. 2004. "Fostering Coexistence in Identity-Based Conflicts: Towards a Narrative Approach." In *Imagine Coexistence*, edited by A. Chayes and M. Minow, 294–310. San Francisco, CA: Jossey Bass.

———. 2013. "Narrative ' Braiding ' and the Role of Public Officials in Transforming the Public's Conflicts (PDF Download Available)." *ResearchGate*. December. https://www.researchgate.net/publication/297403482_Narrative_Braiding_and_the_Role_of_Public_Officials_in_Transforming_the_Public's_Conflicts.

Cobb, Sara, David Laws, and Carlos Sluzki. 2013. "Modeling Negotiation Using 'Narrative Grammar': Exploring the Evolution of Meaning in a Simulated Negotiation." *Group Decision and Negotiation* 23: 1047–65.

Coenen, Harry, and Sjaak Khonraad. 2003. "Inspirations and Aspirations of Exemplarian Action Research." *Journal of Community & Applied Social Psychology* 13: 439–50.

Cohen, Seth B. 2014. "The Challenging Dynamics of Global North-South Peacebuilding Partnerships: Practitioner Stories From the Field." *Journal of Peacebuilding & Development* 9 (3): 65–81. doi:10.1080/15423166.2014.984571.

Collier, Paul. 2001. "Economic Causes of Civil Conflict and Their Implications for Policy." In *Turbulent Peace : The Challenges of Managing International Conflict*, edited by Chester A. Crocker, Fen Osler Hampson, and Pamela R. Aall, 146–66. Washington, DC: United States Institute of Peace Press.

Conciliation Resources. 2012. "Nagorny Karabakh Context." Accessed August 21. http://www.c-r.org/our-work/south-caucasus.

Crenshaw, Kimberle. 1989. "Demarginalizing the Intersection of Race and Sex: A Black Feminist Critique of Antidiscrimination Doctrine, Feminist Theory and Antiracist Politics." *The University of Chicago Legal Forum* 140: 139–67.

Crépeau, François, and Colleen Sheppard, eds. 2013. *Human Rights and Diverse Societies: Challenges and Possibilities*. Newcastle upon Tyne: Cambridge Scholars Publishing.

Creswell, John W., and Dana L. Miller. 2000. "Determining Validity in Qualitative Inquiry." *Theory Into Practice* 39 (3): 124–30. doi:10.1207/s15430421tip3903_2.

De Waal, Thomas. 2013. *Black Garden: Armenia and Azerbaijan through Peace and War*. 10th-year anniversary edition, revised and updated ed. New York; London: New York University Press.

———. 2015. "The Karabakh Truce Under Threat." February 12. http://carnegie.ru/eurasiaoutlook/?fa=59049.

Demmers, Jolle. 2012. *Theories of Violent Conflict: An Introduction*. Contemporary Security Studies. London; New York: Routledge.

Diamond, Louise. 1996. *Multi-Track Diplomacy: A Systems Approach to Peace*. West Hartford, CT: Kumarian Press.

Duffield, Mark. 2007. *Development, Security and Unending War*. Cambridge: Polity.

Ellis, Carolyn, Tony E. Adams, and Arthur P. Bochner. 2010. "Autoethnography: An Overview." *Forum Qualitative Sozialforschung / Forum: Qualitative Social Research* 12 (1). http://www.qualitative-research.net/index.php/fqs/article/view/1589.

Fairclough, Norman. 2001. *Language and Power*. 2nd ed. Language in Social Life Series. Harlow; New York: Longman.

———. 2010. *Critical Discourse Analysis : The Critical Study of Language*. Harlow: Pearson.

Fisher, Roger, William Ury, and Bruce Patton. 1991. *Getting to Yes: Negotiating Agreement without Giving in*. 2nd ed. Boston, MA: Houghton Mifflin.

Fisher, Ronald J., and Loraleigh Keashly. 1991. "The Potential Complementarity of Mediation and Consultation within a Contingency Model of Third Party Intervention." *Journal of Peace Research* 28 (1): 29–42. doi:10.1177/0022343391028001005.

Fitzduff, Mari, and INCORE. 2002. *Beyond Violence : Conflict Resolution Process in Northern Ireland*. Tokyo; New York: United Nations University Press.

Fontan, Victoria. 2012. *Decolonizing Peace*. Lake Oswego, OR: World Dignity University Press.

Frankenberg, Ruth. 1993. "Growing up White: Feminism, Racism and the Social Geography of Childhood." *Feminist Review* 45: 51–84. doi:10.2307/1395347.

Galtung, Johan. 1969. "Violence, Peace, and Peace Research." *Journal of Peace Research* 6 (3): 167–91.

———. 1990. "Cultural Violence." *Journal of Peace Research* 27 (3): 291–305.

Gamaghelyan, Philip. 2005. "Intractability of the Nagorno-Karabakh Conflict: A Myth or a Reality?" *Peace and Conflict Monitor, UN University for Peace*, July. www.monitor.upeace.org/innerpg?id_article+285.

———. 2013. "A Caution against Framing Syria as an Assad-Opposition Dichotomy." *Turkish Policy Quarterly*, 103–11.

———. 2017. "Cynical Politics of Fluid Memory in Contemporary Armenian-Turkish Relations." In *Education and Conflicts in the Post-Soviet Space — Institutions, Narratives, Dominant Discourses and Historical Myths*, edited by Sergey Rumyansev. Georg Eckert Institute for Textbook Research.

Gamaghelyan, Philip, and Christopher Littlefield. 2012. "Facilitator Co-Debriefing." In *Beyond Intractability*, edited by Guy Burgess and Heidi Burgess. Conflict Information Consortium, University of Colorado, Boulder. November. http://www.beyondintractability.org/essay/facilitator-co-debriefing.

Gamaghelyan, Philip, Sevil Huseynova, Maria Karapetyan, and Sergey Rumyansev, eds. 2016. *The South Caucasus and Its Neighborhood: From Politics and Economics to Group Rights*. Istanbul. http://caucasusedition.net/wp-content/uploads/2016/08/Caucasus-Edition-July-2016.pdf.

Garagozov, Rauf. 2006. "Collective Memory in Ethnopolitical Conflicts: The Case of Nagorno- Karabakh." *Central Asia and the Caucasus* 5 (41): 145–55.

Garb, Paula, and Susan Allen Nan. 2006. "Negotiating in a Coordination Network of Citizen Peacebuilding Initiatives in the Georgian-Abkhaz Peace Process." *International Negotiation* 11 (1): 7–35. doi:10.11 63/157180606777835748.

Giddens, Anthony. 1986. *The Constitution of Society : Outline of the Theory of Structuration*. Berkeley: University of California Press.

— — —. 1993. *New Rules of Sociological Method : A Positive Critique of Interpretative Sociologies*. Stanford, CA: Stanford University Press.

Greiff, Jacquie L., Matthew Graville Bricker, Philip Gamaghelyan, Margarita Tadevosyan, and Shu Deng. 2015. "Debriefing in Peacemaking and Conflict Resolution Practice: Models of Emergent Learning and Practitioner Support." *Reflective Practice*, February, 1–15. doi:10.1080/14623943.2015.1005589.

Halpern, Jodi, and Harvey M. Weinstein. 2004. "Rehumanizing the Other: Empathy and Reconciliation." *Human Rights Quarterly* 26: 561.

Handbook of Action Research: The Concise Paperback Edition. 2006. London; Thousand Oaks, CA: SAGE.

Hansen, Toran. 2007. "The History of the Professionalization of Social Work: Lesson for the Field of Conflict Resolution." *Peace and Conflict Studies* 14 (2). Available at: http://nsuworks.nova.edu/pcs/vol14/iss2/1.

Heron, John, and Peter Reason. 2006. "The Practice of Co-Operative Inquiry: Research 'With' rather than 'On' People." In *Handbook of Action Research: The Concise Paperback Edition*, edited by Peter Reason and Hilary Bradbury, 144–55. London; Thousand Oaks, CA: SAGE.

Herr, Kathryn, and Gary L. Anderson. 2015. *The Action Research Dissertation: A Guide for Students and Faculty*. Thousand Oaks, CA: SAGE Publications, Inc.

Hobsbawm, E. J., and T. O. Ranger. 2012. *The Invention of Tradition*. Cambridge: Cambridge Univ Press.

Hopmann, P. Terrence, and I. William Zartman. 2010. "Overcoming the Nagorno-Karabakh Stalemate." *International Negotiation* 15 (1): 1–6. doi:10.1163/157180610X488155.

Horowitz, Donald. 2000. *Ethnic Groups in Conflict*. 2nd ed. University of California Press.

Huffington Post, and Jack Sommers Assistant News Editor. 2016. "This Video Brilliantly Explains How Syria's Civil War Became So Complicated." *The Huffington Post*. 38: 01. http://www.huffingtonpost.co.uk/201 5/11/28/syrian-civil-war_n_8672068.html.

Hunter, Dale, Anne Bailey, and Bill Taylor. 1995. *Zen of Groups*. Boston MA: Da Capo Press.

ICG. 2009. "Nagorno-Karabakh: Risking War—International Crisis Group." http://www.crisisgroup.org/en/regions/europe/south-caucasus/azerbaijan/187-nagorno-karabakh-risking-war.aspx.

Illich, Ivan, ed. 1987. *Disabling Professions*. Ideas in Progress. New York: M. Boyars : Distributed in the U.S. by Kampmann.

International Crisis Group. 2017. "Syria." *Crisis Group*. Accessed March 19. https://www.crisisgroup.org/middle-east-north-africa/eastern-mediterranean/syria.

Jabri, Vivienne. 2006. "Revisiting Change and Conflict: On Underlying Assumptions and the De-Politicisation of Conflict Resolution." *Berghof Research Center for Constructive Conflict Management*. Berghof Handbook Dialogue No. 5 (August).

Jones, Peter L. 2015. *Track Two Diplomacy in Theory and Practice*. Stanford, CA: Stanford University Press.

Kant, Immanuel. 2007. *Perpetual Peace*. [s. l.]: Filiquarian.

Kelman, Herbert. 1972. "The Problem-Solving Workshop in Conflict Resolution." In *Communication in International Politics*, edited by R. L. Merritt, 168–204. Urbana: University of Illinois Press.

———. 2005. "Interactive Problem Solving in the Israeli Palestinian Case." In *Paving the Way: Contributions of Interactive Conflict Resolution to Peacemaking*, edited by Ronald J. Fisher. Lanham, MD: Lexington Books.

Kelman, Herbert C., and Stephen P. Cohen. 1976. "The Problem-Solving Workshop: A Social-Psychological Contribution to the Resolution of International Conflicts." *Journal of Peace Research* 13 (2): 79–90. doi:10.1177/002234337601300201.

Keohane, Robert O. 2005. *After Hegemony: Cooperation and Discord in the World Political Economy*. 1st Princeton classic ed. A Princeton Classic Edition. Princeton, NJ: Princeton University Press.

Knudsen, Susanne. 2006. "Intersectionality—a Theoretical Inspiration in the Analysis of Minority Cultures and Identities in Textbooks." In *Caught in the Web or Lost in the Textbook*, edited by Éric Bruillard, Mike Horsley, Bente Aamotsbakken, et al., 140: 139–67. https://iartemblog.files.wordpress.com/2012/03/8th_iartem_2005-conference.pdf.

Kriesberg, Louis. 2003. "Identity Issues." *Beyond Intractability*. July. http://www.beyondintractability.org/bi-essay/identity-issues.

Lazarus, Ned. 2011. "Evaluating Peace Education in the Oslo-Intifada Generation: A Long-Term Impact Study of Seeds of Peace 1993–2010." Ph.D., District of Columbia: The American University. http://search.proquest.com.mutex.gmu.edu/pqdtft/docview/883388293/abstract/13A380114DBB409351/1?accountid=14541.

Lederach, John Paul. 2008. *Preparing for Peace: Conflict Transformation Across Cultures*. Syracuse, NY: Syracuse Univ. Press.

Lincoln, Yvonna S., and Egon G. Guba. 1985. *Naturalistic Inquiry*. Beverly Hills, CA: Sage Publications.

Lukes, Steven. 2004. *Power: A Radical View*. 2nd ed. Houndmills, Basingstoke, Hampshire : New York: Palgrave Macmillan.

Lund, Michael S., and Steve McDonald, eds. 2015. *Across the Lines of Conflict: Facilitating Cooperation to Build Peace*. Washington, DC: Woodrow Wilson Center Press/Columbia University Press, New York Chichester, West Sussex.

Lutz, Ellen, Eileen Babbitt, and Hurst Nannum. 2003. "Human Rights and Conflict Resolution from the Practitioners' Perspectives." *The Fletcher Forum of World Affairs* 27 (1): 173–93.

Marshall, Catherine, and Gretchen B. Rossman. 2011. *Designing Qualitative Research*. Los Angeles, CA: Sage.

Marutyan, Harutyun Tirani. 2009. *Iconography of Armenian Identity*. Anthropology of Memory 2. Yerevan: "Gitutyun" Pub. House of NAS RA.

Maslow, Abraham. 1943. "A Theory of Human Motivation." *Psychological Review* 50 (4): 370–96. doi:http://dx.doi.org/10.1037/h0054346.

McClelland, C. 1971. "Power and Influence." In *Power*, edited by Champlin, 35–65. New York: Atherton Press.

McLennan, Gregor. 1997. "Critical or Positive Theory? A Comment on the Status of Anthony Giddens' Social Theory." In *Anthony Giddens : Critical Assessments*, edited by Christopher G. A Bryant and David Jary. London; New York: Routledge.

McMillan, Susan M. 1997. "Interdependence and Conflict." *Mershon International Studies Review* 41 (1): 33–58. doi:10.2307/222802.

Mearsheimer, John J. 2003. *The Tragedy of Great Power Politics*. New York, NY: W.W. Norton.

Mertus, Julie, and Jeffrey W. Helsing, eds. 2006. *Human Rights and Conflict: Exploring the Links between Rights, Law, and Peacebuilding*. Washington, DC: United States Institute of Peace Press.

Meulen, Emily van der. 2011. "Participatory and Action-Oriented Dissertations: The Challenges and Importance of Community-Engaged Graduate Research." *The Qualitative Report* 16 (5): 1291–303.

Mitchell, Christopher. 2005a. "Conflict, Social Change and Conflict Resolution. An Enquiry." Berghof Research Center. http://www.berghof-handbook.net/documents/publications/dialogue5_mitchell_lead-1.pdf.

Mitchell, Christopher R. 2005b. "Conflict Analysis, Conflict Resolution and 'Politics': A Reflection." In *Berghof Research Center for Constructive Conflict Management/ Berghof Handbook for Conflict Transformation*. Berlin. http://www.berghofhandbook.net/documents/publications/dialogue5_mitchell_resp.pdf.

Morgenthau, H. J. 1974. *Scientific Man versus Power Politics*. [S.l.]: Univ of Chicago Press.

Morgenthau, Hans Joachim. 1978. *Politics among Nations*. New York: A. A. Knopf.

Nader, Laura. 1993. *Harmony Ideology: Justice and Control in a Zapotec Mountain Village*. Stanford, CA: Stanford University Press.

Naím, Moisés. 2007. "Democracy's Dangerous Impostors." *The Washington Post*, April 21, sec. Opinions. http://www.washingtonpost.com/wp-dyn/content/article/2007/04/20/AR2007042001594.html.

New York Times, and Max Fisher. 2016. "Straightforward Answers to Basic Questions About Syria's War." *The New York Times*, September 18. https://www.nytimes.com/2016/09/19/world/middleeast/syria-civil-war-bashar-al-assad-refugees-islamic-state.html.

Newman, Louise Michele. 1999. *White Women's Rights: The Racial Origins of Feminism in the United States*. Oxford University Press.

Ortega, Mariana. 2006. "Being Lovingly, Knowingly Ignorant: White Feminism and Women of Color." *Hypatia* 21 (3): 56–74. doi:10.1111/j.1527-2001.2006.tb01113.x.

Park, P. 1993. "What Is Participatory Research? A Theoretical and Methodological Perspective." In *Voices of Change: Participatory Research in the United States and Canada*, edited by Peter Park, Mary Brydon-Miller, Budd Hall, and Ted Jackson, 1–21. Westport, CT: Bergin & Garvey.

Pearson d'Estrée, Tamra, Larissa Fast, Joshua Weiss, and Monica Jakobsen. 2001. "Changing the Debate About 'Success' in Conflict Resolution Efforts." *Negotiation Journal* 17 (2): 101–13. doi:10.1023/A:1013275324492.

Plous, Scott. 1993. *The Psychology of Judgment and Decision Making*. McGraw-Hill Series in Social Psychology. New York: McGraw-Hill.

Ray, James Lee. 1998. *Democracy and International Conflict: An Evaluation of the Democratic Peace Proposition*. Columbia, SC: University of South Carolina Press.

Richmond, Oliver P. 2011. "De-Romanticising the Local, de-Mystifying the International: Hybridity in Timor Leste and the Solomon Islands." *The Pacific Review* 24 (1): 115–36. doi:10.1080/09512748.2010.546873.

Roccas, S., and Brewer M. B. 2002. "Social Identity Complexity." *Personality and Social Psychology Review* 6: 88–106.

Ross, Marc Howard. 2001. "Action Evaluation in the Theory and Practice of Conflict Resolution." *Peace and Conflict Studies* 8 (1): 94.

Rossman, Gretchen B., and Sharon F. Rallis. 2010. "Everyday Ethics: Reflections on Practice." *International Journal of Qualitative Studies in Education* 23 (4): 379–91. doi:10.1080/09518398.2010.492813.

Roth, Benita. 2004. *Separate Roads to Feminism: Black, Chicana, and White Feminist Movements in America's Second Wave.* Cambridge University Press.

Rothman, Jay, and Marie L. Olson. 2001. "From Interests to Identities: Towards a New Emphasis in Interactive Conflict Resolution." *Journal of Peace Research* 38 (3): 289–305.

Russell, Bertrand. 1962. *Power — A New Social Analysis.* Unwin Books.

Sartre, Jean-Paul. 2004. "Preface to Frantz Fanon's Wretched of the Earth." In *Violence in War and Peace*, edited by Nancy Scheper-Hughes and Philippe I. Bourgois, 229–36. Malden, MA: Blackwell Pub.

Schon, Donald A. 1984. *The Reflective Practitioner: How Professionals Think In Action.* 1st ed. Basic Books.

Shaw, Rosalind, Lars Waldorf, and Pierre Hazan, eds. 2010. *Localizing Transitional Justice: Interventions and Priorities after Mass Violence.* Stanford Studies in Human Rights. Stanford, CA: Stanford University Press.

Stones, Rob. 2005. *Structuration Theory.* Houndmills, Basingstoke, Hampshire; New York: Palgrave Macmillan.

Sword, Deborah. 2009. "Professionalization Of Conflict Resolvers." *Everyting Mediation.* July. http://www.mediate.com/articles/swordL7.cfm.

"Syria's Mutating Conflict — International Crisis Group." 2013. Accessed June 1. http://www.crisisgroup.org/en/regions/middle-east-north-africa/egypt-syria-lebanon/syria/128-syrias-mutating-conflict.aspx.

Tajfel, Henri. 2010. *Social Identity and Intergroup Relations.* Cambridge: Cambridge University Press.

Themnér, Lotta, and Peter Wallensteen. 2011. "Armed Conflict, 1946–2010." *Journal of Peace Research* 48 (4): 525–36. doi:10.1177/0022343311415302.

Ury, William, and William Ury. 2000. *The Third Side: Why We Fight and How We Can Stop.* New York: Penguin Books.

Van Dijk, Teun Adrianus. 2009. *Society and Discourse: How Social Contexts Influence Text and Talk.* Cambridge, UK: Cambridge University Press. http://www.myilibrary.com/.

Waltz, Kenneth N. 2010. *Theory of International Politics*. Long Grove, IL: Waveland Press.

Wedge, Bryant, and Dennis Sandole. 1982. "Conflict Management: A New Venture into Professionalization." *Peace & Change: A Journal of Peace Research* 8 (2–3): 129–38.

"What's Happening in Syria?—CBBC Newsround." 2017, February 27. http://www.bbc.co.uk/newsround/16979186.

White, S. J. 2001. "Auto-Ethnography as Reflexive Inquiry: The Research Act as Self-Surveillance." In *Qualitative Research in Social Work*, edited by Ian Shaw and Nick Gould, 100–16. Introducing Qualitative Methods. London: Sage.

Winslade, John, and Gerald Monk. 2000. *Narrative Mediation : A New Approach to Conflict Resolution*. San Francisco, CA: Jossey-Bass.

Zartman, I. William, and Maureen R Berman. 1982. *The Practical Negotiator*. New Haven: Yale University Press.

Index

A

Abasov, Ali 131, 187
Abkhazia 35, 175, 220
Alewites 22, 23, 39, 119, 120, 121, 122, 205, 206, 215
Allen, Susan 11, 17, 44, 45, 46, 68, 232
Anderson, Benedict 63, 69, 80, 183, 232
Armenian-Turkish 67, 77, 91, 163
Assad regime 22, 23, 38, 39, 110, 120, 123, 125, 160
Assad supporters 111, 113, 121, 123, 185, 205, 215, 258
Avruch, Kevin 21, 48, 57, 252

B

Binary frame 5, 32
Brubaker, Rogers 49, 50, 52, 53, 54, 55, 67, 161, 168, 169, 171, 263
Burton, John 26, 42, 108
Butler, Judith 194

C

Civil society 118
Cobb, Sara 50, 161, 172
Co-debriefing 115
Conflict transformation 254
Critical Discourse Analysis 19, 50, 56, 94, 176, 186, 198, 207, 210, 216, 249, 262

D

De Waal, Thomas 86, 131

F

Fairclough, Norman 56, 58, 210
Fisher, Roger 42, 43, 47, 156
Fitzduff, Mari 45
Free Syrian Army 22, 38, 39, 118

G

Gamaghelyan, Philip 15, 71, 93, 101, 115, 116, 131, 160, 213
Georgia 16, 35, 47, 169, 175, 180, 182, 187, 189, 221, 245, 256, 261
Georgian-Abkhazian 46
Georgian-South Ossetian 15, 67, 77, 163
Giddens, Anthony 32, 59, 60, 171

H

Hirsch, Susan 11

I

Illich, Ivan 58, 218, 227
Imagine Center for Conflict Transformation 8, 12, 19, 64, 69, 70, 71, 72, 73, 78, 80, 83, 93, 94, 101, 105, 135, 139, 144, 174, 175, 177, 178, 181, 195, 211, 212, 214, 228, 229, 236, 237, 239, 240, 241, 242, 244, 247, 250, 255, 256, 261
Islamic State of Levant 19, 22, 39, 40

K

Kurds 22, 38, 39, 120, 122, 162, 205, 206, 215, 226

L

Lesbian, Gay, Bisexual, Transgender, Intersex 19, 82, 170, 182, 191, 192, 202, 203, 212, 213, 264

M

Minorities 118, 257, 258
Minority 191

N

Nagorno-Karabakh Autonomous Oblast 19, 85, 130, 148
Nakhichevan 130
NK Analytic Initiative 130, 132, 135, 140, 141, 142, 143, 147, 148, 150, 151, 158, 185, 186, 187, 189, 191, 251, 255, 259, 261
Non-Governmental Organization 19, 188, 204, 222, 229, 232, 242, 264
North Atlantic Treaty Organization 19, 139

P

Participatory Action Research 9, 16, 17, 19, 26, 32, 61, 63, 65, 68, 69, 71, 74, 79, 81, 82, 83, 84, 155, 175, 177, 186, 192, 195, 199, 201, 208, 218, 224, 243, 251, 255
Problem-Solving Workshop 7, 19, 21, 42, 43, 44, 101, 102, 107, 108, 120, 133, 136, 141, 164, 175, 177, 204, 234, 258

R

Russia 36, 37, 40, 94, 117, 131, 138, 139, 180, 187, 213

S

Safarov 139, 164, 166
School for Conflict Analysis and Resolution of George Mason University 11, 12, 19, 93
South Ossetia 15, 35, 67, 71, 94, 134, 182, 187, 220, 223, 256, 258, 261
Soviet Socialist Republic 19, 85, 130
Srikantia, Jessica 11, 224
Sunni 23, 121, 205

T

Track 1 5, 40, 41, 45, 129, 138, 147, 149, 156, 157, 158, 186, 231
Track 2 7, 33, 40, 41, 42, 138, 147, 148, 156, 157, 160, 163, 186, 190, 254
Track 3 41, 157
Turkey 92, 94, 117, 163, 175, 176, 179, 180, 181, 209, 213, 245, 256, 260
Turkish-Armenian 67, 91, 93, 102, 160, 163, 165, 174, 176, 178

U

United States 22, 35, 36, 37, 40, 41, 48, 54, 103, 117, 131, 132, 133, 134, 135, 138, 139, 162, 169, 198, 203, 229, 234, 236

Z

Zangezur 130
Zartman, William 37, 131

SOVIET AND POST-SOVIET POLITICS AND SOCIETY

Edited by Dr. Andreas Umland

ISSN 1614-3515

1   Андреас Умланд (ред.)
    Воплощение Европейской
    конвенции по правам человека в
    России
    Философские, юридические и
    эмпирические исследования
    ISBN 3-89821-387-0

2   Christian Wipperfürth
    Russland – ein vertrauenswürdiger
    Partner?
    Grundlagen, Hintergründe und Praxis
    gegenwärtiger russischer Außenpolitik
    Mit einem Vorwort von Heinz Timmermann
    ISBN 3-89821-401-X

3   Manja Hussner
    Die Übernahme internationalen Rechts
    in die russische und deutsche
    Rechtsordnung
    Eine vergleichende Analyse zur
    Völkerrechtsfreundlichkeit der Verfassungen
    der Russländischen Föderation und der
    Bundesrepublik Deutschland
    Mit einem Vorwort von Rainer Arnold
    ISBN 3-89821-438-9

4   Matthew Tejada
    Bulgaria's Democratic Consolidation
    and the Kozloduy Nuclear Power Plant
    (KNPP)
    The Unattainability of Closure
    With a foreword by Richard J. Crampton
    ISBN 3-89821-439-7

5   Марк Григорьевич Меерович
    Квадратные метры, определяющие
    сознание
    Государственная жилищная политика в
    СССР. 1921 – 1941 гг
    ISBN 3-89821-474-5

6   Andrei P. Tsygankov, Pavel
    A.Tsygankov (Eds.)
    New Directions in Russian
    International Studies
    ISBN 3-89821-422-2

7   Марк Григорьевич Меерович
    Как власть народ к труду приучала
    Жилище в СССР – средство управления
    людьми. 1917 – 1941 гг.
    С предисловием Елены Осокиной
    ISBN 3-89821-495-8

8   David J. Galbreath
    Nation-Building and Minority Politics
    in Post-Socialist States
    Interests, Influence and Identities in Estonia
    and Latvia
    With a foreword by David J. Smith
    ISBN 3-89821-467-2

9   Алексей Юрьевич Безугольный
    Народы Кавказа в Вооруженных
    силах СССР в годы Великой
    Отечественной войны 1941-1945 гг.
    С предисловием Николая Бугая
    ISBN 3-89821-475-3

10 Вячеслав Лихачев и Владимир
    Прибыловский (ред.)
    Русское Национальное Единство,
    1990-2000. В 2-х томах
    ISBN 3-89821-523-7

11 Николай Бугай (ред.)
    Народы стран Балтии в условиях
    сталинизма (1940-е – 1950-е годы)
    Документированная история
    ISBN 3-89821-525-3

12 Ingmar Bredies (Hrsg.)
    Zur Anatomie der Orange Revolution
    in der Ukraine
    Wechsel des Elitenregimes oder Triumph des
    Parlamentarismus?
    ISBN 3-89821-524-5

13 Anastasia V. Mitrofanova
    The Politicization of Russian
    Orthodoxy
    Actors and Ideas
    With a foreword by William C. Gay
    ISBN 3-89821-481-8

14 Nathan D. Larson
    Alexander Solzhenitsyn and the
    Russo-Jewish Question
    ISBN 3-89821-483-4

15 Guido Houben
    Kulturpolitik und Ethnizität
    Staatliche Kunstförderung im Russland der
    neunziger Jahre
    Mit einem Vorwort von Gert Weisskirchen
    ISBN 3-89821-542-3

16 Leonid Luks
    Der russische „Sonderweg"?
    Aufsätze zur neuesten Geschichte Russlands
    im europäischen Kontext
    ISBN 3-89821-496-6

17 Евгений Мороз
    История «Мёртвой воды» – от
    страшной сказки к большой
    политике
    Политическое неоязычество в
    постсоветской России
    ISBN 3-89821-551-2

18 Александр Верховский и Галина
    Кожевникова (ред.)
    Этническая и религиозная
    интолерантность в российских СМИ
    Результаты мониторинга 2001-2004 гг.
    ISBN 3-89821-569-5

19 Christian Ganzer
    Sowjetisches Erbe und ukrainische
    Nation
    Das Museum der Geschichte des Zaporoger
    Kosakentums auf der Insel Chortycja
    Mit einem Vorwort von Frank Golczewski
    ISBN 3-89821-504-0

20 Эльза-Баир Гучинова
    Помнить нельзя забыть
    Антропология депортационной травмы
    калмыков
    С предисловием Кэролайн Хамфри
    ISBN 3-89821-506-7

21 Юлия Лидерман
    Мотивы «проверки» и «испытания»
    в постсоветской культуре
    Советское прошлое в российском
    кинематографе 1990-х годов
    С предисловием Евгения Марголита
    ISBN 3-89821-511-3

22 Tanya Lokshina, Ray Thomas, Mary
    Mayer (Eds.)
    The Imposition of a Fake Political
    Settlement in the Northern Caucasus
    The 2003 Chechen Presidential Election
    ISBN 3-89821-436-2

23 Timothy McCajor Hall, Rosie Read
    (Eds.)
    Changes in the Heart of Europe
    Recent Ethnographies of Czechs, Slovaks,
    Roma, and Sorbs
    With an afterword by Zdeněk Salzmann
    ISBN 3-89821-606-3

24 Christian Autengruber
    Die politischen Parteien in Bulgarien
    und Rumänien
    Eine vergleichende Analyse seit Beginn der
    90er Jahre
    Mit einem Vorwort von Dorothée de Nève
    ISBN 3-89821-476-1

25 Annette Freyberg-Inan with Radu
    Cristescu
    The Ghosts in Our Classrooms, or:
    John Dewey Meets Ceauşescu
    The Promise and the Failures of Civic
    Education in Romania
    ISBN 3-89821-416-8

26 John B. Dunlop
    The 2002 Dubrovka and 2004 Beslan
    Hostage Crises
    A Critique of Russian Counter-Terrorism
    With a foreword by Donald N. Jensen
    ISBN 3-89821-608-X

27 Peter Koller
    Das touristische Potenzial von
    Kam''janec–Podil's'kyj
    Eine fremdenverkehrsgeographische
    Untersuchung der Zukunftsperspektiven und
    Maßnahmenplanung zur
    Destinationsentwicklung des „ukrainischen
    Rothenburg"
    Mit einem Vorwort von Kristiane Klemm
    ISBN 3-89821-640-3

28 Françoise Daucé, Elisabeth Sieca-
    Kozlowski (Eds.)
    Dedovshchina in the Post-Soviet
    Military
    Hazing of Russian Army Conscripts in a
    Comparative Perspective
    With a foreword by Dale Herspring
    ISBN 3-89821-616-0

29 Florian Strasser
    Zivilgesellschaftliche Einflüsse auf die
    Orange Revolution
    Die gewaltlose Massenbewegung und die
    ukrainische Wahlkrise 2004
    Mit einem Vorwort von Egbert Jahn
    ISBN 3-89821-648-9

30 Rebecca S. Katz
    The Georgian Regime Crisis of 2003-
    2004
    A Case Study in Post-Soviet Media
    Representation of Politics, Crime and
    Corruption
    ISBN 3-89821-413-3

31 Vladimir Kantor
    Willkür oder Freiheit
    Beiträge zur russischen Geschichtsphilosophie
    Ediert von Dagmar Herrmann sowie mit
    einem Vorwort versehen von Leonid Luks
    ISBN 3-89821-589-X

32 Laura A. Victoir
    The Russian Land Estate Today
    A Case Study of Cultural Politics in Post-
    Soviet Russia
    With a foreword by Priscilla Roosevelt
    ISBN 3-89821-426-5

33 Ivan Katchanovski
    Cleft Countries
    Regional Political Divisions and Cultures in
    Post-Soviet Ukraine and Moldova
    With a foreword by Francis Fukuyama
    ISBN 3-89821-558-X

34 Florian Mühlfried
    Postsowjetische Feiern
    Das Georgische Bankett im Wandel
    Mit einem Vorwort von Kevin Tuite
    ISBN 3-89821-601-2

35 Roger Griffin, Werner Loh, Andreas
    Umland (Eds.)
    Fascism Past and Present, West and
    East
    An International Debate on Concepts and
    Cases in the Comparative Study of the
    Extreme Right
    With an afterword by Walter Laqueur
    ISBN 3-89821-674-8

36 Sebastian Schlegel
    Der „Weiße Archipel"
    Sowjetische Atomstädte 1945-1991
    Mit einem Geleitwort von Thomas Bohn
    ISBN 3-89821-679-9

37 Vyacheslav Likhachev
    Political Anti-Semitism in Post-Soviet
    Russia
    Actors and Ideas in 1991-2003
    Edited and translated from Russian by Eugene
    Veklerov
    ISBN 3-89821-529-6

38 Josette Baer (Ed.)
    Preparing Liberty in Central Europe
    Political Texts from the Spring of Nations
    1848 to the Spring of Prague 1968
    With a foreword by Zdeněk V. David
    ISBN 3-89821-546-6

39 Михаил Лукьянов
    Российский консерватизм и
    реформа, 1907-1914
    С предисловием Марка Д. Стейнберга
    ISBN 3-89821-503-2

40 Nicola Melloni
    Market Without Economy
    The 1998 Russian Financial Crisis
    With a foreword by Eiji Furukawa
    ISBN 3-89821-407-9

41 Dmitrij Chmelnizki
    Die Architektur Stalins
    Bd. 1: Studien zu Ideologie und Stil
    Bd. 2: Bilddokumentation
    Mit einem Vorwort von Bruno Flierl
    ISBN 3-89821-515-6

42 Katja Yafimava
    Post-Soviet Russian-Belarussian
    Relationships
    The Role of Gas Transit Pipelines
    With a foreword by Jonathan P. Stern
    ISBN 3-89821-655-1

43 Boris Chavkin
    Verflechtungen der deutschen und
    russischen Zeitgeschichte
    Aufsätze und Archivfunde zu den
    Beziehungen Deutschlands und der
    Sowjetunion von 1917 bis 1991
    Ediert von Markus Edlinger sowie mit einem
    Vorwort versehen von Leonid Luks
    ISBN 3-89821-756-9

44 *Anastasija Grynenko in Zusammenarbeit mit Claudia Dathe*
Die Terminologie des Gerichtswesens der Ukraine und Deutschlands im Vergleich
Eine übersetzungswissenschaftliche Analyse juristischer Fachbegriffe im Deutschen, Ukrainischen und Russischen
Mit einem Vorwort von Ulrich Hartmann
ISBN 3-89821-691-8

45 *Anton Burkov*
The Impact of the European Convention on Human Rights on Russian Law
Legislation and Application in 1996-2006
With a foreword by Françoise Hampson
ISBN 978-3-89821-639-5

46 *Stina Torjesen, Indra Overland (Eds.)*
International Election Observers in Post-Soviet Azerbaijan
Geopolitical Pawns or Agents of Change?
ISBN 978-3-89821-743-9

47 *Taras Kuzio*
Ukraine – Crimea – Russia
Triangle of Conflict
ISBN 978-3-89821-761-3

48 *Claudia Šabić*
"Ich erinnere mich nicht, aber L'viv!"
Zur Funktion kultureller Faktoren für die Institutionalisierung und Entwicklung einer ukrainischen Region
Mit einem Vorwort von Melanie Tatur
ISBN 978-3-89821-752-1

49 *Marlies Bilz*
Tatarstan in der Transformation
Nationaler Diskurs und Politische Praxis 1988-1994
Mit einem Vorwort von Frank Golczewski
ISBN 978-3-89821-722-4

50 *Марлен Ларюэль (ред.)*
Современные интерпретации русского национализма
ISBN 978-3-89821-795-8

51 *Sonja Schüler*
Die ethnische Dimension der Armut
Roma im postsozialistischen Rumänien
Mit einem Vorwort von Anton Sterbling
ISBN 978-3-89821-776-7

52 *Галина Кожевникова*
Радикальный национализм в России и противодействие ему
Сборник докладов Центра «Сова» за 2004-2007 гг.
С предисловием Александра Верховского
ISBN 978-3-89821-721-7

53 *Галина Кожевникова и Владимир Прибыловский*
Российская власть в биографиях I
Высшие должностные лица РФ в 2004 г.
ISBN 978-3-89821-796-5

54 *Галина Кожевникова и Владимир Прибыловский*
Российская власть в биографиях II
Члены Правительства РФ в 2004 г.
ISBN 978-3-89821-797-2

55 *Галина Кожевникова и Владимир Прибыловский*
Российская власть в биографиях III
Руководители федеральных служб и агентств РФ в 2004 г.
ISBN 978-3-89821-798-9

56 *Ileana Petroniu*
Privatisierung in Transformationsökonomien
Determinanten der Restrukturierungs-Bereitschaft am Beispiel Polens, Rumäniens und der Ukraine
Mit einem Vorwort von Rainer W. Schäfer
ISBN 978-3-89821-790-3

57 *Christian Wipperfürth*
Russland und seine GUS-Nachbarn
Hintergründe, aktuelle Entwicklungen und Konflikte in einer ressourcenreichen Region
ISBN 978-3-89821-801-6

58 *Togzhan Kassenova*
From Antagonism to Partnership
The Uneasy Path of the U.S.-Russian Cooperative Threat Reduction
With a foreword by Christoph Bluth
ISBN 978-3-89821-707-1

59 *Alexander Höllwerth*
Das sakrale eurasische Imperium des Aleksandr Dugin
Eine Diskursanalyse zum postsowjetischen russischen Rechtsextremismus
Mit einem Vorwort von Dirk Uffelmann
ISBN 978-3-89821-813-9

60 *Олег Рябов*
    «Россия-Матушка»
    Национализм, гендер и война в России XX века
    С предисловием Елены Гощило
    ISBN 978-3-89821-487-2

61 *Ivan Maistrenko*
    Borot'bism
    A Chapter in the History of the Ukrainian Revolution
    With a new introduction by Chris Ford
    Translated by George S. N. Luckyj with the assistance of Ivan L. Rudnytsky
    ISBN 978-3-89821-697-5

62 *Maryna Romanets*
    Anamorphosic Texts and Reconfigured Visions
    Improvised Traditions in Contemporary Ukrainian and Irish Literature
    ISBN 978-3-89821-576-3

63 *Paul D'Anieri and Taras Kuzio (Eds.)*
    Aspects of the Orange Revolution I
    Democratization and Elections in Post-Communist Ukraine
    ISBN 978-3-89821-698-2

64 *Bohdan Harasymiw in collaboration with Oleh S. Ilnytzkyj (Eds.)*
    Aspects of the Orange Revolution II
    Information and Manipulation Strategies in the 2004 Ukrainian Presidential Elections
    ISBN 978-3-89821-699-9

65 *Ingmar Bredies, Andreas Umland and Valentin Yakushik (Eds.)*
    Aspects of the Orange Revolution III
    The Context and Dynamics of the 2004 Ukrainian Presidential Elections
    ISBN 978-3-89821-803-0

66 *Ingmar Bredies, Andreas Umland and Valentin Yakushik (Eds.)*
    Aspects of the Orange Revolution IV
    Foreign Assistance and Civic Action in the 2004 Ukrainian Presidential Elections
    ISBN 978-3-89821-808-5

67 *Ingmar Bredies, Andreas Umland and Valentin Yakushik (Eds.)*
    Aspects of the Orange Revolution V
    Institutional Observation Reports on the 2004 Ukrainian Presidential Elections
    ISBN 978-3-89821-809-2

68 *Taras Kuzio (Ed.)*
    Aspects of the Orange Revolution VI
    Post-Communist Democratic Revolutions in Comparative Perspective
    ISBN 978-3-89821-820-7

69 *Tim Bohse*
    Autoritarismus statt Selbstverwaltung
    Die Transformation der kommunalen Politik in der Stadt Kaliningrad 1990-2005
    Mit einem Geleitwort von Stefan Troebst
    ISBN 978-3-89821-782-8

70 *David Rupp*
    Die Rußländische Föderation und die russischsprachige Minderheit in Lettland
    Eine Fallstudie zur Anwaltspolitik Moskaus gegenüber den russophonen Minderheiten im „Nahen Ausland" von 1991 bis 2002
    Mit einem Vorwort von Helmut Wagner
    ISBN 978-3-89821-778-1

71 *Taras Kuzio*
    Theoretical and Comparative Perspectives on Nationalism
    New Directions in Cross-Cultural and Post-Communist Studies
    With a foreword by Paul Robert Magocsi
    ISBN 978-3-89821-815-3

72 *Christine Teichmann*
    Die Hochschultransformation im heutigen Osteuropa
    Kontinuität und Wandel bei der Entwicklung des postkommunistischen Universitätswesens
    Mit einem Vorwort von Oskar Anweiler
    ISBN 978-3-89821-842-9

73 *Julia Kusznir*
    Der politische Einfluss von Wirtschaftseliten in russischen Regionen
    Eine Analyse am Beispiel der Erdöl- und Erdgasindustrie, 1992-2005
    Mit einem Vorwort von Wolfgang Eichwede
    ISBN 978-3-89821-821-4

74 *Alena Vysotskaya*
    Russland, Belarus und die EU-Osterweiterung
    Zur Minderheitenfrage und zum Problem der Freizügigkeit des Personenverkehrs
    Mit einem Vorwort von Katlijn Malfliet
    ISBN 978-3-89821-822-1

75 **Heiko Pleines (Hrsg.)**
Corporate Governance in post-
sozialistischen Volkswirtschaften
ISBN 978-3-89821-766-8

76 *Stefan Ihrig*
Wer sind die Moldawier?
Rumänismus versus Moldowanismus in
Historiographie und Schulbüchern der
Republik Moldova, 1991-2006
Mit einem Vorwort von Holm Sundhaussen
ISBN 978-3-89821-466-7

77 *Galina Kozhevnikova in collaboration
with Alexander Verkhovsky and
Eugene Veklerov*
Ultra-Nationalism and Hate Crimes in
Contemporary Russia
The 2004-2006 Annual Reports of Moscow's
SOVA Center
With a foreword by Stephen D. Shenfield
ISBN 978-3-89821-868-9

78 *Florian Küchler*
The Role of the European Union in
Moldova's Transnistria Conflict
With a foreword by Christopher Hill
ISBN 978-3-89821-850-4

79 *Bernd Rechel*
The Long Way Back to Europe
Minority Protection in Bulgaria
With a foreword by Richard Crampton
ISBN 978-3-89821-863-4

80 *Peter W. Rodgers*
Nation, Region and History in Post-
Communist Transitions
Identity Politics in Ukraine, 1991-2006
With a foreword by Vera Tolz
ISBN 978-3-89821-903-7

81 *Stephanie Solywoda*
The Life and Work of
Semen L. Frank
A Study of Russian Religious Philosophy
With a foreword by Philip Walters
ISBN 978-3-89821-457-5

82 *Vera Sokolova*
Cultural Politics of Ethnicity
Discourses on Roma in Communist
Czechoslovakia
ISBN 978-3-89821-864-1

83 *Natalya Shevchik Ketenci*
Kazakhstani Enterprises in Transition
The Role of Historical Regional Development
in Kazakhstan's Post-Soviet Economic
Transformation
ISBN 978-3-89821-831-3

84 *Martin Malek, Anna Schor-
Tschudnowskaja (Hrsg.)*
Europa im Tschetschenienkrieg
Zwischen politischer Ohnmacht und
Gleichgültigkeit
Mit einem Vorwort von Lipchan Basajewa
ISBN 978-3-89821-676-0

85 *Stefan Meister*
Das postsowjetische Universitätswesen
zwischen nationalem und
internationalem Wandel
Die Entwicklung der regionalen Hochschule
in Russland als Gradmesser der
Systemtransformation
Mit einem Vorwort von Joan DeBardeleben
ISBN 978-3-89821-891-7

86 *Konstantin Sheiko in collaboration
with Stephen Brown*
Nationalist Imaginings of the
Russian Past
Anatolii Fomenko and the Rise of Alternative
History in Post-Communist Russia
With a foreword by Donald Ostrowski
ISBN 978-3-89821-915-0

87 *Sabine Jenni*
Wie stark ist das „Einige Russland"?
Zur Parteibindung der Eliten und zum
Wahlerfolg der Machtpartei
im Dezember 2007
Mit einem Vorwort von Klaus Armingeon
ISBN 978-3-89821-961-7

88 *Thomas Borén*
Meeting-Places of Transformation
Urban Identity, Spatial Representations and
Local Politics in Post-Soviet St Petersburg
ISBN 978-3-89821-739-2

89 *Aygul Ashirova*
Stalinismus und Stalin-Kult in
Zentralasien
Turkmenistan 1924-1953
Mit einem Vorwort von Leonid Luks
ISBN 978-3-89821-987-7

90   Leonid Luks
     Freiheit oder imperiale Größe?
     Essays zu einem russischen Dilemma
     ISBN 978-3-8382-0011-8

91   Christopher Gilley
     The 'Change of Signposts' in the
     Ukrainian Emigration
     A Contribution to the History of
     Sovietophilism in the 1920s
     With a foreword by Frank Golczewski
     ISBN 978-3-89821-965-5

92   Philipp Casula, Jeronim Perovic
     (Eds.)
     Identities and Politics
     During the Putin Presidency
     The Discursive Foundations of Russia's
     Stability
     With a foreword by Heiko Haumann
     ISBN 978-3-8382-0015-6

93   Marcel Viëtor
     Europa und die Frage
     nach seinen Grenzen im Osten
     Zur Konstruktion ‚europäischer Identität' in
     Geschichte und Gegenwart
     Mit einem Vorwort von Albrecht Lehmann
     ISBN 978-3-8382-0045-3

94   Ben Hellman, Andrei Rogachevskii
     Filming the Unfilmable
     Casper Wrede's 'One Day in the Life
     of Ivan Denisovich'
     Second, Revised and Expanded Edition
     ISBN 978-3-8382-0044-6

95   Eva Fuchslocher
     Vaterland, Sprache, Glaube
     Orthodoxie und Nationenbildung
     am Beispiel Georgiens
     Mit einem Vorwort von Christina von Braun
     ISBN 978-3-89821-884-9

96   Vladimir Kantor
     Das Westlertum und der Weg
     Russlands
     Zur Entwicklung der russischen Literatur und
     Philosophie
     Ediert von Dagmar Herrmann
     Mit einem Beitrag von Nikolaus Lobkowicz
     ISBN 978-3-8382-0102-3

97   Kamran Musayev
     Die postsowjetische Transformation
     im Baltikum und Südkaukasus
     Eine vergleichende Untersuchung der
     politischen Entwicklung Lettlands und
     Aserbaidschans 1985-2009
     Mit einem Vorwort von Leonid Luks
     Ediert von Sandro Henschel
     ISBN 978-3-8382-0103-0

98   Tatiana Zhurzhenko
     Borderlands into Bordered Lands
     Geopolitics of Identity in Post-Soviet Ukraine
     With a foreword by Dieter Segert
     ISBN 978-3-8382-0042-2

99   Кирилл Галушко, Лидия Смола
     (ред.)
     Пределы падения – варианты
     украинского будущего
     Аналитико-прогностические исследования
     ISBN 978-3-8382-0148-1

100 Michael Minkenberg (ed.)
     Historical Legacies and the Radical
     Right in Post-Cold War Central and
     Eastern Europe
     With an afterword by Sabrina P. Ramet
     ISBN 978-3-8382-0124-5

101 David-Emil Wickström
     Rocking St. Petersburg
     Transcultural Flows and Identity Politics in
     the St. Petersburg Popular Music Scene
     With a foreword by Yngvar B. Steinholt
     Second, Revised and Expanded Edition
     ISBN 978-3-8382-0100-9

102 Eva Zabka
     Eine neue „Zeit der Wirren"?
     Der spät- und postsowjetische Systemwandel
     1985-2000 im Spiegel russischer
     gesellschaftspolitischer Diskurse
     Mit einem Vorwort von Margareta Mommsen
     ISBN 978-3-8382-0161-0

103 Ulrike Ziemer
     Ethnic Belonging, Gender and
     Cultural Practices
     Youth Identitites in Contemporary Russia
     With a foreword by Anoop Nayak
     ISBN 978-3-8382-0152-8

104 Ksenia Chepikova
‚Einiges Russland' - eine zweite KPdSU?
Aspekte der Identitätskonstruktion einer postsowjetischen „Partei der Macht"
Mit einem Vorwort von Torsten Oppelland
ISBN 978-3-8382-0311-9

105 Леонид Люкс
Западничество или евразийство? Демократия или идеократия?
Сборник статей об исторических дилеммах России
С предисловием Владимира Кантора
ISBN 978-3-8382-0211-2

106 Anna Dost
Das russische Verfassungsrecht auf dem Weg zum Föderalismus und zurück
Zum Konflikt von Rechtsnormen und -wirklichkeit in der Russländischen Föderation von 1991 bis 2009
Mit einem Vorwort von Alexander Blankenagel
ISBN 978-3-8382-0292-1

107 Philipp Herzog
Sozialistische Völkerfreundschaft, nationaler Widerstand oder harmloser Zeitvertreib?
Zur politischen Funktion der Volkskunst im sowjetischen Estland
Mit einem Vorwort von Andreas Kappeler
ISBN 978-3-8382-0216-7

108 Marlène Laruelle (ed.)
Russian Nationalism, Foreign Policy, and Identity Debates in Putin's Russia
New Ideological Patterns after the Orange Revolution
ISBN 978-3-8382-0325-6

109 Michail Logvinov
Russlands Kampf gegen den internationalen Terrorismus
Eine kritische Bestandsaufnahme des Bekämpfungsansatzes
Mit einem Geleitwort von Hans-Henning Schröder
und einem Vorwort von Eckhard Jesse
ISBN 978-3-8382-0329-4

110 John B. Dunlop
The Moscow Bombings of September 1999
Examinations of Russian Terrorist Attacks at the Onset of Vladimir Putin's Rule
Second, Revised and Expanded Edition
ISBN 978-3-8382-0388-1

111 Андрей А. Ковалёв
Свидетельство из-за кулис российской политики I
Можно ли делать добро из зла?
(Воспоминания и размышления о последних советских и первых послесоветских годах)
With a foreword by Peter Reddaway
ISBN 978-3-8382-0302-7

112 Андрей А. Ковалёв
Свидетельство из-за кулис российской политики II
Угроза для себя и окружающих
(Наблюдения и предостережения относительно происходящего после 2000 г.)
ISBN 978-3-8382-0303-4

113 Bernd Kappenberg
Zeichen setzen für Europa
Der Gebrauch europäischer lateinischer Sonderzeichen in der deutschen Öffentlichkeit
Mit einem Vorwort von Peter Schlobinski
ISBN 978-3-89821-749-1

114 Ivo Mijnssen
The Quest for an Ideal Youth in Putin's Russia I
Back to Our Future! History, Modernity, and Patriotism according to Nashi, 2005-2013
With a foreword by Jeronim Perović
Second, Revised and Expanded Edition
ISBN 978-3-8382-0368-3

115 Jussi Lassila
The Quest for an Ideal Youth in Putin's Russia II
The Search for Distinctive Conformism in the Political Communication of Nashi, 2005-2009
With a foreword by Kirill Postoutenko
Second, Revised and Expanded Edition
ISBN 978-3-8382-0415-4

116 Valerio Trabandt
Neue Nachbarn, gute Nachbarschaft?
Die EU als internationaler Akteur am Beispiel ihrer Demokratieförderung in Belarus und der Ukraine 2004-2009
Mit einem Vorwort von Jutta Joachim
ISBN 978-3-8382-0437-6

117 Fabian Pfeiffer
Estlands Außen- und Sicherheitspolitik I
Der estnische Atlantizismus nach der
wiedererlangten Unabhängigkeit 1991-2004
Mit einem Vorwort von Helmut Hubel
ISBN 978-3-8382-0127-6

118 Jana Podßuweit
Estlands Außen- und Sicherheitspolitik II
Handlungsoptionen eines Kleinstaates im
Rahmen seiner EU-Mitgliedschaft (2004-2008)
Mit einem Vorwort von Helmut Hubel
ISBN 978-3-8382-0440-6

119 Karin Pointner
Estlands Außen- und Sicherheitspolitik III
Eine gedächtnispolitische Analyse estnischer
Entwicklungskooperation 2006-2010
Mit einem Vorwort von Karin Liebhart
ISBN 978-3-8382-0435-2

120 Ruslana Vovk
Die Offenheit der ukrainischen
Verfassung für das Völkerrecht und
die europäische Integration
Mit einem Vorwort von Alexander
Blankenagel
ISBN 978-3-8382-0481-9

121 Mykhaylo Banakh
Die Relevanz der Zivilgesellschaft
bei den postkommunistischen
Transformationsprozessen in mittel-
und osteuropäischen Ländern
Das Beispiel der spät- und postsowjetischen
Ukraine 1986-2009
Mit einem Vorwort von Gerhard Simon
ISBN 978-3-8382-0499-4

122 Michael Moser
Language Policy and the Discourse on
Languages in Ukraine under President
Viktor Yanukovych (25 February
2010–28 October 2012)
ISBN 978-3-8382-0497-0 (Paperback edition)
ISBN 978-3-8382-0507-6 (Hardcover edition)

123 Nicole Krome
Russischer Netzwerkkapitalismus
Restrukturierungsprozesse in der
Russischen Föderation am Beispiel des
Luftfahrtunternehmens "Aviastar"
Mit einem Vorwort von Petra Stykow
ISBN 978-3-8382-0534-2

124 David R. Marples
'Our Glorious Past'
Lukashenka's Belarus and
the Great Patriotic War
ISBN 978-3-8382-0574-8 (Paperback edition)
ISBN 978-3-8382-0675-2 (Hardcover edition)

125 Ulf Walther
Russlands "neuer Adel"
Die Macht des Geheimdienstes von
Gorbatschow bis Putin
Mit einem Vorwort von Hans-Georg Wieck
ISBN 978-3-8382-0584-7

126 Simon Geissbühler (Hrsg.)
Kiew – Revolution 3.0
Der Euromaidan 2013/14 und die
Zukunftsperspektiven der Ukraine
ISBN 978-3-8382-0581-6 (Paperback edition)
ISBN 978-3-8382-0681-3 (Hardcover edition)

127 Andrey Makarychev
Russia and the EU
in a Multipolar World
Discourses, Identities, Norms
With a foreword by Klaus Segbers
ISBN 978-3-8382-0629-5

128 Roland Scharff
Kasachstan als postsowjetischer
Wohlfahrtsstaat
Die Transformation des sozialen
Schutzsystems
Mit einem Vorwort von Joachim Ahrens
ISBN 978-3-8382-0622-6

129 Katja Grupp
Bild Lücke Deutschland
Kaliningrader Studierende sprechen über
Deutschland
Mit einem Vorwort von Martin Schulz
ISBN 978-3-8382-0552-6

130 Konstantin Sheiko, Stephen Brown
History as Therapy
Alternative History and Nationalist
Imaginings in Russia, 1991-2014
ISBN 978-3-8382-0665-3

131 Elisa Kriza
Alexander Solzhenitsyn: Cold War
Icon, Gulag Author, Russian
Nationalist?
A Study of the Western Reception of his
Literary Writings, Historical Interpretations,
and Political Ideas
With a foreword by Andrei Rogatchevski
ISBN 978-3-8382-0589-2 (Paperback edition)
ISBN 978-3-8382-0690-5 (Hardcover edition)

132 Serghei Golunov
The Elephant in the Room
Corruption and Cheating in Russian
Universities
ISBN 978-3-8382-0570-0

133 Manja Hussner, Rainer Arnold (Hgg.)
Verfassungsgerichtsbarkeit in
Zentralasien I
Sammlung von Verfassungstexten
ISBN 978-3-8382-0595-3

134 Nikolay Mitrokhin
Die "Russische Partei"
Die Bewegung der russischen Nationalisten in
der UdSSR 1953-1985
Aus dem Russischen übertragen von einem
Übersetzerteam unter der Leitung von Larisa Schippel
ISBN 978-3-8382-0024-8

135 Manja Hussner, Rainer Arnold (Hgg.)
Verfassungsgerichtsbarkeit in
Zentralasien II
Sammlung von Verfassungstexten
ISBN 978-3-8382-0597-7

136 Manfred Zeller
Das sowjetische Fieber
Fußballfans im poststalinistischen
Vielvölkerreich
Mit einem Vorwort von Nikolaus Katzer
ISBN 978-3-8382-0757-5

137 Kristin Schreiter
Stellung und Entwicklungspotential
zivilgesellschaftlicher Gruppen in
Russland
Menschenrechtsorganisationen im Vergleich
ISBN 978-3-8382-0673-8

138 David R. Marples, Frederick V. Mills
(eds.)
Ukraine's Euromaidan
Analyses of a Civil Revolution
ISBN 978-3-8382-0660-8

139 Bernd Kappenberg
Setting Signs for Europe
Why Diacritics Matter for
European Integration
With a foreword by Peter Schlobinski
ISBN 978-3-8382-0663-9

140 René Lenz
Internationalisierung, Kooperation
und Transfer
Externe bildungspolitische Akteure in der
Russischen Föderation
Mit einem Vorwort von Frank Ettrich
ISBN 978-3-8382-0751-3

141 Juri Plusnin, Yana Zausaeva, Natalia
Zhidkevich, Artemy Pozanenko
Wandering Workers
Mores, Behavior, Way of Life, and Political
Status of Domestic Russian Labor Migrants
Translated by Julia Kazantseva
ISBN 978-3-8382-0653-0

142 David J. Smith (eds.)
Latvia – A Work in Progress?
100 Years of State- and Nation-Building
ISBN 978-3-8382-0648-6

143 Инна Чувычкина (ред.)
Экспортные нефте- и газопроводы
на постсоветском пространстве
Анализ трубопроводной политики в свете
теории международных отношений
ISBN 978-3-8382-0822-0

144 Johann Zajaczkowski
Russland – eine pragmatische
Großmacht?
Eine rollentheoretische Untersuchung
russischer Außenpolitik am Beispiel der
Zusammenarbeit mit den USA nach 9/11 und
des Georgienkrieges von 2008
Mit einem Vorwort von Siegfried Schieder
ISBN 978-3-8382-0837-4

145 Boris Popivanov
Changing Images of the Left in
Bulgaria
The Challenge of Post-Communism in the
Early 21st Century
ISBN 978-3-8382-0667-5

146 Lenka Krátká
A History of the Czechoslovak Ocean
Shipping Company 1948-1989
How a Small, Landlocked Country Ran
Maritime Business During the Cold War
ISBN 978-3-8382-0666-0

147 Alexander Sergunin
Explaining Russian Foreign Policy
Behavior
Theory and Practice
ISBN 978-3-8382-0752-0

148 Darya Malyutina
     Migrant Friendships in a Super-Diverse City
     Russian-Speakers and their Social Relationships in London in the 21st Century
     With a foreword by Claire Dwyer
     ISBN 978-3-8382-0652-3

149 Alexander Sergunin, Valery Konyshev
     Russia in the Arctic
     Hard or Soft Power?
     ISBN 978-3-8382-0753-7

150 John J. Maresca
     Helsinki Revisited
     A Key U.S. Negotiator's Memoirs on the Development of the CSCE into the OSCE
     With a foreword by Hafiz Pashayev
     ISBN 978-3-8382-0852-7

151 Jardar Østbø
     The New Third Rome
     Readings of a Russian Nationalist Myth
     With a foreword by Pål Kolstø
     ISBN 978-3-8382-0870-1

152 Simon Kordonsky
     Socio-Economic Foundations of the Russian Post-Soviet Regime
     The Resource-Based Economy and Estate-Based Social Structure of Contemporary Russia
     With a foreword by Svetlana Barsukova
     ISBN 978-3-8382-0775-9

153 Duncan Leitch
     Assisting Reform in Post-Communist Ukraine 2000–2012
     The Illusions of Donors and the Disillusion of Beneficiaries
     With a foreword by Kataryna Wolczuk
     ISBN 978-3-8382-0844-2

154 Abel Polese
     Limits of a Post-Soviet State
     How Informality Replaces, Renegotiates, and Reshapes Governance in Contemporary Ukraine
     With a foreword by Colin Williams
     ISBN 978-3-8382-0845-9

155 Mikhail Suslov (ed.)
     Digital Orthodoxy in the Post-Soviet World
     The Russian Orthodox Church and Web 2.0
     With a foreword by Father Cyril Hovorun
     ISBN 978-3-8382-0871-8

156 Leonid Luks
     Zwei „Sonderwege"? Russisch-deutsche Parallelen und Kontraste (1917-2014)
     Vergleichende Essays
     ISBN 978-3-8382-0823-7

157 Vladimir V. Karacharovskiy, Ovsey I. Shkaratan, Gordey A. Yastrebov
     Towards a New Russian Work Culture
     Can Western Companies and Expatriates Change Russian Society?
     With a foreword by Elena N. Danilova
     Translated by Julia Kazantseva
     ISBN 978-3-8382-0902-9

158 Edmund Griffiths
     Aleksandr Prokhanov and Post-Soviet Esotericism
     ISBN 978-3-8382-0903-6

159 Timm Beichelt, Susann Worschech (eds.)
     Transnational Ukraine?
     Networks and Ties that Influence(d) Contemporary Ukraine
     ISBN 978-3-8382-0944-9

160 Mieste Hotopp-Riecke
     Die Tataren der Krim zwischen Assimilation und Selbstbehauptung
     Der Aufbau des krimtatarischen Bildungswesens nach Deportation und Heimkehr (1990-2005)
     Mit einem Vorwort von Swetlana Czerwonnaja
     ISBN 978-3-89821-940-2

161 Olga Bertelsen (ed.)
     Revolution and War in Contemporary Ukraine
     The Challenge of Change
     ISBN 978-3-8382-1016-2

162 Natalya Ryabinska
     Ukraine's Post-Communist Mass Media
     Between Capture and Commercialization
     With a foreword by Marta Dyczok
     ISBN 978-3-8382-1011-7

163 *Alexandra Cotofana,*
James M. Nyce (eds.)
Religion and Magic in Socialist and Post-Socialist Contexts I
Historic and Ethnographic Case Studies of Orthodoxy, Heterodoxy, and Alternative Spirituality
With a foreword by Patrick L. Michelson
ISBN 978-3-8382-0989-0

164 *Nozima Akhrarkhodjaeva*
The Instrumentalisation of Mass Media in Electoral Authoritarian Regimes
Evidence from Russia's Presidential Election Campaigns of 2000 and 2008
ISBN 978-3-8382-1013-1

165 *Yulia Krasheninnikova*
Informal Healthcare in Contemporary Russia
Sociographic Essays on the Post-Soviet Infrastructure for Alternative Healing Practices
ISBN 978-3-8382-0970-8

166 *Peter Kaiser*
Das Schachbrett der Macht
Die Handlungsspielräume eines sowjetischen Funktionärs unter Stalin am Beispiel des Generalsekretärs des Komsomol Aleksandr Kosarev (1929-1938)
Mit einem Vorwort von Dietmar Neutatz
ISBN 978-3-8382-1052-0

167 *Oksana Kim*
The Effects and Implications of Kazakhstan's Adoption of International Financial Reporting Standards
A Resource Dependence Perspective
With a foreword by Svetlana Vlady
ISBN 978-3-8382-0987-6

168 *Anna Sanina*
Patriotic Education in Contemporary Russia
Sociological Studies in the Making of the Post-Soviet Citizen
With a foreword by Anna Oldfield
ISBN 978-3-8382-0993-7

169 *Rudolf Wolters*
Spezialist in Sibirien
Faksimile der 1933 erschienenen ersten Ausgabe
Mit einem Vorwort von Dmitrij Chmelnizki
ISBN 978-3-8382-0515-1

170 *Michal Vít,*
Magdalena M. Baran (eds.)
Transregional versus National Perspectives on Contemporary Central European History
Studies on the Building of Nation-States and Their Cooperation in the 20th and 21st Century
With a foreword by Petr Vágner
ISBN 978-3-8382-1015-5

171 *Philip Gamaghelyan*
Conflict Resolution Beyond the International Relations Paradigm
Evolving Designs as a Transformative Practice in Nagorno-Karabakh and Syria
With a foreword by Susan Allen
ISBN 978-3-8382-1057-5

ibidem-Verlag

Melchiorstr. 15

D-70439 Stuttgart

info@ibidem-verlag.de

www.ibidem-verlag.de
www.ibidem.eu
www.edition-noema.de
www.autorenbetreuung.de